CAUGHT IN THE CROSSFIRE

CAUGHT IN THE CROSSFIRE

Children of Divorce

DEBBIE BARR

Pyranee Books

Zondervan Publishing House
Grand Rapids, Michigan

Caught in the Crossfire

This is a Pyranee Book
Published by the Zondervan Publishing House
1415 Lake Drive, S.E., Grand Rapids, Michigan 49506

Copyright © 1986 by The Zondervan Corporation

Library of Congress Cataloging in Publication Data

Barr, Debbie.
    Caught in the crossfire.

    "Pyranee books."
    Bibliography: p.
    1. Children of divorced parents. 2. Family—Religious life.
3. Children of divorced parents—United States. I. Title.
HQ777.5.B375   1986   646.7'8   85-26420
ISBN 0-310-28561-5

Unless otherwise indicated, the Scripture text used is the New American Standard Bible, copyright © 1960, 1962, 1963, 1968, 1971, 1972 by the Lockman Foundation, La Habra, California.

All rights reserved. No part of this publication may be reproduced, stored in a retrieval system, or transmitted in any form or by any means—electronic, mechanical, photocopy, recording, or any other—except for brief quotations in printed reviews, without the prior permission of the publisher.

Masculine pronouns are sometimes used generically when gender is irrelevant.

Edited by James E. Ruark and Lisa Garvelink
Designed by Carole B. Parrish

Printed in the United States of America

86 87 88 89 90 91 / 10 9 8 7 6 5 4 3 2 1

To Darrell

CONTENTS

PART ONE
When the Bough Breaks

1. The Children of Divorce — 15
2. A Death in the Family — 27

PART TWO
How Children Respond to Divorce

3. Babies and Toddlers — 45
4. Preschoolers (Three-to-Five-Year-Olds) — 56
5. Six-to-Eight-Year-Olds — 68
6. Preadolescents (Nine-to-Twelve-Year-Olds) — 80
7. Teenagers — 92

PART THREE
Tell Me Where It Hurts

8. Mirror, Mirror: Divorce and Self-Esteem — 111
9. The Grandparent Connection — 120
10. Report Card Blues — 127
11. Blaming God — 135
12. Money Matters — 146

PART FOUR
Family Ties

13. Woe is One — 163
14. The Case of the Missing Father (Single-Mother Families) — 178
15. When Mom Bails Out (Single-Father Families) — 192
16. Family Heirlooms — 203

PART FIVE
Healing Propositions

17.	A Modern Ministry	229
18.	A Pound of Cure	239
19.	Prescription for Parents	261
20.	Divorce and the Great Commission	276
21.	An Ounce of Prevention	289
	Appendix A. Books to Help Children Through Divorce	304
	Appendix B. How To Know God in a Personal Way	308
	Bibliography	312
	Notes	314

MATTHEW AND STEPHANIE
A Read-Aloud Story for Children

1.	Bad News!	327
2.	Is It My Fault?	331
3.	Why Do I Feel So Bad?	335
4.	Will Mommy and Daddy Get Back Together?	339

ACKNOWLEDGMENTS

I wish to express my gratitude and appreciation for the many people who made special contributions to this book.

My sincere thanks goes first of all to my "panel of experts"—the twenty-six children of divorce and single parents who graciously and openly shared their personal experiences and thoughtful insights on the subject of divorce. Their lives and words have been woven into the heart of this book and into my own heart as well. Throughout the book their names have been changed, and on this page they remain anonymous, except to say that they hail from nine different states—Tennessee, Nebraska, North Carolina, Florida, Pennsylvania, Georgia, Arkansas, Wisconsin, and Louisiana. To the best of my knowledge, all follow Christ as Lord.

Applause and appreciation go to my friends Pam Harrelson, Sheryl Fink, Judy Couchman, Tim Wilkins, Liz and Joe May, Christine Gale, Andrea Buczynski, Diane Serge, and Loraine Clewis for their efforts in locating many of the children and single parents to be interviewed by mail and/or phone.

I am indebted to several authors whose works especially stimulated my thinking and provided a wealth of information about children's responses to divorce: Judith S. Wallerstein and Joan Berlin Kelly (*Surviving the Breakup*), Linda Bird Francke (*Growing Up Divorced*), Archibald Hart (*Children and Divorce*), and Henry B. Biller (*Paternal Deprivation; Father, Child and Sex Role; Father Power*).

I am similarly appreciative of the following friends who shared their professional expertise with me: attorney Christine Gale, Christian counselors David Martin and Don Mann, and teacher Jan Hipp. I would also like to thank John Schweighart of WSJS radio and Steve Finnegan of

WSEZ for their help in tracking down the song used in chapter 4.

A special thank-you goes to those who took time from their busy schedules to read the manuscript and offer many valuable suggestions and a great deal of encouragement: Sharon Fausch, Ruth Moore, Dr. Gary Chapman, Dr. Dan Meyer, David Martin, Don Mann, and Darrell Barr. Special thanks also to Dave and Sue Imbrock for the loan of their personal computer for several months and to Maureen Stahle for typing most of the manuscript.

Finally, I would like to express my appreciation for those special people who have encouraged my writing in so many different ways: my mother Sylvia Greenly, whom God called home before this book could be completed; my husband Darrell, without whose love, support, and patience this book could never have been written; Judy and Ron Kessinger, Martha Saunders, Dr. Gary Chapman, and many other friends whose thoughtful kindnesses and words of encouragement always seemed to come just when I needed them most.

"Feel the dignity of a child. Do not feel superior to him, for you are not."

—Robert Henri

PART ONE

WHEN THE BOUGH BREAKS

1 The Children of Divorce

I think divorce is now a normal part of life. It's hard for kids nowadays, but most kids can adjust. But some kids can't.
—Anna, age 17

Todd is not quite three years old, but he knows how it feels when a mommy and a daddy get divorced. It's scary and lonely. It makes you cry. It's so hard to understand where Mommy is and why she doesn't come back home where she belongs. Divorce isn't much fun, but it sure helps to have an older brother and a daddy and a grandpa who stick close to you through it all.

Ten-year-old Paige knows a lot about divorce. Her family got a separation five years ago and then they got a divorce a few years later. It really hurts when your mom and dad don't see eye to eye on the most important things in life, and it can cause some terrible problems. Especially financial ones. It's hard, too, when your daddy doesn't call you for months on end and even forgets your birthday! It sort of makes you wonder if he cares.

Sarah has some definite opinions about divorce in general and about her parents' divorce in particular. At fifteen, it's hard not to judge her father when it seems that what he's done is so obviously wrong. Seeing her mom cry makes her cry too. Sometimes she feels scared, and sometimes she feels bitter. Depression comes and goes. "It's really weird for me to hate and love somebody at the same time," she admits.

Things in Terry's family never were really right. His

parents separated when he was a baby and finally divorced when he was thirteen. Now in his late twenties, Terry would be the first to admit that he is still bothered by the way his parents' relationship affected his childhood. In fact, he still feels uneasy, as if something very important was never really settled. Trying to figure out just what went wrong and how to avoid making the same mistakes can be a major preoccupation. The hurt just never seems to go away, no matter how many years go by.

Todd, Paige, Sarah, and Terry are part of one of our nation's fastest growing population groups. They are the children of divorce.

THE FACTS

In just two short decades we have managed to increase our rate of divorce by 250 percent,[1] crowning our nation with perhaps its most dubious distinction: the highest rate of divorce in the world. Sixty percent of all divorce cases involve children,[2] and since 1972 more than *one million* children have seen their parents divorce each year. Today an estimated one out of every six children is a child of divorce.

As the rate of divorce increases, so does the number of single-parent families. Fully half of the children growing up now in this country will see their parents separate and/or divorce.[3] A majority of these will spend at least some of their childhood in a single-parent family. One-parent families are already increasing at a rate twenty times faster than two-parent families, giving evidence to the dramatic way in which American family life is changing.[4]

Though many of us would still describe the typical American family as one in which the father is the sole breadwinner and the mother stays at home to raise the children, the surprising truth is that today only 7 percent of the population fits this description.[5] Our spiraling rate of divorce, of course, has been a key element in this shift away from the "Father Knows Best" sort of family that typified our nation during the 1950s.

The Children of Divorce

The reasons for divorce are myriad, but one thing that has contributed to its current popularity is the notion that it really isn't all that harmful to children. Proponents of this line of thinking maintain that if adults see divorce as the answer to their marriage problems, their children will see it that way too. After all, if the adults aren't happy in the marriage, the children can't be happy either. A second, equally comforting thought is that children are resilient. They bounce back as quickly from divorce as they do from a skinned knee. Even if they don't like the idea of parental divorce at first, they soon change their minds. They're young, so they will probably adjust even better than their parents will.

As reassuring as these ideas are, the unfortunate fact is that they are false. Before the late teen years, virtually no children will be in agreement with their parents' decision to divorce. Furthermore, a recent study has shown that very few children (less than 10 percent) experience relief of any kind when their parents divorce. What they do experience is unpleasant and far from insignificant. For them divorce is an emotional earthquake, an unparalleled crisis that roars through their lives making sweeping changes without their consent.

Divorce researchers Judith Wallerstein and Joan Kelly* found that even five years after divorce 56 percent of

---

*In 1971 psychologists Judith S. Wallerstein and Joan B. Kelly began a comprehensive study of the effects of divorce on children and their families. Sixty families were involved in their research, including 131 children ranging in age from two to eighteen. All these families were from the same geographic location (Marin County, California) and were predominantly white (88 percent) and middle class. They had responded to advertising for a free six-week divorce counseling service and consented to participate in the research undertaking which came to be known as the California Children of Divorce Project.

Initially a psychologist or psychiatric social worker interviewed each adult six times and each child three or four times. They were interviewed one year later and again at the five-year mark. At the latter, 101 of the 131 participated, enabling the researchers to trace the effects of divorce over time. This study was the first to examine the long-range effects of divorce on children and as yet has no Western counterpart in either its scope or its duration. Because of this I refer to the study frequently in this book.

the children in their study felt that divorce had made little or no improvement in their family life. These same researchers also made an eye-opening discovery: only about a third of the children they observed had bounced back with the kind of resiliency that most adults expect to see. The 101 children who were interviewed five years after their parents' divorces varied widely in their adjustment. From a psychological point of view, 34 percent "appeared to be doing especially well," 29 percent "were in the middle range of psychological health," and 37 percent were "consciously and intensely unhappy and dissatisfied with their life in the postdivorce family."[6]

These findings illuminate the facts that every divorce is different and that every child is different too. Even children in the same family do not necessarily respond in the same way to parental divorce. In very general terms, the younger the child, the more hostile the relationship between parents, and the more stresses and changes that confront a child at once, the harder it will be for him or her to bear up under divorce. Boys typically take it harder than girls do, but all children need extra emotional support during the crisis of divorce.

The great and sad irony is that just as a child's needs for security and reassurance are escalating in the face of impending divorce, parental capacity for meeting those needs is greatly diminishing. Brandon, a divorced father of two, reflected on the time just before he and his wife separated. He said, "The problem with that time is that your whole mind and all your efforts are pointed in the direction of trying to work things out or trying to figure out what's going on. So I think you tend to neglect your kids at that time. You're very short with them. You just don't give them the time that you normally do. They don't know what's going on. The only thing that could really be better—and I don't know if it's humanly possible—is to try to think of them more and try to spend more time with them and not be so short-tempered. I think that's probably the time they suffered the most."

Understandably, parents in great emotional distress

have trouble dealing with the pain of their children. Even when they consciously recognize that a child is hurting, parents may not be able to muster enough emotional energy to lay their own concerns aside and reach out to the child. There may also be a tendency to downplay what the child is feeling in order to keep the child's pain from adding guilt to the hurt and anxiety already burdening the parent: "Come on! It's not the end of the world, you know."

At other times parents are completely unaware of what their children are experiencing. Preoccupied with their own problems, they may interpret quietness, withdrawal, or unusually good behavior as good adjustment or nonchalance on the part of the child. This is unlikely to be so, but parents often have a strong need to believe it anyway—at least until they regain their own equilibrium.

Discovering later how a child actually experienced the divorce may be unsettling. When *Newsweek* reporter Linda Francke began to research the topic of divorce and children, she decided to interview her own daughters. Although she knew that they had been unhappy about her divorce from their father three years before, she was aghast to discover that they had experienced a real crisis. In her book *Growing Up Divorced,* she recalls her reaction after interviewing her younger daughter. "I was struck dumb by my maternal ignorance. How could I have failed to pick up the distress signals that she must have been sending out? I could have comforted her, reassured her, at least *listened* to her. And why hadn't she told me all this before? 'Because you never asked,' she said with a grin."

That night was a difficult one for Linda. "Long after the children were asleep," she writes, "I lay awake, wondering whether other divorced or separated parents knew what their children were thinking, feeling, fantasizing, scheming, suffering. For even though my children and I led very close and interdependent lives, I never had a clue any of this was going on."[7]

Wallerstein and Kelly found that the parental depression that often accompanies divorce makes it difficult for parents to console their children. They report, "Sometimes in attempting to comfort the child, the parent would reexperience his own anguish and sob along with the grieving offspring. Children might then become alarmed at the impact of their distress on their parents, and learn to refrain from expressing their sadness or seeking solace."[8]

More than half of the children in the study felt that their fathers were "entirely insensitive to their distress" and more than one-third felt this way about their mothers.[9] They also found that younger children tended to be better cared for than older ones, and these older children "were acutely aware of the lapses in parenting and felt aggrieved and neglected."[10] Almost every nine-or-ten-year-old boy felt completely neglected by his father, and many girls felt that their mothers had emotionally abandoned them.[11]

Christian psychologist Archibald Hart has termed parental divorce "the most serious and complex mental health crisis facing the children of the eighties."[12] This seriousness and complexity, in my opinion, is compounded by the fact that many of these children essentially suffer alone. Divorce presents many children with an unprecedented problem. In other upsetting times such as a bad storm, an illness, or an argument with a playmate, the child has turned to the parents for consolation. Now the parents are the *source* of his trauma and are increasingly unavailable to him as comforters. Not only is he facing the greatest crisis of his young life, but he is doing so without the kind of emotional support he is used to receiving from his parents. Other significant adults in the child's life— teachers, neighbors, relatives, Sunday school teachers— may be unaware of the child's plight, or if aware, they may have no idea how to help him cope. Often there is no adult at all to whom a child feels he can turn, and so he hobbles along emotionally, dealing as best he can with a situation that may make almost no sense to him.

All in all, divorce is often a very scary, lonely, miserable time for a child. Life is full of stress and confusion. Adults suddenly seem remote. God may seem far away. Nothing is certain, and security is nowhere to be found. In this climate a child's coping skills are often taxed to their limit.

SUPPLYING SUPPORT

Ultimately a child's adjustment to divorce hinges on three things. First and most important is the way his parents handle the divorce and interact with each other and the child; second, the way the child perceives his parents' behavior and the losses and changes that divorce brings his way; and third, the support he does or does not receive from others both during and after the divorce. Thus the parents, the child himself, and other people outside the family unit but within the child's circle of relationships all play a part in mediating the child's adjustment. What happens within the home is far more critical than what happens outside of it; outside relationships, no matter how wholesome and positive, cannot make up for a troubled home. Yet a child lacking outside support may cope far less well than he otherwise might. To look at it another way, the less support a child is receiving at home, the more important outside support becomes. In light of this, it is my strong feeling that God would have His people play a far greater role in the lives of children of divorce than is typical at present.

What can be done? Happily, a great many things. But let's take a realistic look at two prerequisites for helping the children.

Loving Attitudes

Many attitudes about divorce exist among Christian people. Some feel that divorce is wrong under any circumstances. Others feel that divorce is legitimate only when there has been adultery and a lack of repentance on the part of the unfaithful partner. Still others think that divorce is also permissible whenever there has been physical abuse or desertion. Some have added "irreconcilable differences" to that list.

No matter where we stand on the issue of divorce, it is critical that we do not forget that the bottom line of every divorce is *people*—people whom Christ loves and for whom He died. As representatives of Christ we have a

God-given responsibility to love them, accept them, and extend a helping hand in their direction with no strings attached. It is sad but true that many have instead responded with condemnation and rejection. As a result, the church is often the last place the wounded survivors of divorce turn—or return.

When it comes to the children of divorce, the way we respond is of vital importance. In the 1980s, divorce is an omnipresent fact of life. A whole generation of children has begun to absorb its impact. These children are almost always innocent bystanders, not willing participants, when their parents divorce. Most of them strongly oppose parental divorce, but they are powerless to stop it.

Even more than adults, children need acceptance, love, and encouragement when divorce divides their homes. Through no fault of their own, their life's path has suddenly been littered with debris that God never intended to be there. When the path is not well lit, it is easy for them to trip over the obstacles in their way. Psalm 119:105 says, "Thy word is a lamp to my feet, and a light to my path." The Living Bible puts it this way: "Your words are a flashlight to light the path ahead of me, and keep me from stumbling." Our loving attitudes and actions toward children of divorce can help determine the way they will come to view the future, themselves, and the Word of God.

Understanding

Adults naturally look at divorce from an adult point of view. It is natural for us to try to look at the corollary issue of children and divorce in the same way. But we need to try to view it as if we were standing in a child's shoes. Understanding how it feels to him, what he fears, what he is angry about, and what behaviors are likely to result are prerequisites to helping him. We need to know what his immediate and long-term needs may be. We should be aware of the prognosis for his future. We need to understand that divorce can influence a child's concept of self, trust in God, academic performance, sexual adjustment, and ability to relate to others. We should be aware that it can affect his views on marriage and family and even influence the way he will one day raise his own children. In short, we need to understand as much as possible about the way a child experiences divorce so that our efforts in his behalf will count.

Beyond a factual understanding, we need empathy. *Webster's New World Dictionary* defines empathy as "the projection of one's own personality into the personality of another in order to understand him better; ability to share in another's emotions or feelings." We may find it easier to be empathic toward fellow adults because we can relate to them on a similar level of maturity, verbal ability, and cognitive development. It's harder with a child, especially a very young one. His perceptions of reality and fantasy, of good and bad, and being loved or not are far different from an adult's.

A major difference in the way children and adults cope with divorce may have to do with memory. Adults, even those who have been married for a great many years, can recall a time in their lives before marriage. They can even remember a point at which they had not yet met their spouses. So even when they sense that life after divorce will not be easy, adults at least remember that it is possible.

A child, however, has no such assurance. He can recall no time in his life when he lived without father or mother. In fact, just trying to imagine life apart from a parent may be nearly impossible for him to do. One of his greatest natural fears has always been that of being abandoned and left to fend for himself. When separation and divorce breathe life into that fear, an unprecedented crisis can occur. For some, life will never really be the same again. Most of us would like to deny that this is so, but we must accept it as fact, laying aside the temptation to assume or assign blame. Instead, we need to focus on understanding what it really means to be a child of divorce. For many it means

- Looking at the calendar and remembering your parents' anniversary and then realizing that there is nothing to celebrate anymore
- Spending Christmas with Mom and then having another Christmas at Dad's
- Having to worry about money
- Wondering deep down inside whether you are really the cause of your parents' unhappiness
- Having to go through a period of grief and anger
- Giving up your dreams about all the things you had hoped to do together as a family
- Crying yourself to sleep at night
- Wondering if God really cares
- Feeling insecure and worried about the future
- Losing some of your childish innocence and trust
- Praying and pleading and trying with all your might to change the situation, but failing in your attempt
- Wondering if you'll get married when you grow up, and if you'll get divorced too

When we understand divorce from a child's eye-view and can lovingly empathize with him, we are ready to help.

In ministering specifically to children, what can be done depends a great deal on the age of the child and the kind of relationship we have both with the child and with the parents. The amount of time we have with the child makes a difference too. For example, a schoolteacher who sees the child five days a week has opportunities that an aunt or uncle in another city does not have, and vice versa. Every caring adult in the child's circle of relationships can play a unique role in his adjustment to divorce.

I once heard someone say, "Life is *relationships*." I think both biblical and secular wisdom supports that idea. Relating to others is what brings joy, meaning, and fulfillment to life. Sharing and communicating with other people helps us know who *we* are and stimulates us intellectually, emotionally, and spiritually. A healthy network of interpersonal relationships that meets our need for love and acceptance frees us to look beyond ourselves to consider the needs of others.

Unhealthy or broken relationships have the opposite effect. Whether we are estranged from our Creator, a brother, or a spouse, a broken relationship makes it hard to feel good about ourselves or about life in general. It's hard to think of the needs of others—sometimes just hard to think at all—until there is restoration, forgiveness, and healing.

Life *is* relationships, and this is as true for children as for adults, but not in the same way. For children, life is primarily—sometimes exclusively—family relationships. The younger the child, the fewer relationships he has formed apart from mother and father, sisters and brothers. When divorce permanently alters that network of relationships, life goes topsy-turvy. Feeling good again may be a long time in coming, since there is not likely to be the kind of restoration, forgiveness, and healing between Mom and Dad that normally mends other interpersonal conflicts. Learning to live with, instead of repairing, a broken relationship becomes the task of the whole family. It's not easy because it's not natural.

It is in this context that we can reach out with love and encouragement. Children's perceptions of relationships per se and their trustworthiness of adults in general may have been dimmed by the divorce that has rocked their household. Because of this, patience and a warm personal touch—smiles, hugs, a listening ear—are essential. Because life *is* relationships, we must take care not to institutionalize our outreach too much. On one hand, because of their professionally trained staffs and larger resources, churches, schools, clinics, and social service agencies can do many things that no private individual could hope to do.

On the other hand, there are many things that close friends, neighbors, and relatives can do that would never mean as much coming from a pastor or counselor. Most children would undoubtedly adjust better and faster if help were available from both qualified professionals and caring laypeople. Ideally both parents, the child's teacher, Sunday school teacher, a professional counselor, friends, and extended family should all offer informed support and encouragement to varying degrees. But when this does not happen, even just one person who is genuinely concerned and willing to really listen can make all the difference in the world.

Perhaps you can be that person.

2 A Death in the Family

The death of my parents' marriage has shown me that the union of a man and a woman is indeed the creation of a new life. Marriages are living things. And sometimes they die.
—Bruce Yoder, pastor [1]

In the original scheme of things, marriages—like men and women—were not supposed to die. But both men and marriage have fallen under sin's sentence of death. There is a difference, however. All men will die whether or not they are prepared for it, whether or not they consent to it. Marriages, on the other hand, don't just die of their own accord. They are either starved to death or dealt an intentional deathblow by one or both of the partners. Otherwise, marriages live as long as the spouses do.

Divorce is the legal means by which husbands and wives pull the plug on the marital life-support system. To some, it is a mercy killing. To others, it is nothing short of murder. Either way, the marriage dies. When it does, the children who mourn its passing are thrust into a sort of no man's land of grief: the marriage is dead, but the parents live. Family members are the same, but life is very different. Contradictions like these make divorce one of the hardest griefs for a child to bear.

THE LOSSES OF DIVORCE

We usually associate the word "grief" with the physical death of a loved one or friend. But grief is not limited to death. Anything perceived as a loss, big or small, tangible or intangible, can evoke grief. Denting the fender on a brand-new car, losing a valuable ring, or missing out on the family reunion on account of having the flu—all these can cause grief.

The depth of a person's grief depends on how significant he perceives his loss to be. Much depends on how great an emotional investment he had in what was lost. Thus a loss that seems slight to one person may be seen as quite major by another. We may feel that a child is overreacting to his parents' divorce, yet only that child knows how it feels to be the son or daughter of these particular parents and to be losing the things he or she feels are being lost through their divorce.

The losses sustained can be incredible. Tangible losses sometimes include

- The permanent removal of one of his parents from the home, or from his life altogether
- A brother or sister who goes to live with the other parent in cases of split custody
- The family home, which may have to be sold
- Reduced income, which means fewer clothes, toys, family outings, etc.
- Moving away from familiar surroundings—school, classmates, neighborhood friends, after-school activities, church involvement
- Aunts and uncles, cousins, or grandparents who will never be seen again
- The after-school or evening companionship and supervision of Mother, who must now work outside the home
- A pet or hobby that can no longer be afforded or made to fit into an apartment lifestyle

Intangible losses are keenly felt too. Some of these losses include

- Security
- Self-esteem
- A stable home environment

- Respect and status in the eyes of others
- Happiness and a sense of well-being
- Trust in adults
- Faith in God
- The ability to concentrate in school
- A sense of being able to control one's own life
- The identity that comes from seeing oneself as a part of a normal family
- Hopes and dreams of family times to come

Beyond these things, a child may feel embarrassed about the divorce, rejected by the parent who left, lonely, guilty, fearful, and confused—all at once.

Unlike any other experience that can befall children, divorce has the power to inflict cataclysmic and simultaneous losses that would never otherwise confront them in so short a time. The fact that these things are happening because one or both parents are *choosing* to get a divorce adds insult to injury. The parents' aim, of course, is not to hurt the children, but to gain relief from what is viewed as an intolerable situation. But even when they are old enough to recognize this, few children will be greatly comforted by this knowledge. Instead, they grieve.

Grief is a normal, God-given response to loss. In grief, we withdraw to ponder what has been lost. As we comprehend what has happened we begin to adjust. Slowly we emerge to cope with life again, minus what has been lost. Grief is not only natural, but necessary. To suppress it, deny it, or defer it is to interfere with our emotional healing.

Barbara Spence, a divorced mother of three, discovered that this is true for adults and children alike. She wrote,

> If only I had been allowed to go through the stages of grief, holding tightly to my faith in a loving God, I could have been healed much more quickly.
>
> But I'm not the only one who was suffering because of the divorce. My children were, too. . . .

I learned that they need to be allowed to grieve too. They have lost a part of themselves. Their lives, which had been safe and snug up to this point, were completely uprooted. They are young, but they know that something terribly important has been lost to them forever.

But who allows the children to grieve? So many parents want to "protect" their children by telling them half-truths or vague realities. And it's easy to be so overwhelmed by your *own* pain and guilt that the children and their pain take a back seat. It's tragic and it's wrong, but it happens.[2]

Children need to grieve the losses of divorce. No child should ever be punished for grieving or be pressured to hurry through the process. Verbally denying that the child has lost anything of value, or refusing to allow him to sort through his feelings and experience his grief, is detrimental to his emotional and psychological well-being. Those who are not permitted to deal with their losses as they occur will likely confront them again at a later date, perhaps as adults. Even when the predivorce relationship between a parent and a child has not been an especially positive one, there is still likely to be grief. In these situations a child may feel that part of what he is losing through divorce is the potential for developing a future good relationship with the parent. This may shatter with finality his dreams about someday having a happy family. Whether or not a child feels that his home was happy, and whether or not he had a healthy relationship with either parent, the divorce experience is still likely to trigger some degree of grief.

Individual children have their own timetable for adjustment. If allowed to follow it, most will be able to cope with their losses, adjust reasonably well, embrace whatever realities now exist, and go on with life. On the way to emotional healing, both adults and children pass through various stages, known as the grief cycle. Some experts feel that younger children do not grieve in the same sense that adults do, but they still experience pain in loss. The sequence of the grief cycle is

DENIAL: "This isn't really happening."

ANGER: "Why, why, why?"

BARGAINING: "I promise I'll be extra good, if only. . . ."
ACCEPTANCE: "This *is* happening, and I can cope."
GROWTH: "I'm going to be stronger because of this."

Others believe the sequence is a little different, suggesting shock as a first response, followed by denial, anger, self-pity, and acceptance. Put perhaps more simply, any person who sustains a loss can respond in one of three ways. He can try to avoid it, try to change or undo it, or accept it. A grieving person typically goes all three routes, arriving eventually at acceptance. People progress at different rates through the stages of grief, sometimes cycling back through stages again and again before finally accepting the loss.

Avoid it is a typical child's first reaction to divorce because the news is too hard to digest. It really can't be true! Very young children may avoid dealing with the idea of divorce by pretending that the absent parent is just at work or on a long trip. This denial functions as a cushion that keeps the awful truth from hurting them. As long as a child continues to deny the inevitable, however, he can move neither backward nor forward. He cannot go backward because what was no longer exists; he cannot move forward because he has not yet accepted what has become reality. He is suspended in a fantasy of avoidance. This is not abnormal but it is usually short-lived.

Change it is almost always the desire of a child who learns that his parents plan to divorce. He argues, reasons, and pleads with them. He may pray earnestly, perhaps trying to bargain with God. He may become super-good and unusually cooperative. But to no avail. Everything is going to change and none of it is what he wants.

Accept it is what the child has been fighting against. It may be a long, hard road for some, but as the truth sinks in—that he can neither run from reality nor change the circumstances—acceptance gradually takes place. Along the road to acceptance, many different feelings and reactions can occur, varying with the age and personality of the child. These varying responses all characterize what we call grief.

Depression

Depression is the classic sign of grief. In depression, it is almost as if the child shifts into low gear in order to absorb at a more tolerable pace everything that is confronting him. He withdraws, preferring to be alone rather than with friends or family. He may spend a lot of time thinking and may cry easily. His ability to concentrate in school may suffer. He may not feel like eating, or he may overeat. He may have trouble sleeping at night or may feel constant restlessness during the day. Self-confidence shrinks, and decision making becomes difficult.

Anxiety

Anxiety is really a form of fear. Many things that previously felt secure and could be taken for granted now seem uncertain. What is going to happen next? Will people laugh at us? Will Mommy leave me too? Are we going to be poor? Do I have to change schools?

An anxious child is apt to be a very busy child as he tries to bury his uncertainty and fear in a flurry of activity. He may have nightmares, temper tantrums, and physical manifestations of his anxiety such as stomachaches, diarrhea, headaches, asthma, or chest pains. He may begin to bite his nails or wet the bed. He may be afraid to let his custodial parent out of his sight and may worry about that parent getting sick, dying, or otherwise abandoning him.

Anger

Practically every child will be angry about his parents' divorce. Because something so dramatic is occurring entirely against his will and outside his control, he will feel frustration and insecurity. Anger is the result, and it's a normal part of the grieving and healing process.

Children who cannot verbally express their anger or are prevented from expressing it may turn to indirect or "passive-aggressive" outlets for their rage. Instead of being open about their anger and finding acceptable outlets for it, these children express it in masked ways such as bad attitudes, disobedience, being critical of others, not doing well in school, or harming pets or property. This kind of anger is not healthy and needs rechanneling with the help of an experienced counselor.

Unhealthful anger has two faces: guilt and blame. Guilt can result from anger turned inward: "This is all *my* fault." Anger turned outward results in blaming others for what happened: "Why did *you* let this happen?" Younger children, as we shall see in the next chapter, are particularly prone to self-blame when parents divorce. Their guilt is, of course, unfounded; but to the child it is real and burdensome. Older children may blame God, their parents, the "other woman" or "other man," or circumstances.

GRIEVING DIVORCE

According to child psychologist Lee Salk, divorce ranks second only to parental death among childhood traumas. "Divorce is, in a way, worse than death," said Patty, forty-four, a divorced mother of two. "Death is a natural part of life—we know it will happen. We never suspect that divorce will occur as we march down the aisle on the wedding day." Children never suspect it will occur either, and in at least five ways, divorce *is* actually worse than if a parent had physically died.

No Ceremony

To begin with, marital death, unlike physical death, has no socially accepted ritual that eases the grief of the survivors. Joseph T. Bayly has written, "The viewing and funeral are our sole concession to death. As a result, they must bear a heavy weight of grief-expression, death-affirmation and memorialization."[3] A divorce is often as heart-rending as a death, especially to a child. But where is the ceremony that bears the "heavy weight of grief-expression, death-affirmation and memorialization" of the marriage? There is none. The reasons are not hard to comprehend.

Unlike death, divorce is often an embarrassment to the family. Unlike death, it is a choice. And unlike death, the divorcing parties hardly wish to memorialize the "deceased," even though children often feel differently. So there is a death in the family, but no viewing, no funeral, no ceremony, and quite often no fellow mourners to surround the family with understanding and consolation. As a result, the grief a child experiences when parents divorce can be more severe than when a parent dies.

No Clean Break

Physical death, with its funeral ceremony and burial, releases the family to start afresh. First there is grief, then healing, and then closure of the wound. It is over. The person is gone. A new chapter in life begins in which the deceased person has no role except in memory. There is sometimes a sense of relief: "Mommy doesn't have to suffer with her cancer anymore. Now she is with Jesus."

Divorce is seldom like that. There has been a death, but not a total break. Like death the loss is permanent, but unlike death it is only a partial loss. Both parents live and continue to play out their parental roles according to revised scripts. There may be also ongoing disagreement about custody, child support, visitation and other issues, making it hard to start afresh.

Ironically it is only the marriage that has produced children that can never be declared completely dead. Because of the children, the parents must continue to interact, make decisions, and still behave toward each other in many ways as if they were still married.

Much of what a child mourns is the way divorce continues to affect him on a day-to-day and week-to-week basis. The ambivalence of having lost something yet still having it makes the grief that follows divorce an off-again, on-again process. That is, as the child grows older he continues to discover more ways in which the divorce has affected his life. When he realizes something he was previously unaware of, he may grieve afresh at that time; wounds can be reopened at various stages of life. Time spent with a friend's intact family, the seemingly conspicuous absence of his second parent at a special school function, or the annual reminder of Christmas or Father's Day may trigger fresh grief.

False Hopes

A third way in which divorce and parental death differ has to do with hope. Because the parents have not died, but actually do live, there is always the possibility in the child's mind that they will reunite. Almost every child characteristically clings to the notion of parental reconciliation following divorce. Common fantasies are usually variations on the same theme: Mom and Dad realize that they really do love each other after all. They reconcile their differences and get back together, and the family lives happily ever after. That this is so universal a response suggests that divorce, like death, was never meant to be.

But even death holds the promise of a resurrection. All who die will live again. Those who have trusted Christ will spend a joy-filled eternity with Him; those who have rejected the Savior-Messiah will be eternally separated from God. Children instinctively believe that a dead marriage can live again too. But marital resurrection rarely occurs, and the childish hopes that flourish after divorce are almost certain to lead to disappointment and disillusionment.

In her book *Where Has Grandpa Gone?* Ruth Kopp notes, "Any loss that is expected to be temporary is more difficult to mourn than one perceived and accepted as permanent."[4] Thus the tendency to cling to the ideal of reconciliation hinders children in the important task of grieving.

Compounded Losses

Divorce multiplies grief upon grief. As we have already seen, there are both tangible and intangible losses. Many of these losses *by themselves* would be sufficient to produce a period of grief. Thus divorce can bring about a multifaceted grief deeper than the grief of death.

Isolation

When a family member dies, the rest of the family huddles closer for mutual support and consolation. People outside the family reach out with expressions of sympathy and kindness. The mourners are thereby assured of several things. First, they are assured that it's normal to be feeling loss and emptiness. Second, they know their grief is understood and accepted by others. Third, there is the confirmation that they are loved and cared about by a circle of concerned friends and family members. By contrast, a child whose parents divorce rarely receives adequate comfort from either family members or outsiders.

In her book *Which Way Is Home?* Leslie Williams writes, "In grieving over a death, the family members pull together in their suffering. They get closer, and they support and love each other through the trauma. In a divorce, you also feel a need to pull together as a family. *But there's no family.* You end up grieving for the very thing you need but can't have. Knowing that you can never again have the support of the family makes the grief more intense."[5]

There is a tendency for those outside the family to refrain from reaching out when divorce occurs. They don't know what to say, and it's hard to know what to do—it doesn't seem right to send flowers or take food the way one would if there had been a death. After all, it's always *possible* that the family may be *happy* about the divorce. Consequently many people feel less at ease with a loss sustained through divorce than they would with one sustained through death. Often the result is a complete avoidance of both the people and the problem.

I remember reading about one woman and her son who experienced this reaction. The woman wrote that when her first husband had died, her church responded immediately with gifts of food, phone calls, sympathy cards, visits to their home, and other demonstrations of love. Her young son was much impressed and moved by this, as was the woman herself. Later the woman married again, but the marriage was troubled and ended in divorce. After her husband left the home, no one called or came by. There were no gifts of food or encouraging cards or notes. There was only silence. The boy remembered vividly the response other Christians had given when his father had died. Now he had lost a second father and no one seemed to care. It puzzled him greatly. "When will the people from church be by?" he asked his mother. She tried to help him understand that yes, divorce is a lot like death, but it is different too. In divorce you bear your grief alone.

Experts agree that a sense of isolation serves to compound grief. Because of the dynamics within the family at the time of divorce and the hesitation of those outside the home to become involved, divorce very often creates an isolated grief.

SUGGESTIONS FOR HELPING CHILDREN COPE WITH THE GRIEF OF DIVORCE

1. Realize that a child will view divorce as a loss even if the parents do not. Do not try to minimize a child's losses: "I can't see why you're so upset. It's not that big of a deal. You will probably see your dad more now than you did before." Instead, let him know you understand: "I know you really miss your dad. I realize that this isn't an easy time for you, but try to remember that both your dad and I love you very much, no matter what has happened between us."

2. Allow the child to spend time by himself, but offer to keep him company. For example, a parent, grandparent, or baby-sitter could read or do needlework in the same room as the child but should not force him to talk or participate in any activity. He should be *invited* to take part, however, if others are going to play a game, take a walk, or engage in other activity.

3. Do not punish the child for moping or being depressed. Recognize that he is going through a necessary healing

process. At the same time, it is important to maintain discipline and see that chores and homework assignments are accomplished. He still needs the security of boundaries, rules, and responsibilities. Do be gentle and understanding, though, knowing that it may actually be more difficult for him to feel motivated and to make decisions.

4. Allow the child to talk about his other parent. This may be trying, but talking about the parent and times past can help him accept his present losses, just as talking about one who is deceased helps family members accept the death.

5. Pray with the child understandingly, not patronizingly. God may seem far away, so help him tap into his heavenly Father's comfort and love. Let him know you're praying *for* him daily too. (See chapter 11 for additional suggestions.)

6. Let him know, above all, that you *accept* him and his feelings. Let him know it's OK to cry and it's OK to want to be alone. Assure him that if he wants to talk, you're a good listener, but it's also all right if he doesn't want to talk. With smaller children, physical comfort is especially important. Holding them, rocking them, tucking them into bed, or just sitting close by can be comforting.

7. The child may emerge periodically from his grief and seem to be fine. This is the time for distractions—fun outings, reading a joke book together, trying out a new box of crayons or paints, learning to bake brownies, or whatever else interests him. Do not be dismayed if he lapses into grief again, however. This is not unusual. Be patient.

8. Change as little as possible in the child's environment and lifestyle. The fewer changes that confront him at once, the less overwhelmed he will feel. For example, postpone moving to a new neighborhood or going to

work for the first time, if possible, for as long as you can.

9. Passive-aggressive anger, excessive anxiety, or prolonged depression may call for professional help. A parent who is himself experiencing prolonged grief or depression will probably benefit from counseling as well. This will help the child in the long run, too, since hurting parents find it hard to be sensitive to their children's needs. If you have trouble locating a Christian family and child therapist in your area, a pastor or an association such as the Christian Association of Psychological Studies may be able to give you direction.

10. Friends should *not* avoid the subject of divorce. Let both parent and child know of your sincere concern and your willingness to listen or help in practical ways. Encouraging cards, notes, phone calls, and visits are entirely appropriate expressions of love.

PART TWO

HOW CHILDREN RESPOND TO DIVORCE

This section touches on some of the most typical responses to divorce in particular age groups of children. Age at the time of divorce is significant for two reasons. First, children vary according to age in their ability to comprehend divorce and deal with the stresses it imposes on a family. Second, the child's age at the time of divorce determines how great a portion of his life will be affected by divorce. Infants whose parents divorce will know nothing of the "before" and "after" lifestyles that a fifteen-year-old child can point to. Also, the younger the child is at the time of divorce, the greater is the percentage of his life that will be consumed by the divorce-resolution period. Typically about three years elapse from the time a couple divorces until the time when the members of the family could be said to have readjusted to a postdivorce lifestyle. A child who was three years old at the time of divorce will be six when the adjustments are completed. Thus a full 50 percent of his young life will have been affected by stresses relating to his parents' divorce.

For a child of any age, much depends on how quickly his parents regain their emotional stability, how well or how poorly they continue to relate to each other, and the degree to which each of them maintains a positive, affirming relationship with the child. Parental maturity and unselfishness at the time of divorce may be difficult, yet the long-term benefits for the child are well worth any effort and self-control required.

Most experts on divorce and children would probably agree with Sandy, a divorced mother of three:

> If there's no reconciliation possible—he's going his way and she's going hers—they need to realize that those kids need as much emotional stability in the very beginning as they can get. The number one priority is for the kids: what's

best for them? If the parents can really sit down and think through in their own individual situation what is best for that child and act upon that, then the child or the children are going to be all right.

Understanding a child's age-related needs and probable responses at the point of divorce is the first step toward minimizing its stresses on him. Regardless of age, every child is a unique individual facing a unique set of circumstances, and no two will respond in exactly the same manner when divorce occurs. The following chapters, therefore, will be most useful when seen as an overview of possible common responses rather than as an attempt to stereotype children of divorce at their various stages of development.

3 Babies and Toddlers

My five-year-old was only ten months old when the separation occurred. How or if he has been affected, I cannot surmise.
— Patty, 44, single mother of two

THE PREGNANCY DIVORCE

At first thought it seems almost impossible that a baby still in his mother's womb could be affected by the divorce of his parents. Yet because they are inseparably connected, whatever affects the mother affects the baby too.

Divorce may cause an expectant mother to experience a variety of intense emotions. She may be depressed at one point and fearful, anxious, angry, or grief-stricken at other times. Her body is often in a state of alert as extra chemicals go charging through her system.

When high-level stress continues through a significant portion of pregnancy, the fetus is affected by the chemicals in the mother's bloodstream. Research reported by Linda Francke indicates that the stress transferred from a mother can cause fetal activity to increase as much as 300 percent. Premature births and low birth weights are likely to result, and the babies are often squirmers who are harder to care for. They have trouble sleeping, cry more, and experience digestive problems.[1]

New mothers with unhappy babies and even unhappier ex-husbands need a great deal of emotional and tangible support from others if they are to make a good adjustment to their new mothering role.

All the information in the following section typically applies to mothers and babies when divorce occurs during pregnancy or infancy.

BABIES

Babies whose parents divorce are affected in several ways that may not be readily apparent. Because of divorce, their earliest life experiences may differ widely from those of other infants. But it may be what babies do not experience because of divorce that may actually be most significant.

Father-Care

Virtually all infants will remain in their mothers' custody following divorce. As a result, one of the things infants usually do not experience is routine care and play from their fathers.

Fathers' patterns of interaction with infants are measurably different from those of mothers. Men have deeper voices, wear different kinds of clothing, have larger and more muscular bodies, and actually respond differently to babies than women do. Infants of divorce miss out on masculine nurture and the benefits of two complimentary kinds of stimulation. Studies have shown that

- Fathers are "significantly more likely" than mothers to "rock, vocalize with, and imitate" their babies.
- Fathers spend more time holding babies for play, while mothers are "far more likely to hold them for caretaking purposes."
- Fathers tend to play in more physically stimulating ways with babies than mothers do. By contrast, mothers tend to play in a more intellectual style with their infants.
- Infants respond differently to fathers. One study showed that "infants' response to play with their fathers was significantly more positive than their response to play with mothers."

- Fathers provide more tactile stimulation, while mothers provide more verbal stimulation.
- Fathers who participate in the early care of their infants may experience the same sort of bonding with the baby that is known to occur between mothers and babies.[2]

Many researchers feel that infants experience not merely more stimulation from their fathers, but a qualitatively different pattern. Babies who receive care exclusively from their mothers and other women, which is often the case following divorce, do not benefit from the distinctively different style of care that their fathers would have provided.

Breast-Feeding

Another benefit usually removed from babies of divorced parents is long-term breast-feeding. Breast milk is easy for the baby to digest and offers various benefits. Breast-fed babies are less likely to suffer from colic and stomach upsets. They catch fewer colds and develop fewer allergies, ear infections, and dental problems. Nursing enhances facial development and lessens a baby's urge to suck his thumb. A breast-fed baby is more likely to feel secure and to cry less than a bottle-fed baby due to the positive effects of close physical contact with the mother.[3]

The relative merits of breast- versus bottle-feeding are certainly subject to any mother's circumstances and personal preferences. The point here is not to unduly exalt breast-feeding but to suggest that the stress of divorce may interfere with a woman's ability to succeed at breast-feeding or her desire to attempt it. If able to nurse, she may find that as a working mother—which most divorced mothers are—it is difficult to manage more than a few initial weeks of breast-feeding. She may find that expressing her milk at work and transporting it home requires more motivation than she can muster, given the demands of her job, her commuting schedule, and her emotional pressures.

Daytime Nurture

Most of these same infants are likely to experience institutional day care or care from a sitter rather than care at home from their mothers during the workweek. Of course, many babies are placed in the care of others by married, working couples. The point is, again, that the single working mother often has little choice in the matter.

There is a notable lack of enthusiasm among many professionals regarding the practice of leaving babies in the care of someone other than the parent. Dr. Rene Spitz, professor of psychology at the University of Colorado Medical Center, is quoted by La Leche League as follows:

> Working mothers who return to their jobs shortly after the birth of a baby are endangering the future lives of their children. . . . The biggest cause of . . . failure in adulthood is the lack of a normal mother-child relationship in the first year of life. . . .

Dr. Joyce Brothers is similarly quoted:

> Do you believe the studies that say children need their own mothers during the first few years of life? I realize that the economic necessities of life often force us to do things differently than we would like. But when it comes to child raising, I am convinced that a woman should make every possible effort to spend the first 3 years with her child.

Divorced working moms often feel trapped in a kind of Catch-22. If they don't work, how will they support their children? If they do work, how can they heed the advice given by experts like Spitz and Brothers?

Mother-Care

A fourth way in which infants are affected by divorce is one that may be highly significant. Studies have shown that mothers who do not have supportive husbands tend to behave differently toward their infants than those who do. Thus, not only do these babies miss a father's masculine care style, but they may also experience a different sort of mothering. Studies[4] indicate that

Babies and Toddlers

- One of the most important roles of the father is "to provide emotional and economic support to the mother and thereby enhance the mother-infant relationship."
- When a husband is emotionally supportive of his wife and they enjoy a mutually satisfying marriage relationship, the mother is more competent in her mothering role and has a greater sense of well-being.
- An encouraging and supportive husband enhances a mother's "sensitivity and adaptation to the needs of the infant."
- Mothering "skills and warmth in handling the baby" have been related to the "anxiety level, age, and marital satisfaction" of the father.
- Both the father's attitudes about the pregnancy and the mother's perceptions of his emotional and physical support have been "consistently correlated with . . . the mother's involvement and responsiveness with the child" throughout the first four years of his life.
- "When mothers were with their husbands, they were more likely to explore the baby and smile at the baby than when they were alone with the newborn."[5]

AT THE STARTING LINE

During his first year a child develops basic perspectives on life that are either generally trusting or distrusting. The depth of his emotional relationship with his parents or the person who cares for him most of the time has a tremendous impact on the formation of this basic outlook on life.

In a baby's first six months of life, when his cries bring the food, cuddling, or dry diapers he desires, he quickly learns that the world is a responsive place. His actions bring reactions, and he develops competence, security, and trust as a result. But babies whose cries seem to make little difference in the way they are cared for learn that there is no connection between what they do and what happens to them. Their actions do not bring reactions, and according to research, these babies actually cry more often than those who are frequently tended to. Dr. Paul Chance has summed up the issue by saying, "A responsive environment . . . inclines a child toward competence, while an unresponsive environment inclines a child toward helplessness."[6]

Divorce and its accompanying depression and stress sometimes make it hard for a new mother to provide a highly responsive environment for her baby. Babies pose a challenge even in the best of circumstances, when both mother and father are present, getting along well, and mutually committed to nurturing their little one. A newly divorced mother can feel overwhelmed by the needs of her infant when there is no husband to provide encouragement and support. Physically and emotionally drained, she may sometimes feel as much like crying as the baby who is screaming in the next room. At times she may find it extremely difficult to put her own feelings aside to concentrate on her baby's needs. Yet her ability to nurture and respond is very important to the infant's development.

During the second half of a baby's first year many exciting things begin to take place. He develops the ability to discriminate between familiar and unfamiliar faces and thus becomes better able to recognize the people in his life as individuals. For this same reason he may become anxious in the company of strangers. As his mobility increases he also begins to develop some independence. And, around seven or eight months of age, he becomes especially attached to the most constant person in his life, usually his mother.[7] He wants to be with this person constantly and feels most secure and happy in her presence. In a sense, it is almost as though this person is a part of him. Because of this, he has a deep-seated fear of becoming separated from this parent. When separation is forced upon him, he experiences separation anxiety. He clings, cries, screams, and becomes exceedingly fearful when it appears that this person intends to physically leave him.

There is reason to believe that babies of divorced parents may experience greater separation trauma than other babies. Psychologist Henry Biller cites data showing that "infants who had little contact with their fathers were more likely to experience greater separation anxiety from their mothers and more negative reactions to strangers."[8]

This attachment bond and the resulting separation anxiety are normal stages in a child's development. They are biologically based responses and have nothing to do with a child's being spoiled, as some parents may be tempted to think. Many authorities on child development feel that this first emotional attachment forms the basis for all of the child's future relationships. Through the mother-baby relationship he learns how to give and receive love and how to relate emotionally to another person. Children develop at different rates, and Dr. George MacLean, staff psychiatrist at Montreal Children's Hospital, believes that this attachment-separation process peaks somewhere between eighteen months and three years of age.[9]

Children who can form attachments to both parents seem to have the greatest social advantages later in life. Biller writes, "Our observations have suggested that children who are able to form strong attachments to both their mothers and fathers during infancy have more positive self-concepts and success in their interpersonal relationships than children who have only an attachment to their mother."[10] Since divorce tends to hinder strong attachment to fathers, these children typically bond only with their mothers. Those who are frustrated in this very first emotional attachment with Mother may have trouble in their relationships with others as they grow older. Some search for affection at random; others want to avoid emotional involvements of any sort.

Divorce may interfere with a baby's attachment bonding by forcing a daily separation between mother and baby as Mom leaves to go to work. It becomes a greater nightmare if the child must leave his mother for overnight or weekend visits with his noncustodial father.

TODDLERS

Between a child's first and second birthdays his basic developmental task is that of learning self-confidence. He becomes a little explorer, investigating, climbing, and poking his nose into everything that captures his interest. Too much interference and thwarting of his natural curiosity and desire for independence may serve to undermine his self-confidence, rather than building it up.

Sometimes emotionally hurting parents are tempted to cling to a small child as a sort of security blanket in the wake of a divorce. Their own emotional neediness or the fear of losing the child to the other parent through a custody dispute may cause them to stifle the child, rather than to free him to discover and explore the world around him. This period in a child's life is critical to his intellectual and social development, and stimulation from all sorts of places, things, and people is very important. Researchers for Harvard University's Preschool Project found that "providing a rich social life for a twelve-to-fifteen-month-old child is the best thing you can do to guarantee a good mind."[11] They also discovered that those permitted to explore the living areas of their homes freely progressed faster than those who were restricted.

The period between the ages of two and three, notoriously known as "the Terrible Twos," marks the beginning of a transition from babyhood to childhood. In many ways it is as great a psychological upheaval as the transition from adolescence to adulthood.

"No!" is the favorite word of every healthy two-year-old. He is demanding, hard to please, hard to compromise with. Temper tantrums and tears are common. His behavior, while normal, is quite aggravating. Adults in the midst of a divorce may find their patience pushed to the limit by this little rebel. Developmentally he is striving to establish his own identity. To do this he must resist social control in a sort of purposeful rebellion.

In spite of his rebellion, he also craves security, and divorce can be a devastating experience for a two-year-old.

Boys in particular have a difficult time. Henry Biller reports research showing that "boys who became father absent before age 2 were found to be less trusting, less industrious, and to have more feelings of inferiority than boys who became father absent between the ages of 3 and 5."[12] Without the presence of their fathers in the home, boys may feel insecure and vulnerable. Fears can loom very large, and since a child this age cannot adequately verbalize what he is afraid of, bad dreams may become the outlet for the scary things on his mind. Bedtimes are hard anyway because one of the things he fears is that his remaining parent might disappear while he is sleeping. With the onset of nightmares, going to bed may become a real ordeal for him.

Sometimes two-year-olds regress in their behavior when their parents divorce. Regression is like a timeout. The child is basically saying, "Hold it, folks! I can't handle this. Let's go back to the way things used to be when life was secure and I felt pretty good about growing up." He reverts to more infantile behavior because going back in time suddenly seems safer than forging ahead into unknown territory.

Separation anxiety still plagues many two-year-olds. He knows that his parents are a unit; the departure of one implies the departure of the other. Being left with a sitter or dropped off at Grandma's can send him into a panic state.

My husband and I observed full-blown separation anxiety when a recently separated friend brought his children, two-year-old Todd and three-year-old Jan, for a weekend visit with us. From the moment the children set foot in our home they seemed fearful. Though they had been in our company several times before, they became terrified when their father went outside for a moment to bring the suitcases from the car. They screamed and cried and tried desperately to prevent him from going out the door. Left with us, they clung to each other and wept hysterically. Nothing we could say or do was of the slightest comfort. When their father returned with the luggage, they latched onto him in relief, their little bodies heaving with sobs. The obvious depth of their anxiety and misery was heartbreaking. They were terrified to think that Daddy might walk out the door and not come back, like Mommy.

Babies and toddlers are the age groups least ready for any sort of shared custody. Experts recommend that the noncustodial parent visit the child instead shuffling him back and forth between parental homes. Infants and toddlers are most secure in a consistent, familiar environment—same blankets, same toys, same colors and shapes in their rooms. Obviously, parental kidnapping is an extremely poor practice for the same reasons.

SUGGESTIONS FOR HELPING BABIES AND TODDLERS

1. Expectant mothers need all the emotional support they can get during divorce. Because of the potential impact of high-level stress on an unborn baby, professional counseling may be important in helping a pregnant woman deal with her emotions and anxieties. Expressions of love, concern, and tangible support from others can be invaluable. She may need a patient listener, a shoulder to cry on, or a very practical help like getting her nursery ready or finding a Lamaze coach. Any ministry to the mother is, in the long run, also a ministry to the infant.

2. When it is possible and practical, arrange for trustworthy and mature male baby-sitters rather than female to provide babies and toddlers with the opportunity to experience a masculine carestyle in the absence of the father. Grandfathers, uncles, and other relatives can provide masculine nurture whether they are baby-sitting or not.

3. Maintain a consistent, stable, familiar environment for the child. Household routine is important. The same person should function as the child's caretaker in the

absence of the mother, preferably in the child's home rather than at a day-care facility.

4. Emotionally stressed parents should be aware of the need to balance their interaction with the child. They must not fail to provide a sufficiently nurturing environment, nor must they squelch a toddler's genuine need to explore his environment and to begin in small ways the process of emancipation from parents.

5. The emotional tension in a divorcing household will not go unnoticed by very young children. Babies and toddlers will comprehend little from verbal explanations about divorce since they are experientially rather than verbally oriented. Parental efforts to comfort them should instead be directed toward balancing their negative experiences with positive ones. For example, spending extra time with children, cuddling, rocking, holding, and playing with them will help increase feelings of security.

6. Churches with a significant number of babies and toddlers from divorced homes should consider recruiting men as well as women nursery teachers.

4 Preschoolers (Three-to-Five-Year-Olds)

People don't understand that divorce is very hard on the children and that most children feel terrible the rest of their lives.
—Benjamin, age 10

Marcie was three years old when her father left. One of her earliest memories is that of waving goodby to him as he boarded a train. She never saw him again. For years she was plagued with a nagging sense of rejection. Why hadn't he come back? What had she done to make him want to leave? Why didn't he love her anymore? It was only after prolonged therapy as a thirty-three-year-old woman that Marcie was able to realize that it was not her, but her mother, whom her father had rejected. When the feelings of guilt lifted, Marcie wept with relief.

Marcie's parents may have cared a great deal about her, but they made a grave error in choosing to handle things as they did. Like most parents of preschool children, they thought, "She's too young to know what's going on," and offered Marcie no explanation whatsoever for her father's leaving. It is true that Marcie was too young to comprehend the reasons behind her parents' breakup, but she was certainly aware that something was going on. Further, the lack of explanation left her at the mercy of her vivid, youthful imagination. Had his train simply disappeared the way things do in cartoons on TV? Was her daddy hurt or sick or hungry? Did he have a place to sleep at night? Such concerns may seem almost silly to adults, but preschoolers may worry about such matters.

A TIME OF CONFUSION

Young children like Marcie have trouble verbalizing their deep concerns and questions about divorce. As a result, divorce can be a time of great mystery and frustration as fact and fantasy swirl together in their thoughts. For this reason, parents should purposely tell their preschool-age children as much as possible about what is happening, since it is quite logical for them to be wondering where their other parent is and why he or she no longer comes home at night. Unfortunately, according to one study, 80 percent of the preschoolers whose parents are divorcing are given no explanation of any sort.[1] One of the two most important people in their lives has seemingly vanished and no one even brings up the subject!

MOM, DAD, AND FEELING GUILTY

Marcie's response to her father's departure was typical for a preschooler: she blamed herself. There are several reasons for this. One is that young children tend to perceive their parents as practically perfect. Therefore, if there is a problem, it cannot be the parents' fault; it must be the child's. Also, preschoolers tend to view life in terms of good and bad. Their rationale is, "Obviously Mom and Dad are getting a divorce because I've been so bad." In an attempt to reverse the situation they may try to become ultra-well-behaved. So doing, they may become burdened with guilt and feel depressed. Self-condemning statements such as "If I wasn't so bad Daddy would come back" may indicate that the child feels responsibility for the breakup.

Dr. E. Mavis Hetherington, who has done extensive research on children of divorce, feels that preschoolers are prone to self-blame because they have such limited contacts outside their own homes and families. Their whole world revolves around family relationships, and when something as serious as divorce occurs they easily assume that they are to blame. They also typically harbor the fear that another family member will leave them.[2]

Another reason why a preschooler may feel guilty when a parent leaves is that he may have wished for exactly that to happen. Small children believe that their thoughts are extremely powerful. If they think it, it can happen. An angry wish that their daddy would just go away, followed coincidentally by his departure from the home, can be interpreted by preschoolers in only one way: the wish came true!

When it is the same-sex parent who leaves, a child's guilt may be intensified and complicated by what is taking place in his developing sexual identity. During the preschool years, a little boy often falls in love with his mother, and a little girl with her dad. These tiny romantics are forming mental models of the kind of person they will someday marry. It is perfectly natural for them to wish that their "competition" would somehow disappear so that they can have the object of their affection all to themselves. In normal, intact families this stage, called "the oedipal phase," resolves itself quite naturally. Under normal circumstances, the "competition" does not go away, of course, and by the time children are six years old the desire for strong relationships with peers of the same sex becomes more prominent. Divorce interferes with this oedipal resolution process in a big way, however. What was once just a safe fantasy wish has now become a scary reality. Little boys left alone with their mothers or little girls left with their fathers have no idea how to handle the "romance" once the parent who served as a buffer has been removed.

Nine times out of ten, it is the father who leaves the home. This is one reason why preschool boys have a more difficult time with divorce than preschool girls do. A boy may be guilt-ridden to think that he has actually won out over his father, as evidenced by his dad's departure.

Deep inside, the victory is anything but sweet. He knows he can never take his father's place, and he really doesn't want to. He wishes desperately that Dad would return.

Besides these uncomfortable feelings, a boy may

wonder whether he too will be banished from the household, since he, like Dad, is male. Perhaps out of a sense of powerlessness, sons typically become very angry with their mothers at this point. And they don't stop with Mom: all adult women become objects of anger that may last even two years or longer.

A boy may also feel confused about his masculine role and the kinds of behaviors he is supposed to display. After all, how is he supposed to learn how to be a man when there are no men around? Consequently many preschool boys adopt a somewhat feminine style of behavior modeled after Mom. Henry Biller reports,

> I found that father-absent five-year-old boys had less masculine sex-role orientations ... and sex-role preferences ... than did father-present boys. Moreover, the boys who became father-absent before the age of four had significantly less masculine sex-role orientations than those who became father-absent in their fifth year.[3]

Mothers sometimes unknowingly aggravate this problem by discouraging their sons from such boyish activities as wrestling and climbing trees. Instead they give approval for passivity and encourage quiet indoor activities like looking at books, watching TV, or coloring. These mothers may naturally be a bit more anxious to ward off accidents and injuries than they might be if life in general were a bit more serene. But by safeguarding their sons' physical safety they may be contributing to an even greater problem psychologically.

There can also be problems if mothers verbally criticize and tear down their ex-husbands in front of their sons. Little boys know that they are males like Dad, and comments such as "Men are so disgusting" or "Men are all alike" will surely be taken to heart by the child, causing him further insecurity about his masculinity.

A preschool girl has a different problem. When her dad leaves, she feels almost jilted. Feeling frustrated and rejected, she may strongly deny that her father has even left. She may boast of her father's love and frequent attention. Wallerstein and Kelly found that preschool girls tend to fantasize about being loved by their fathers because this helps them in "undoing the rejection and in maintaining the self-esteem and sense of their own lovability that was threatened by the father's departure."[4]

Girls who visit with their fathers after divorce can be quite hurt by negative comments from their dads about women in general. "Women are stupid" translates into "Daddy thinks I am stupid!" Since their fathers are still the object of their affections, this wholesale rejection of their sex can be crushing. In the Wallerstein and Kelly study, little girls whose fathers made caustic comments like these cried all the way home after each visit.[5]

Experts on children's responses to divorce feel that the worst time for parents to divorce is the period between the child's third and eighth years. One reason why divorce during the preschool years can be costly lies in the fact that unresolved oedipal tensions are likely to resurface during the teens. Boys who have never understood what it means to be a man or learned how to handle their sexuality may act out their false and immature impressions. Often that means adopting a sort of hypermasculine, exaggerated macho style of behavior. Girls may become sexually promiscuous, unconsciously still reaching out for their fathers' love.

A father's influence in the home has been linked to the child's development of both impulse control (the ability to refrain from doing things he knows he shouldn't do) and delay of gratification (the ability to wait with desires that are better or more properly fulfilled at a later time). Dad's departure from the home during the preschool years may influence a child's development in these areas.

REGRESSION

Preschoolers commonly experience regression when their parents divorce. For a time their development appears to go backward instead of forward. Life has become confused, and the energy that should be applied to maturation is instead focused on trying to figure out what is happening at home. A child who has been independent and pleasant may become a clinging vine who whines and cries a lot. Those who are quite capable of feeding themselves may want to be fed or opt for fingers rather than forks. Thumb-sucking may resume. A child who is potty trained may suddenly forget that he knows where the bathroom is during the day and may wet the bed at night. Baby blankets may be reclaimed along with baby toys. Physical coordination and the ability to learn may regress too.

Regressive children are sad children, and even diversions such as play or being read to may not help. When divorce takes place with relative civility and the household quickly regains much of its former equilibrium, regression does not last long. When life remains in turmoil, however, with hostility seething between parents, some aspects of regression can linger as long as a year. An adult who provides constant reassurance and gets emotionally involved with the child helps ensure that regression will soon run its course.

SEPARATION ANXIETY

Preschool-age children are still prone to separation anxiety. Because of this, visitation with the noncustodial parent can turn out to be a traumatic experience. Steve told me how visitation affected his three-year-old daughter: "When she would come back she would just be terribly upset, almost to a point of being out of control. Of course, since she was as young as she was you couldn't reason too much with her, because she couldn't understand why she had to leave one and live with the other."

Brandon, another single parent, regularly observes separation anxiety in his preschoolers. "I can really see it in the kids each time that they visit their mother and then have to come back to me. I don't know if the words 'torn apart' are exactly the right words to use, but it's like they're torn in different directions. When they go to her, they're being pulled away from me, in a sense. They go through that *every* time they visit."

EXHIBITING MODEL BEHAVIOR

Sometimes children who feel responsible for divorce become exceedingly compliant and well-behaved. Hoping to somehow atone for the crayon marks on the wall or the chocolate ice cream stains on the sofa that must have made the parent angry enough to leave for good, a child will suddenly become a model of good behavior. This child is, in fact, miserable, but the adults in his life are usually more than grateful for his newfound "maturity." Their dead-wrong assumption is that the divorce must actually have somehow been quite beneficial to the child, whose behavior has only improved since that fateful day. The truth is, the child believes that if his very bad behavior sent the parent away, his very good behavior might just bring him back. He needs to be freed from his self-imposed strictures by the realization that he had nothing to do with his parent's decision to leave.

OTHER RESPONSES

Other responses typical of preschool children include bouts of fear, bad temper, crankiness, anger, or frustration. Some begin to sleep fitfully, probably linked to a fear of being abandoned by the remaining parent. Many of the youngest children in the California Children of Divorce Project displayed a generalized emotional neediness. That is, they reached out for attention and affection from any adult at all, even climbing into the laps of strangers.

After his wife left, Brandon noticed an increase in moodiness in his two preschoolers. He soon learned to take this as a cue that their "emotional tanks" were getting empty and they needed increased attention from him.

Usually when I sense this—sometimes it takes a while to catch it—I'll just cancel something for an evening. If I was going to be home that evening anyway to work on stuff at the house, I'll just push it all aside and spend the whole evening with them. And it makes a world of difference in them. It really does.

Anger is part of the mourning process. Some children turn their anger outward, blaming others, while some turn their anger inward and blame themselves. Girls are more likely to turn inward, boys outward. Both may be confused about why they feel as they do. Inward anger may be manifested when the child does things to deliberately harm himself or make himself uncomfortable, perhaps as punishment for causing the divorce. Outward anger includes aggressive or bullyish behavior, which can harm relationships with peers.

Interestingly, as bullyish behavior subsides, girls tend to be welcomed back into their circle of peers, while boys often continue to be ostracized and unforgiven. The boys' only recourse may be to play with girls or children younger then themselves, which fosters immature behavior. Mavis Hetherington feels that during the second year following divorce, boys who have had this problem might benefit from a move to a new neighborhood or playschool. That way, with their adjustment period past, they can make new friends and leave their bad reputations behind them.

PLAYTIME

Anger and fear have a way of showing up in the way a child plays. Because young children are so unskilled at expressing themselves verbally, they will often act out their feelings using dolls or puppets or in their play together in small groups. Observing the way a child holds dolls and the scenarios he acts out with them can be very revealing. Clumping a family of dolls very close together in a bunch might be telltale of how the child feels: he wishes his family could be close again. Earthquakes, fires, and monsters that come out of nowhere to afflict the dolls may be statements about how it feels to be four or five years old when parents get a divorce.

Adults can help children at play to express their feelings by letting dolls or puppets talk about what the child is likely to be feeling. For example, the adult's doll could say to the child's doll, "I cried when Daddy left 'cause it made me feel so bad."

Artwork is also telltale. One child may draw himself suspended between two houses—his mother's and his father's. Another may portray his house about to be swamped by water or eaten by a monster. Yet another may draw a picture of his family with Dad off to the side in a little box. All of them are depicting their feelings about divorce.

Music can stimulate a child to express his feelings too. Sandy recalled how music helped her five-year-old daughter open up for the very first time. She said, "The song, 'Just When I Needed You Most'* by Randy Vanwarmer

---

*You packed in the morning and I
stared out the window and I
struggled for something to say.
You left in the rain without
closing the door.
I didn't stand in your way.
Now I miss you more than I
missed you before and I . . .
Where I'll find comfort, God knows!
'Cause you left me just when I
needed you most.

I wake every morning and I
stare out the window and I
think about where you might be.
I've written you letters that
I'd like to send, if you would
just send one to me.
'Cause I need you more than I
needed before and I . . .
Where I'll find comfort, God knows!
'Cause you left me just when I
needed you most.

was on the radio when we were driving home one day. My daughter sat in the car crying. She said, 'Why did my Daddy have to leave?' In over a year that was the first emotion she showed, she had buried it so deep down."

SUGGESTIONS FOR HELPING PRESCHOOLERS

1. Every preschool child needs a simply worded verbal explanation concerning divorce. Ideally both parents should talk to the child together before the actual separation takes place. It is important to use language that preschoolers can understand. Words like "custody," "irreconcilable differences" or "child support" are probably meaningless to them. They need to know basic information like where they will live and how often they will see their other parent. Preschoolers may not be able to perceive time relationships the way an adult does, so again, it is important to speak their language. Instead of saying, "You'll see Daddy every other weekend and on Wednesdays" tell him he'll see Daddy "a lot."

You packed in the morning and I
stared out the window and I
struggled for something to say.
You left in the rain without
closing the door.
I didn't stand in your way.
Now I love you more than I
loved you before and I . . .
Where I'll find comfort, God knows!
'Cause you left me just when I
needed you most.
Oh yeh, you left me just when I
needed you most.
You left me just when I
needed you most.
© 1978 Fourth Floor Music, Inc.

2. The guilt feelings that these children have following divorces usually arise from false guilt. Yet, to the child these feelings are serious and grievous. Few children at this stage of development are capable of distinguishing between real and false guilt. Because of this, some experts feel that a child should be encouraged to confess his divorce-related "wrongs" to God and ask for forgiveness to try to alleviate the guilt. Others disagree, saying that confession can never relieve false guilt because it is false; that is, there is nothing to be forgiven. Christian counselor Don Mann suggests instead that parents provide repeated assurances that the child is in no way responsible for the breakup. A parent might say something like, "I know you feel bad about the divorce, but the problem is between Mommy and Daddy. It has nothing to do with you. The divorce is not your fault." (Chapter 2 in the read-aloud story, "Is It My Fault?" is intended as a resource for helping a child see that he played no part in the parents' decision to divorce.)

3. Respond to regressive behaviors and moodiness by spending additional time with the child and maintaining an emotionally close relationship.

4. If the father has left the home and does not maintain an adequate involvement with the children, surrogate role models are important, especially for boys. Male relatives, Sunday school teachers, nursery school teachers, friends, and baby-sitters can provide positive examples for boys.

5. Do not discourage rough-and-tumble play by father-absent boys. Consistently giving approval only for quiet or passive behaviors may lead a little boy to believe that typically masculine behaviors are inappropriate for him or even punishable. At the same time, however, it is important to maintain discipline and control and to set standards of conduct.

6. Recognize uncharacteristically compliant behavior as a sign that the child may be trying to make up for causing the breakup. Don't reinforce this ultragood behavior with praise and gratitude. Rather, sensitively draw the child out and emphasize the idea that he did nothing that contributed to the parents' decision to divorce.

7. Spend as much quality time with the child as possible. Physical affection—hugs, stories read on the lap, tucking into bed at night—warmth, positive eye contact, and genuine attention communicate love and acceptance.

8. Refrain from making negative, critical, or condemning statements about the child's other parent when the child is present. Those outside the family should never criticize either parent in the child's hearing. Wholesale putdowns of either sex should likewise be avoided.

9. Utilize paints, clay, crayons, dolls, puppets, and music to help discover how the child is coping and to help him express his feelings.

10. If possible, take the child to the place where his noncustodial parent is living soon after that parent leaves the home. This way the child will see that he has a safe place to live, a bed, and food, and is in no danger. Preschoolers are reassured by this and can also visualize the parent's home from that point on whenever they think about him or her.

11. Fathers who move away from the family residence should make every effort to maintain a close relationship with their preschool-age children.

12. If a preschool boy is having a difficult time getting along with his peers, postpone if possible any move to a new location until the second year after divorce. This way he will be able to start over with a new group of friends once his aggressive behaviors are past. This same principle also applies to school-age children.

5 Six-to-Eight-Year-Olds

What upsets me most about my parents' divorce is the hurt that you get down deep.
— Candace, age 8

The early school years from first to third grades are full of transition. In a major way a child now begins to enjoy relationships and daily experiences that are not held in common with other members of his family. In school he may encounter conditional—rather than unconditional—acceptance for the first time. He can no longer count on being loved and appreciated simply on the basis of who he is as his family regards him; now acceptance and approval by his peers depend increasingly on his performance—in the classroom, on the playground, and in social situations. Consequently, during these years the child begins a quest for mastery in a variety of areas, with peer acceptance as a motivating force. For most children these transitions and challenges are pleasant, and the years from six to eight are often treasured as relatively carefree, serene, and happy.

DIFFICULT DAYS

When divorce occurs during this rather idyllic period in a child's life, it can cast a long shadow on both his ability to be happy and on his sense of well-being. Authorities on divorce and children believe that along with the preschool years, the period between the ages of six and eight is probably the worst time for a child to experience parental divorce. This is because he is able to understand more about what is happening than his younger brothers and sisters, but he does not yet possess the emotional maturity and skills for coping that older children do. Life at this age still revolves around Mother and Father, and he still perceives his own needs to be very much intertwined with the needs of his parents. While he does not feel the guilt that a preschool child feels when parents divorce, he experiences a parent's leaving home as a personal rejection.

SADNESS

Children in this age group, more than any other, experience overwhelming grief when their parents divorce. Wallerstein and Kelly called deep sadness "the most striking response" of these early elementary children. They described them as "more intensely conscious of their sorrow than any other group in the study."[1] This pervasive sadness is not lifted by distractions like recreation, reading, crafts, or other activities. Like the grief that accompanies death, it may linger on and on, coloring all of life with its darker hue until the period of mourning is past.

Many six-to-eight-year-olds respond with panic, sobbing, and great fear when their parents separate. The death of their parents' marriage is a terrifying event. A comment by Gordon Livingston, director of psychiatry at the Columbia Medical Plan in Columbia, Maryland, is especially descriptive when applied to this age group. He said,

> The disillusionment that comes with the knowledge that your parents do not love each other anymore and are not going to stay together is probably as profound as the eventual knowledge that someday you are going to die. It's not only a tremendous blow to a child's conception of the world as an orderly place, but it shakes his fundamental faith in everything. It's the one thing children expect to persist and when it doesn't, it's scary.[2]

Six-to-eight-year-olds characteristically display an intense yearning for their noncustodial parent. Usually this is the father, and it is not uncommon for a child to feel that he has been abandoned by him. One third-grade girl told me, "My father needs to understand that I want him home more than anything in the whole world." Similarly, many of the children interviewed in the California Children of Divorce Project longed for their fathers with an intensity reminding researchers of grief for a dead parent.

COMMITMENT TO FAMILY

Early elementary children tend to remain unswervingly devoted to both parents, no matter how much attention or inattention they receive, or how much one parent may pressure the child to renounce the other. Wallerstein and Kelly felt that about a quarter of the six-to-eight-year-olds in their study were being pressured by their mothers to reject their fathers. They commented, "These youngsters continue to be loyal to both parents, frequently in secret, and often at considerable psychological cost and suffering. Their capacity to do this, despite the pressure, and their courage were often moving and impressive."[3]

Few children at this age are capable of being angry with their fathers, but some direct strong anger toward their mothers for supposedly driving their fathers away. Usually being angry with either parent is hard. Their level of social reasoning tells them that you can't be mad at somebody and love him too. This is evident in peer relationships: "I'm mad at Cynthia and I'm never going to be her friend anymore!" Relationships are pretty much all-or-nothing-at-all. So being mad at Dad or Mom makes little sense because it might mean risking the loss of that parent. And that is the very last thing six-to-eight-year-old children want.

What they *do* want—fervently—is a reunited family. Being with one parent then with the other but never with both at the same time can be quite dissatisfying for many kids. It just doesn't meet their emotional needs. They want both parents, and they want them together. As a result, the reconciliation fantasy is strong.

Seven-year-old Greg, whose family was the subject of a TV documentary on divorce, was typical. He told his interviewer, "I want them back together no matter what. I'm never going to give up."[4] Eight-year-old Mary Beth told me, "I wish my mother would get married to my dad again. I want them to get together and not stay apart." But of course, fairy-tale reconciliations rarely occur, and holding onto the fantasy only strengthens and prolongs a child's grief. The desire to reunite Mom and Dad also makes kids very resistant to the idea of parental dating. Boyfriends or girlfriends of either parent are a direct threat to the cherished dream of reconciliation. Verbal or nonverbal efforts to deter or at least dampen parental dating can be anticipated.

FATHER-LOVE

Noncustodial fathers who are not regularly involved with their six-to-eight-year-olds may not realize how desperately their children desire a relationship with them. Boys miss their fathers tremendously, especially if they are the oldest or only boy in the family. When their fathers disappear from their lives they become father-hungry and are eager to accept father substitutes. Male teachers, neighbors, and others may be sought out in an attempt to fill the void. A boy will tend to overinvest in the relationship, however, creating the potential for disappointment should the prospective father-figure not share his enthusiasm.

Mothers who date a succession of men should be aware of the potential effect on their sons. If a boy becomes emotionally attached to a series of boyfriends only to have them fade out of the picture, he may become disillusioned and learn to shrink back from making emotional commitments as he sustains loss upon loss. His ability and desire to form future good relationships may be hampered in the process.

Girls miss their dads just as much as boys do, but they are less willing to replace them with substitutes. Their affections still belong to Daddy alone, and no one else can really fill his shoes. They willingly cultivate relationships with adult males and enjoy their attention, but they rarely make the kind of emotional investment in potential father surrogates that boys this age so easily do. Instead, when Daddy pays little attention, a girl compensates by fantasizing about his love and devotion to her.

If a father does remain involved with his children after divorce, he is likely to devote more attention to his sons than to his daughters, according to research. Six-to-eight-year-old girls can be deeply hurt by a father's inattention and seeming preference for their brothers. The ache of having felt rejection from the first and most important man in their lives can color future relationships with a sense of being unlovable.

BOTTLED-UP FEELINGS

Some children in this age group have a hard time talking about their feelings. This may be especially true when parents themselves have not made a practice of verbalizing their feelings, not just about the divorce, but about the events that make up normal day-to-day living. The children learn to keep their feelings bottled up inside. When lack of communication is a habit, talking about the painful feelings surrounding divorce is doubly hard. There are more emotions than ever inside, but the cap seems to be sealed on tighter than ever.

Similarly, children whose parents tend to fly off the handle easily soon learn to keep to themselves any information that may upset or anger a parent. In the volatile climate of divorce, they may repress the churning emotions that threaten to provoke some of Mom or Dad's less desirable reactions. A child who is "just fine, thank you" may be far less tranquil than he appears on the surface.

Early elementary children need to talk about what's going on. They need to understand the events that are happening around them and should be given the freedom to express the feelings that naturally result. Parents who cannot or will not discuss the divorce should at least afford their children an opportunity to talk with a therapist, pastor, or teacher who knows how to draw them out. Since children this age fear alienating their parents, even when Mom and Dad are excellent communicators, counseling of some sort is still a good idea because it allows them to share their feelings with a safe adult.

Six-year-old Sheila wasn't talking. Her mother wisely brought her to see a Christian counselor, who soon discovered that Sheila was hiding a lot of grief and sadness behind her withdrawn façade. She didn't want much of anything to do with anyone. In fact, her sole confidant was her teddy bear. David Martin, who was Sheila's counselor, recalls,

> She sat down in that chair and she wouldn't talk to me. And the only thing that really got things going was when I asked her, "If your teddy bear were sitting right next to you now, and you had to tell him how you were feeling, what would you tell him?" She looked at me and then she turned and started talking to this imaginary teddy bear. She was avoiding letting anybody get into her, but she was willing to talk to her teddy bear. Now, for a while that's what we had to do until she started getting to the point where she could trust me.

Sheila, according to David, had lost faith in her parents through the divorce and needed desperately to reestablish trust. Counseling was the right step for her mother to take in her behalf.

FEARS AND RESPONSIBILITIES

Most children have fears regarding divorce or stemming from the experience. The fear of losing the custodial parent is common. Eight-year-old Mary Beth dreads that "we might drive off a bridge." She has other worries too. "It scares me," she said, "when I think that my mom might marry someone mean." Candace, who is also eight, said she gets scared just thinking about her father. She admits, "Sometimes I worry about him coming back and hurting us."

Such fears may or may not be grounded in reality, but they are nonetheless real concerns for the child. Children who are unable to talk to their parents about their divorce-related feelings are especially prone to unrealistic fears, such as a fear of starving or a fear about going to school.

Children who have been told by well-meaning adults that they are now "the man of the house" or "the little homemaker" may be fearful about their ability to take the place of the departed parent. Custodial parents who are depressed or emotionally unstable are most likely to usher the child into this unrealistic role, grateful for the comfort it brings them. Other parents merely think it's cute when a little boy assumes his father's place at the dinner table or when a little girl tries to take over as family cook. Children, of course, cannot adequately assume adult roles and can be filled with anxiety in trying.

Overworked single parents may be tempted to allow their children to assume as much responsibility as they are capable of, both in caring for themselves and in taking care of the house. Children as young as first and second graders may be responsible for getting themselves up on school days, fixing their own breakfast, packing their own lunches, and making sure they catch the right school bus at the right time. After school it is up to them to get home safely, let themselves into the house and amuse themselves until mom gets home. Sometimes six-to-eight-year-olds may be expected to see to the needs of younger brothers or sisters, perhaps making their supper—soup and a hot-dog—and putting them to bed. There may be a number of household tasks that they are expected to accomplish besides.

Children in these situations are apt to feel neglected

and angry that they are not cared for the way their friends are. Some hardly see their parents, who may work odd hours, perhaps moonlighting on a second job, taking night classes, or dating in the evening. Children who have no siblings may spend many lonely hours at home by themselves.

Even the busiest of single parents need to keep in mind that six-, seven-, and eight-year-olds are *children*. They need supervision, guidance, and nurture, if not from parents, then from parent-substitutes who can free the children from enough of their duties and concerns to just let them enjoy childhood. Household tasks assigned to children should not merely help unburden Mom or Dad, but should be especially chosen to help children feel more competent and important. Jobs that they can succeed at in a measurable way are best because they will boost their self-esteem. By contrast, jobs that are really beyond their capabilities ensure their failure or frustration, making them feel discouraged and incompetent.

FEELING DEPRIVED

Six-to-eight-year-olds are deeply affected by the many tangible and intangible losses they sustain through divorce. Feelings of deprivation are not unusual. As a result, some become compulsive overeaters, trying to fill the emotional void with food. Grieving losses on all sides, others compensate by demanding more material possessions— often more than parents can afford to provide. They say they need new clothing, toys, athletic gear, and gadgets that their friends have. When their wishes cannot be fulfilled, some children respond by making up stories about possessions they don't really have or lavish vacations they have never really taken. They seem to feel that if they can't have what they want, they can at least increase their status by pretending they do.

Feelings of deprivation can make children selfish with the things they do possess. Perhaps feeling that they cannot risk the loss of one more item, they may become dead set against sharing anything with others. Feelings of deprivation can even tempt a child to help himself to some of the more desirable items he finds in his friends' possession. The line between what belongs to him and what belongs to another becomes blurred in his effort to make the empty feelings go away. Author Linda Francke writes, "Feelings of deprivation are symptomatic of the anxiety these children feel about the impermanence and the inadequacy of their family support systems. All they see around them is loss—of a parent, of parental attention, of extra money, of a secure future."[5]

SUGGESTIONS FOR HELPING SIX-TO-EIGHT-YEAR-OLDS

1. The parent who moves away from the family home should be aware that six-to-eight-year-old children are apt to perceive his or her departure as rejection. This parent should make every effort to maintain a close relationship with the children following divorce, giving both verbal and tangible assurances of love. Fathers especially need to bear in mind how much their sons need to feel loved by them. Fathers who have both girls and boys should take care not to show preference for sons over daughters.

2. Do everything you can to assure the child of parental love, a secure future, and adequate material provision. Pray with your children about family needs and their personal needs. Let them observe your reliance upon God for both material provision and emotional strength. Recognize that, in spite of God's faithfulness and your good example, grief is still an entirely normal response to the losses the child has sustained.

3. Learn to verbally express your feelings, and be a good listener when your children express theirs. Telling them, "That sure makes me feel bad" or "Boy, am I

tired today" lets the child know that in his family it's OK to say how you are feeling. When parents are open and honest about their feelings and show respect for the feelings of others, the children learn how to talk about what's on their minds. If sharing feelings is awkward, perhaps a few sessions with a counselor will help the family to learn better communication skills. One note of caution: While it is important to work at open communication, maturity and restraint are equally important, especially following divorce. Do not burden a child with adult problems that he is not equipped to handle. Find another adult in whom to confide.

4. Never pressure a child to renounce his loyalty to either parent or even hint that he should do so. It is entirely normal for him to care for both, and he is in fact under biblical mandate to do so—"Honor your father *and* your mother" (Exodus 20:12; Ephesians 6:2). Attempts to turn a child against one parent are likely to backfire anyway. At some point the child will come to resent the parent or other person who pressured him, rather than the parent he was supposed to have turned against.

5. Don't feed the reconciliation fantasy unless it is actually quite probable that the parents will reconcile their marriage. In almost every case it is much kinder to gently remind the child that his parents are divorced and that this is a permanent arrangement. Tell him that the parents' decision to stay apart is final. (Chapter 4 in the read-aloud story, "Will Mommy and Daddy Get Back Together?" may help a child better understand the finality of divorce.)

6. Do some special things from time to time to help take the sting out of feelings of deprivation. Simple and inexpensive gestures can go a long way toward increasing feelings of security. Here are a few ideas:

- Tuck a special "I love you" note into a jeans pocket or lunchbag.
- Surprise the child with a batch of warm chocolate chip cookies.
- Send a greeting card through the mail. (Most six-to-eight-year-olds don't get much mail!)
- Give a small, inexpensive gift for no reason.
- Take him to McDonald's for Saturday lunch.
- Add a slight increase to his allowance.

7. Mother substitutes and father substitutes can never really replace uninvolved parents, but they can provide positive role models and meet many emotional needs that might otherwise go unmet. If the absent parent is not adequately involved in his children's lives, help them cultivate wholesome and rewarding friendships with adults who can in some measure be surrogate parents. If the father is the absent parent, it is especially important that boys develop a friendship with a stable, mature, and trustworthy man. Be aware of the potentially different response to this person by girls in the family.

8. Do not allow the child to try to fill the role of the parent who left the home. When others imply that this is something the child should now do, temper these comments with assurances to the child that he does *not* have this responsibility. While all family members will no doubt have increased responsibilities following divorce, do not expect a first, second, or third grader to carry an adult's share of the workload or to accomplish tasks that are beyond his childish capabilities.

9. Spend as much quality time with the child as possible. Discussing homework and daily events, doing chores together, walking the dog, reading books out loud, playing board games, and so on will help to make the child feel secure and loved. Morning or evening prayers together, regular mealtimes and bedtimes, and

enforceable household rules are also helpful in reestablishing equilibrium following divorce.

10. If you cannot be at home when your child comes home from school, arrange for a sitter or relative to be there in your place, or work out an arrangement whereby your child can stay with a neighbor or at the home of a school friend until you arrive at home. This companionship not only assures greater safety for the child, but it also helps ward off feelings of loneliness and isolation, particularly for only-children.

11. Studies have shown that children need warm, meaningful relationships with both parents to make an optimal adjustment following divorce. Yet six-to-eight-year-olds may not be ready for joint-custody arrangements that require them to divide their week between both parents, spending, for example, three days at one parent's home and then four days with the other. The constant physical and emotional upheaval can be confusing and taxing for some children at this age. A better solution would be for the child to reside with one parent but have easy access to the other whenever he desires. Parents who live within walking or biking distance of each other offer the best potential custody arrangement for a six-to-eight-year-old child.

12. Neighbors or friends knowing of children who are alone after school or during the evenings can invite them to their homes or offer to spend time at the children's home. In some cases it might be appropriate to offer to pay for a regular sitter who can supervise the children in the parent's absence.

13. Pre- or postdivorce counseling for all family members is recommended, especially when there are children under the age of eight.

6 Preadolescents (Nine-to-Twelve-Year-Olds)

I think divorce is terrible and that parents shouldn't be able to do it.
—Benjamin, age 10

Preadolescent children are developing in ways that significantly influence the way they respond to divorce. Around the age of nine children begin to develop more mature coping skills. With these they are able to interpret divorce as something that is solely between their parents, something for which they have no responsibility. They are the first age group capable of feeling any twinge of relief at parental divorce, and they can objectively point out ways in which divorce may have actually benefited their parents. They usually do not experience guilt when parents break up, although they are anything but pleased about what Mom and Dad are doing to the family unit.

Nine-to-twelve-year-olds are still very family oriented with a strong sense of family identity. They are scrutinizing parental behavior and values, subjecting them to typical preadolescent black-and-white thinking. Girls in particular are beginning to mature physically. Socially, preadolescents have had time to build a solid base of support outside the family and to develop a string of achievements in various areas that help boost the self-esteem which divorce so easily threatens to undo.

Thus, in many ways it would appear that preadolescents are in a position to weather the storms of divorce successfully. Yet divorce at this stage in a child's development can be traumatic in entirely different ways than it is for younger children.

ANGER

The most characteristic response to divorce at preadolescence is anger. At this age, cries of "It's not fair!" are apt to resound whenever a child believes that someone is not playing by the rules. Divorce calls forth anger because it breaks all the rules about how parents are supposed to behave. Preadolescent black-and-white thinking does not allow exceptions to the rules, and the rules, both biblical and secular, say that you're supposed to stay married to the same person. You're not supposed to get involved with somebody who is not your spouse. You're supposed to set a good example for your children. And if you're a Christian, you're supposed to forgive each other instead of getting a divorce. So nine-to-twelve-year-olds are embarrassed, outraged, and humiliated when parents break the rules that they themselves may have strongly espoused.

Because children view parental breakup this way, and because they feel so completely powerless to stop it, anger easily bubbles up and boils over into the classroom and into relationships with peers and parents. At school their anger may be reflected in the quality of their work and in their behavior. Friends may be alienated just when the child needs them the most. At home many launch a one-man campaign to stop the divorce, becoming angry tyrants who give orders, try to make the custodial parent feel guilty, and try to sabotage parental attempts at dating. This anger is often directed especially toward the noncustodial parent, making visits anything but pleasant. As a result, visits tend to fall off, making the child even angrier.

Wallerstein and Kelly feel that the removal of the father from the home has a lot to do with this angry-dictator kind of response. The father is generally perceived by children to be the parent whose presence governs discipline and impulse control. When he leaves, children may feel a "sense of moral indignation and outrage that the parent who had been correcting their conduct was behaving in what they considered to be an immoral and irresponsible fashion."[1]

Nine-to-twelve-year-olds, while angry, are often extremely embarrassed by divorce and desire to hide what is happening at home. On the outside they can appear cool even when they are seething on the inside. In response to both their anger and embarrassment, these children often lose themselves in a flurry of activity, which may be either constructive or destructive.

Alignments

Because these children tend to cope with their anger through vigorous activity, those who are emotionally vulnerable can sometimes be incited by one parent to turn against the other parent in a way that is hostile or vindictive. This unhealthy parent-child relationship, termed an "alignment" by Wallerstein and Kelly, fits in nicely with a preadolescent's black-and-white thinking. He can easily be persuaded that the parent with whom he is aligned is the good parent and that the one they are against is the bad parent.

While the stated purpose of an alignment is often that of restoring the marriage, in reality its purpose is to inflict misery and retribution on the former spouse. The "good" parent may enlist the child to spy on or harass or humiliate the "bad" one, all the while fueling the child's indignation.

Findings of the Children of Divorce Project strongly suggest that both adults and children who are willing to form alignments are psychologically unstable, greatly distressed, and highly vulnerable in the wake of divorce. It seems that the child whose "emotional tank" is empty is the most likely candidate for an alignment. The opportunity to experience a special closeness with one parent seems to be worth the price of alienating the other one. In addition, the child feels important and excited about engaging in such exhilarating clandestine activities with the permission and blessing of the "good" parent.

When alignments occur between mother and child, the child is usually a son and the woman is his custodial parent. Typically, according to Wallerstein and Kelly, she is a woman who is feeling rage and hostility about being passed over by her husband for a younger, more attractive woman—often after working to support him while he obtained higher education or professional training. She feels that she was used as a stepping stone to his career goals and then cast aside. Alignments between a custodial mother and her son are often the most destructive kind, sometimes enduring for months and even years after the initial separation, probably due to negative reinforcement day by day in the custodial mother's home.

When an alignment occurs between the noncustodial parent and a child, the child is usually a daughter and the parent is the father. Men who formed alignments, as observed in the Children of Divorce Project, felt that their wives had rejected them and their morality often in favor of younger, less morally principled men. These kinds of alignments tend to fade over time, usually dwindling to a halt by the end of the first year of separation. Not surprisingly, during the alignment period the child experiences a very poor relationship with her mother, the custodial parent.

One of the saddest and most unfortunate aspects of an alignment is the damage it can do to the excluded parent, whose self-esteem may be shaky after the divorce. His own child is employed against him as an agent of ill will. Often this parent attempts earnestly to establish a positive postdivorce relationship with the child, but the child is unable to view him apart from the distorted and hostile perspective of the alignment.

Alignments are particularly destructive in their long-term effects on the children. Wallerstein and Kelly noted that within five years after a divorce, almost all alignments had disappeared. However, they discovered that those who had been angry as nine to twelve-year-olds were now even angrier as teenagers. For boys in particular, the preadolescent anger that went unresolved endured to collide head-on with teenage rebellion. This manifested itself in a number of unhealthy behaviors, including theft, drug use, arson, and promiscuity. Some of the teenagers generalized the anger they had felt toward their parents so that it now encompassed all adults or the world as a whole. In contrast, some others were able to confine their anger to the still excluded parent, enabling them to do well in school, make close friends, and otherwise live successfully.

Children who are psychologically stable and able to resist aligning with one parent or the other may nevertheless bear the brunt of parental anger. Brenda, a divorced mother of children aged twelve and sixteen, observed, "My children are angry that they are the victims of their dad's anger and are often used as a buffer or communicator between their dad and me." Jonathan feels that his son and daughter are angry that "for a long time they were 'used' by both parents in what they already seemed to understand was a selfish, vengeful effort to win their affection. They knew we both loved them so much, but they would rather have been somewhere other than in the middle of the conflict."

When parents have not sufficiently reconciled to the point of speaking face to face, children are sometimes employed by both sides to deliver threats, to spy, to report back on the activities over at the enemy camp, and to keep secrets from each parent. An already angry child who is exposed to the anger of each parent is likely to have his own rage intensified. "In a way I hate them both," said one eleven-year-old. "What they've put on me. What they talk to me about."[2] Clearly, like almost everything else about the divorce, the preadolescent feels strongly that this is not fair. Mental health experts identify children caught in a long-term war between two hostile parents as high suicide risks.

LITTLE ADULTS

Nine-to-twelve-year-olds are often hustled into premature adulthood by busy, tired, or depressed single parents. As with the six-to-eight-year-old group, they may be assigned to a multitude of responsibilities, but they are actually capable of much more. They are old enough to competently do laundry, go shopping, care for younger children, or cook meals in the absence of a parent. But as a result, many of them feel older than their years. Children in this age group, especially girls, may be given a disproportionate share of chores, even when there are other children in the household. Said twelve-year-old Kim,

> It's harder on me because there are only two of us to do the housework. If Mom were there all day she could get it done, but she has to come home from work and get it done. My brother, if my mom asks him, will clean up the kitchen, and sometimes my sister will fold the towels, but mostly my mom and I will do it.

Preadolescents may be able to carry an adult's share of the work, but the fact that they are still children shows up in a recurrence of separation anxiety. They worry: what if mom is killed in a car accident while she is out? What will happen if she gets sick? What if she loses her job? Preadolescents are not equipped to face life without the security and provision of a parent, and the prospects of having to do so can be very scary. Those who come home to empty houses, eat supper alone and go to bed in a house that is spooky-quiet can easily become fearful and feel very alone.

Children who see little of their parents not only take care of themselves physically to a large degree, but they also basically learn to guide themselves in making decisions and forming values and goals. Peer advice, the media, and his own best judgment may form the only basis upon which a child can establish his morality, philosophy of life, and personal life goals. The preadolescent child actually wants parental guidance and the security of discipline and boundaries. In short, he wants rules to live by and a parent to model himself after. He also wants to really know both parents—what they think, what they feel, what they believe. And he wants them to know him in the same meaningful way.

But often there is barely time for the single parent to tend to the necessities of life during nonworking hours—grocery shopping, paying bills, taking the car to be repaired, mowing the lawn. Time for serious parent-child discussions about philosophy of life, morality, and spiritual values is next to nonexistent in many households. Where such conversations do take place, parents deliberately carve out time in the family's schedule to tend to their children's character development and emotional and spiritual needs.

In contrast to the parent who is seldom at home, other parents make little adults out of their children by depending on them excessively for emotional reassurance, comfort, and support. The child then feels responsible to take care of that parent and may feel guilty about leaving him or her in pursuit of his own interests. In a sort of role reversal with the parent, he lays aside his age-appropriate activities to tend to his hurting parent. This makes it very hard for a child to achieve one of the developmental tasks of the preadolescent, that of breaking with childhood and surging toward the teen years when the emancipation from parents is completed.

Everything about the child is telling him to become more independent. His social life is picking up, his intellectual horizons are expanding, even his hormones are telling him that childhood is becoming a thing of the past. But emotionally, a child who feels the burden of parenting his parent will have trouble breaking away. He may feel torn and resentful, realizing that he is being called upon to fill a role he was not meant to fill. When adolescence is finally upon him, he may find it impossible to make the necessary break from his overly dependent parent, which will significantly affect his adult years.

THE RECONCILIATION FANTASY

Ben is ten years old and lives in Louisiana; Paul is twelve and lives in Pennsylvania; nine-year-old Tim lives in Florida. I asked each of them to complete the same sentence any way they wanted to. Their answers leave no doubt that the reconciliation fantasy is alive and well at this age.

BEN: If I could, I would "get my mom and dad back together."

PAUL: If I could, I would "make it so Mom and Dad would get back together."

TIM: If I could, I would "get them together again."

Kimberlee, age twelve, knows of an honest-to-goodness real-life reconciliation of the sort that would spark hope in any preadolescent. She related,

A friend of mine up at school, her parents got a divorce, but they found that they couldn't live without each other. He said he didn't love her anymore, but he really did. They got a divorce, but they got back together 'cause they still loved each other.

While children at this age fervently desire a reunited family, they are also able to temper their desires with reality. Paul, for example, admitted realistically that "there is a slim chance that they'll get back together." Ten-year-old Paige said that she would tell other kids to always keep a hopeful attitude because "they might get together or they might not." Her personal outlook is not so bright, however. She explained matter-of-factly that her own dad "can't come back because he's married to a lady."

SEXUAL TENSION

Preadolescent girls are beginning to mature physically. Many fathers, divorced or not, find themselves pulling back from their daughters at this time in a sort of fatherly self-defense. The child is becoming a woman before his very eyes and he is no longer quite sure how to treat her. Daughters need reassurance about their femininity and their lovability during puberty, and Dad's pulling back causes frustration and self-doubt.

One girl I know compensates for her father's inattention by pretending she doesn't care. "Now that he's stayed away," she told me unconvincingly, "I don't miss him at all, not really, anymore. This year I said, 'If he doesn't care, I'm not going to miss him.' Because if that's the way he wants to come through this, then he's going to have to serve the consequences for it. It's not going to hurt me. It's hurting him worse than it is me."

Eleven-and-twelve-year-old girls have an especially strong need to feel approved by their fathers. Dr. Ross Campbell has said that paternal approval is "absolutely essential" if a girl is going to feel *self*-approved in her feminine role.[3] Divorce often takes fathers and daughters even further apart than usual, and the awkwardness that is felt on both sides can be heightened by infrequent contact.

A daughter who feels somewhat distant from her father is apt to feel quite jealous when he begins to date. Seeing Dad with someone other than safe, comfortable Mom illuminates a disturbing fact: Dad is a sexual being. This is something that is normally masked in intact homes and something that most preadolescents would prefer not to think about. The result is often a strong dislike for the woman in Dad's life and sometimes outright hostility. Said one daughter, "When he saw us he would bring his girlfriend along with him. That upset us like crazy. I could not stand it." For this very reason, experts say that the period between a child's ninth and fifteenth birthdays is the worst time for a parent to remarry. The child and a stepparent are likely to be at odds, and sexual jealousy is one of the central factors in the discord.

If a girl knows or suspects that her father is sexually active, the tension between her and her father and between her and his girlfriend can grow even worse. She is apt to lose respect for him, hold his partner in highest disdain, and refuse to visit him when the girlfriend is present or when she will be spending the night.

Having to confront parental sexuality at a time when her own sexual awareness is beginning to blossom can complicate matters for a girl. Not only can she become excessively focused on sex, she may start to seek out a faster, more mature group of friends and perhaps become sexually active herself. She may also begin to view men that her mother dates as fair game, openly flirting with them and competing with her mother for their affection.

Boys at this age do not have the same problems as girls. Most have not yet entered puberty, so their concerns during this time in their lives center mainly on whether parental behavior is moral and ethical. When they conclude that it is not, they can become quite upset and disillusioned. An awareness of sexual activity by either parent, especially before the divorce is final, can be especially distressing.

Wallerstein and Kelly found that practically every nine-or-ten-year-old boy in their study felt completely neglected by his father. This is most unfortunate since a boy at this level of development needs a good relationship with his dad. Fathers are particularly important as role models and disciplinarians. Psychological studies reveal that ten-and-eleven-year-old boys are more prone to aggression and disobedience if their parents are divorced. Good parenting, especially from their fathers, can counteract their tendency to wander into trouble. As always, a civil and workable relationship between parents gives a boy the best chance at a good adjustment to divorce. One reason for this is that boys at this age are especially prone to believe that their mother's anger with their fathers is directed at them as well.

SUGGESTIONS FOR HELPING NINE-TO-TWELVE-YEAR-OLDS

1. Do not draw your child into an alignment against your former spouse no matter how angry you may feel toward him or her and no matter how justified you

believe you are. Seek professional help if your anger is eating at you, but don't feed your child's anger with your own. Children at this age need help in defusing, not fueling, their anger.

Try to verbally build up the image of the other parent before your child, rather than taking potshots. Everyone has good points as well as bad. Don't add to your child's struggle with anger by continually reinforcing how bad your "ex" really is. Your child's self-concept is drawn from two major sources, his mother and his father. *For the sake of your child,* verbally focus on the good things about his other parent and draw positive comparisons. Intelligence, appearance, sense of humor, talent, and athletic ability can all be cited as positive characteristics that the child has inherited from his other parent.

2. Remember that preadolescents are still children, not pint-sized adults. Don't allow them to become overburdened by asking them to support you emotionally beyond their capabilities. Rather than allowing them to parent you, let them be children. Console them in their worries about your welfare. Talking about what would happen if you were killed in an accident or if you were to become ill is an excellent idea. Make provisions in your will for their custody and care, and discuss what kind of finances might be available for their college education, wedding, etc. If these are unresolved issues, take steps that will put them to rest for both you and your children. You may need to consult a lawyer or to confer with your former spouse.

3. Personally teach your child God's standards of morality and discuss the ways these conflict with the standards of our culture. If you feel ill-prepared for this task, enlist the help of a concerned pastor or Sunday school teacher. Ask them to suggest resources. Remember that while others can provide guidance, this is a parental responsibility. It is critical that your words and your conduct are not in conflict. Preadolescents are not only

listening, but also watching. Seek out spiritual guidance for yourself if you are confused about these issues. If the child's other parent is promiscuous, model and teach biblical morality, but do not verbally condemn him or her.

4. The involvement of fathers is still of vital importance. Boys need them as behavioral models, and girls need their affection to feel self-approved. Fathers should not back away from their children during this preadolescent period. They need good fathering more than ever. At least initially, fathers of preadolescent girls should not involve their girlfriends in their visits with the children.

5. Don't use your children as informers regarding your former spouse's lifestyle or activities. Don't use them to carry messages back and forth between parents. Do your own talking and work hard to keep the lines of communication open.

6. Parents who lead especially busy or hectic lives need to take time to be alone with individual children, putting forth special effort to help them feel loved and cared for. Saying, "That's OK, Sue, I'll do the dishes tonight" may help her feel like a twelve-year-old again. Taking her out to dinner or doing something special just for her can be a real boost.

   Make time to talk about the things in life that are really important, such as values and goals, as well as the more mundane happenings of each day. A daily habit of talking things over is best. At the dinner table or before bed each night allow each family member to share two or three things that happened in his life that day, including how he felt about what happened and what he may have learned from it. This simple practice can help extra busy families stay in touch with one another's lives.

7 Teenagers

I wish my mother would understand that it's hard on us kids and not just her.
—Anna, age 17

The teen years mark the beginning of the passage from childhood into adulthood. During the early teens, boys mature physically. Both boys and girls become very socially oriented, with a keen interest in the opposite sex. Each year is different from the last, bringing new challenges and new steps toward independence.

13 At thirteen, the parent-child relationship is often stormy, even when optimum conditions prevail at home. The fledgling adolescent is apt to be moody and tends to guard his privacy. He is contemplating himself, his world, and how he fits into the social pecking order of his peer group.

14 Fourteen is a sociable year. Boys spend time with boys, girls with girls, much of it on the phone. The opinions of friends are very important, since teens' evaluations of themselves are largely based on these. Sexual awareness blooms. Patterns of behavior and morality formed at fourteen may be around for a long time to come.

15 Fifteen can be a year of turmoil. There may be an identity crisis in process. Again, there is moodiness and possibly criticism and rejection aimed at adults.

Thoughts turn to the future, sex, religion, and other important topics.

16 Sixteen is generally a year of equilibrium and self-confidence. People this age are outgoing and happy to be with friends. Emotionally they are maturing and stabilizing.

17 On the brink of adulthood, the seventeen-year-old begins the important break from parents and home. His concerns for the future are serious and important. His basic approach to life has already been settled, and much of his future will hinge on the decisions he will make this year.[1]

When the slow process of emancipation and maturation is finally drawing to a close, both parent and child breathe a sigh of relief. The teen years are often stormy and tumultuous, and never easy. While the teenager has more outside support, more personal maturity, and far more outlets for his tension and anxiety than a younger child, divorce—whether it occurred last week or long ago—makes the teen years all the more complex.

IDENTITY

One reason for this complexity has to do with the teenager's quest to secure his personal identity. He needs to know who he is and what his heritage is, religious, social, genetic, and otherwise. Both parents and their backgrounds are probed for clues that might help him answer the "Who am I?" question. A recent divorce forces him to make adjustments to his own longstanding identity and his sense of family identity. If he identified closely with his same-sex parent, divorce may challenge his self-image. It also causes him to reinterpret his understanding of commitment and relationships. The fact that parents who used to love each other no longer do implies that even the most well-intentioned commitments aren't necessarily forever. Moreover, the very people he thought he could always count on to be the same have now changed dramatically in their relationship with each other. He wonders if he is destined to reenact his parents' divorce one day.

A divorce that took place in years past is now significant in ways that mattered little before. As he looks back at his childhood with nostalgia, a teenager may suddenly feel angry and view his life as abnormal because his childhood memories do not include the kind of happy times with both parents that he would have liked. He may feel that he missed out on something he should rightfully have had; he may be upset that his parents did not try harder to resolve their differences.

A teenager whose noncustodial parent walked out of his life when he walked out of the marriage may feel an almost instinctive urge to locate that parent, much as an adoptive child searches for his biological parents. Feelings of rejection may resurface. Some children attempt to emulate the absent parent's characteristics, basing their adaptations on memory or speculation. Of course, the more years that have passed since parent and child have been in touch, the less correct the child's perceptions are likely to be.

Whether a teenager's parents divorced recently or many years ago, he may scour old photo albums, scrapbooks. and yearbooks, asking questions designed to provide evidence that his parents' love was once real and that he was loved and wanted by them both. Wise parents will furnish proof and assurances that this was indeed the case. Some unthinkingly have instead provided the teenager with the awful knowledge that their marriage was forced by an unwanted pregnancy—him—and doomed from the start. Even when this is the truth, a parent can still comfort the child with the basic assurance he is looking for, using kindness, love, and a careful choice of words. A refusal to temper the brutal truth, perhaps out of the parent's own lingering resentment, can leave a teenager feeling responsible for his parents' unhappiness and apologetic about his very existence.

Parents are sometimes mystified when a teenager begins to dig through the ruins of the marriage. Many make no connection between what happened in the family years ago and what is now taking place in the child's life. Equally baffling are the changes in behavior that may occur at the same time. Christian counselor David Martin said that teenagers are

> starting to develop their own concept of who they are and what they are, and if they have to handle mother and father divorcing, I think what you have is another added problem. Some teenagers that I've dealt with have handled it very well. But in other instances I can see dropping grades and a loss of motivation, a rebellious attitude. And the parents seem to have no concept of why their children are doing this. This may be three or four years after the divorce and all of a sudden now, they're starting to be like this. They come in to me and say, "Why is my son, why is my daughter like this?" It's because now they've put the pieces together. Now they're finding out: "It wasn't all mom's fault or all dad's fault and somewhere in the picture I've got to find out where I am as a person." And that's rough! It's hard enough trying to change gears from childhood to adulthood with a growing healthy family, let alone having to deal with a malfunctioning one.

SECURITY

Sixteen-year-old Angela said, "I think divorce is good for people that can't communicate and live a normal life. I'm happy that my parents are divorced rather than living with the stress and resentment." Jennifer, age seventeen, said, "Divorce is not right, but sometimes necessary." Even though many teenagers like Angela and Jennifer are more likely than younger children to view divorce as a reasonable solution to serious marital problems, many also feel strongly that their parents are selfish for pursuing divorce at this stage in the teenager's life. Why not wait just another few years, until the child is out on his own? Why add more complication to his life at a time when it is already more complex than he ever dreamed it would become?

One of the most significant ways that divorce complicates a teenager's life is by knocking out the supports of home at a time when he needs them critically. Teens normally progress toward adulthood by taking two steps forward into the unknown and sometimes frightening world of growing up, then one step back toward the safety and security of home and parents. With the knowledge that home and family are always there if he needs them, a teenager edges his way little by little toward his destination: independence. Divorce throws a roadblock in the way of emancipation by crumbling the security of home and forcing the child to plunge into the real world all at once.

Wallerstein and Kelly state flatly, "The toppling of the family structure at this time burdens . . . normal developmental processes and threatens to derail them. The adolescents who came to us felt that the change in the family had limited or entirely removed the family as a safe base for refueling."[2]

The teenager of divorcing parents suddenly finds that he is more on his own than he would like to be. But there is nothing he can do about it. Mom and Dad are more wrapped up in their emancipation from each other than in his emancipation from them. The bewildering emotions and concerns of the adolescent must take a back seat to the family's turmoil. The teenager no longer sees his parent as someone to whom he can turn. Ready or not, he is on his own. But teenagers are not usually ready for instant independence.

They're not ready, either, to go from the status of child within the family structure to the role of adviser and confidant overnight. While many teens no longer feel that they can go to their parents with problems and questions, some find that their parents are now coming to them with their very adult divorce-related concerns. Most teenagers are naturally flattered to be consulted on such matters; the sense of being needed is gratifying. Yet teenagers are rarely equipped for this role reversal. Added to their own adolescent struggles, the concerns of a divorcing parent may overburden them to the point of despair.

Teenagers often feel a conflicting sense of loyalty to both parents. They feel duty-bound to be what each parent wants and needs them to be. This task used to be easier. When parents were a unit instead of two distinct people, it wasn't as hard to know how to please them. They expected certain things and had certain requirements. They felt certain ways about things, went certain places, did certain things. Divorce breaks that dependable and somewhat predictable unit into separate entities in separate households, often with differing sets of standards, rules, and requests with which the child must comply or fall into disfavor.

Some teenagers bend over backward to please both, even to their own hurt. Sixteen-year-old Bob told me that "trying to live up to both their standards and expectations" was one of the hardest things about the divorce. Some, like seventeen-year-old Jennifer, have decided which parent has which rights. Her father hasn't been able to get the picture though. She said, "I wish my father would understand that since he doesn't live with us any more he has given up some of the rights a parent has—like making rules." Other teens give up completely on the task of trying to obey and please two parents, figuring that if they are as on their own as they seem to be, parental wishes and demands simply don't matter much anymore. No matter where they fall on the parental loyalty spectrum, divorce can cause teenagers to feel insecure and very much outside the nest they have been accustomed to living in.

ANGER AND GRIEF

Anger and grief go hand in hand, as we have seen. Teenagers of divorced parents are likely to experience both. The feeling of having been pushed out of the nest before they were ready to go often calls forth anger. They may deeply resent the fact that their parents' needs have upstaged their own and left them feeling alone and unable to rely on their families. Moreover, the inability to do anything to put the family back together brings anger and frustration.

In her book *Which Way Is Home?* Leslie Williams describes her feelings of anger as a college student whose parents divorced. She writes,

> This volcano of anger! Where does it come from? This is shocking. I didn't know I had so much hostility inside me. Now that I start thinking about it, I realize I am mad because our family has broken up. I am angry because our parents couldn't work out their problems, angry because I am unhappy and miserable on account of something that isn't my fault. I am just mad as hell. . . . The nights are still bad. I'm still having bad dreams, and I wake up sometimes with my fists clenched and my heart pounding. I simply do not know how to handle this anger, this unfocused stream of emotion. How do you handle being angry at a 'situation'? You can't talk to a situation or hit it, or get back at it, or change it in any way.[3]

Angry teenagers can sometimes be pulled into an alignment with one parent against the other. But unlike the alignments that preadolescent children may form, parent-teen alignments do not usually have staying power. Most dissolve rapidly. Perhaps this is due to an older child's ability to see virtues as well as flaws in both parents. Or perhaps it is because teenagers more often want to please both parents and are unable to deliberately alienate one and give preference to the other without causing internal conflict. A teenager under pressure from one parent to turn against the other is likely to resolve the dilemma by backing away from both parents, allowing the anger on all sides to cool.

Backing away is a common response by many teenagers and one that Wallerstein and Kelly discovered is not without purpose. In their study, both teens who had been close to their families before the separation and those who had been emotionally distant were observed to pull back from the conflict at home. For those who had already been distant, the divorce served to push them into total independence. Those who had been close were initially a source of concern for researchers: would this experience make them self-centered and uncaring about others? One year later, they were pleased to learn that this had been a strategic withdrawal. They reported,

> Creating distance from the parents at the height of the struggle saved these youngsters from overwhelming anguish, humiliation and emotional depletion, and enabled them at a later date . . . to be supportive, empathic and sensitive to needy parents. Thus their withdrawal served to maintain the integrity of their development.[4]

The sources of teenage anger in a divorce situation are as varied as the households from which teenagers come. Jennifer, age seventeen, is angry that she cannot relax and be herself around either parent. She says she always has to "be careful what I say to one or the other of them because if there's a problem, my dad blames it on my mom or vice versa."

Brett, fifteen, says that his father's noninvolvement with him and his sisters makes him angry. He said, "It hurts—we haven't seen him for two years. I've played the guitar for five years and he's never heard me play. And he hasn't called us for our birthdays or Christmas, sent us a card or anything!"

Angela, who is sixteen, is upset that her father "expects me to communicate to Mom for him."

Fifteen-year-old Sarah's anger stems mostly, she says, from "what my father's done to himself and how blind he's acting. Sometimes I think he acts like a two-year-old. I just can't figure him out and it sort of makes me mad." She is especially angry that her father lied about the affair he was having. He is now married to his girlfriend, who is expecting his child. The sight of her bulging tummy, says Sarah, "just makes me mad."

The sensation of suddenly losing one's childhood—often against one's wishes—can trigger not only anger but also deep grief. When divorce forces a child to grow up in many ways almost overnight, he may simultaneously mourn the death of his childhood along with the death of his family. The selling of the family home, with its cargo of memories—birthday parties, Christmas Eves, measles, braces, puppies, skinned knees—may symbolize that what once was no longer is. The page from childhood to adulthood has been turned. Grief is not an uncommon response.

Bad dreams, difficulty in concentrating, depression, feelings of emptiness, and chronic fatigue may indicate that the teenager is in the midst of the grieving process. Teenagers may not recognize that the depth of their emotional response is basically grief. They may just know that they are miserable, angry, and feeling sorrow and loss.

SEXUALITY

Most teenagers are vitally concerned about their ability to relate well to the opposite sex. Sex itself is also a monumental concern, occupying much of their thought life. Divorce frequently heightens a teenager's preoccupation and anxiety about both sex and dating.

One of the first surprises many teenagers have after their parents divorce is the sudden seeming youthfulness of their heretofore outdated parents. Mom and Dad may begin to wear the same kind of clothing that the teenager wears and may choose younger hairstyles or develop a new proficiency in teen jargon. In the starting-over mentality that often follows divorce, a parent may be grappling with the same issues as the teenager: "Who am I? What is my purpose in life? What are my standards for relating to the opposite sex? Is sex outside marriage OK? What occupation should I pursue?" Instead of having stable, reliable parents whom he had hoped could guide him through these same issues, many a teenager finds that he has parents who are asking the same questions that he is asking while leaning on him and competing with him on his turf.

In the lonely and confusing aftermath of divorce, many adults seek out sexual encounters, particularly during the second year of their new life. Some, of course, are sexually involved even before the marriage ends. When either parent is sexually active, teenagers are bound to be aware of it. When youth-conscious parents choose partners who are perilously close to the age of a teenage son or daughter, the child may feel extremely uncomfortable. Seeing Mom or Dad with someone who is a part of his generation rather than the parent's may induce sexual fantasies about the parent, making it most distressing to be in his company. Some may cope by seeking to avoid the parent altogether.

The younger the teenager, the more apt he is to become extremely upset by the knowledge that a parent is engaging in sex outside of marriage. Some feel almost betrayed, responding with disgust and embarrassment. Others use the stumbling block of parental immorality to rationalize sexual involvements of their own.

Studies have shown that teenagers from divorced homes are more likely than other teenagers to become sexually active, to have more partners, and to begin their sexual encounters at an earlier age. Some are perhaps just seeking warmth and physical comfort as a diversion from the problems at home. Others may be subconsciously trying to start a family of their own to replace the one that has fallen apart. Girls may unwittingly continue the search for the love of a father who has long since chosen not to be an affectionate and involved part of their lives.

In a study conducted with teenage girls who regularly attended a particular community center, Mavis Hetherington compared girls whose fathers were absent from their lives due to death or divorce with those whose fathers lived at home. She found that girls whose fathers were absent interacted in a different way with men and male peers than the other girls did. There was a difference between those who were daughters of widows and those who were daughters of divorcees, however. Reporting Hetherington's research, Henry Biller writes,

> The daughters of divorcees tended to be aggressive and forward with males whereas the daughters of widows tended to be extremely shy and timid in interacting with males. . . . Daughters of divorcees sought more attention from men and tried to be near and have physical contacts

> with male peers. The daughters of widows, however, avoided male areas and preferred to be with females.... The daughters of widows sat as far away from male interviewers as possible, whereas the daughters of divorcees tended to sit as close as possible. (The girls from intact families generally sat at an intermediate distance.)[5]

Hetherington found that the girls who had the most difficulty in relating properly to boys and men were those whose fathers had been absent from their lives before they were five years old.

While divorce may cause some girls to be more forward in their dealings with boys, it may cause some boys to be almost the opposite. In a sort of revival of his preschool oedipal attachment to his mother, sometimes an adolescent boy in the custody of his mother begins to focus more on her than he does on girls his age. This teenager gladly steps into the role of his absent father, screening her phone calls, escorting her when she goes out, becoming jealous of her other friendships, and comforting her when she is depressed or upset. Lonely single mothers are most likely to encourage this behavior, thankful that their sons, unlike their ex-husbands, want to take such good care of them. Wise mothers, however, will encourage their sons to become more socially active and to concentrate on girls their own age, recognizing that while the boy's intentions are good, neither mother nor son will really benefit from such an arrangement in the long run.

In the shadow of their parents' failed marriages many teenagers come to expect failure in their own relationships with the opposite sex. Many of the teenagers in the Children of Divorce Project took it for granted that they would fail both as marriage partners and as sex partners. The researchers in this study described the outlook of these teens as an "unquestioning acceptance" of the fact that these failures would characterize their lives.

Almost as if meeting a self-fulfilling prophecy, many teenagers of divorced homes find that they are unable to maintain long-term dating relationships. Some, out of a fear of losing yet another person whom they care for, become overly possessive, demanding far too much loyalty and suffocating the relationship. Others find that long-term relationships make them uneasy, so they move from one relationship to another, preferring to end a friendship rather than resolve a conflict.

LEAVING THE NEST

Divorce frequently helps a teenager become more deliberate and thoughtful about the choices he or she makes. In one study, a third of the teens observed were thought to have been stimulated to greater emotional and intellectual maturity as a result of seeing their parents divorce. They became more responsible and dependable and were able to make better decisions. They began to ponder seriously their own futures, giving consideration to what had gone wrong in their parents' lives and what might have been done to avoid the breakup.

Divorce has few positive aspects, but the maturity and wisdom it brings to some teenagers are certainly beneficial. Those who are able to learn from their parents' experiences are likely to view marriage as a serious undertaking and to think about the qualities that build good, workable relationships. Financial responsibility, morality, career choices, and other important concerns are likely to be given careful thought by the teenager for whom divorce has served as a tutor.

Yet, divorce does not always inspire maturity. Some teenagers, in the face of anger, grief and the worries of facing adulthood so soon, allow immaturity to rise up in protest. Without their family supports intact, some are incapable of making the kind of wise and well-thought-out decisions that would benefit them most. Some turn to alcohol, drugs, or promiscuity for escape and solace. Some drop out of high school; twice as many dropouts come from divorced homes as from intact homes.

Boys in particular may become overly aggressive without a solid father-son relationship to temper their behavior. Some, perhaps because of parental sexual activity, become sophisticated beyond their years. Others may do exactly the opposite and regress in their behavior, pursuing relationships with younger, more childish companions. A regressive teenager may even return to doll play or become childishly attached to the custodial parent, preferring his or her company over the company of friends. Regression is usually of short duration, but emotionally needy parents can complicate matters if they encourage teens to stay at home with them instead of getting involved in age-appropriate activities. The discovery of a parent's extramarital sexual activity can sometimes trigger severe regression, according to Wallerstein and Kelly.

As a teenager gets closer and closer to the time when he or she will actually leave for college, move away from home to take a job, or marry, many internal struggles may ensue. Guilt about leaving the custodial parent may rise up accusingly: "She needs you—how can you leave her?" The parent may add to this guilt by implying that he or she cannot make it without the teenager or that alimony may be cut off if he leaves. Concerns about how the parent really will get along without his daily presence may loom large in his mind. Worries about how college expenses will be met may burden both parent and child.

There may be a real difference, too, in the way the teenager, the noncustodial parent, and the custodial parent think the teenager should be educated. One parent may feel that the child should attend a prominent four-year college; the other may feel that he belongs in the local community college so that he can live at home. The teenager may have strong preferences one way or the other, but often this dispute is settled practically—the parent paying the bills has the final say-so. A boy who was all but ignored by his father as he was growing up may now find that Dad not only suddenly wants a relationship with him, but that he has his own ego wrapped up in what the boy accomplishes academically, athletically, and vocationally. Boys may understandably have mixed emotions at this time.

Once the teenager enrolls in college, every semester

break and summer vacation presents the same problem: how to divide his time between both parents in a way that will make them both happy. The problem is intensified if parents live geographically distant from each other. How can he hold a job in the summer and still get to see them both? What if he wants to spend his semester break on a hiking trip with friends? Many teenagers feel obligated to spend their vacations, not as they would like, but rather bouncing between parental homes. When both parents want him to spend the same block of time with them and refuse to compromise, the teenager may decide to do something entirely apart from either to avoid having to choose between them.

Most of the teenagers who shared their personal divorce experiences with me had coped fairly well. Even though they are still hurt, angry, and grieving in some regards, they are also able to see ways in which divorce has contributed to their emotional and spiritual maturity. Most see the need to proceed with great caution toward future marriage, harboring apprehension about their chances for a successful and lasting relationship. They are painfully aware that the odds for any marriage are not especially encouraging today, but having observed their parents' mistakes, they want desperately to succeed. Here are some of their comments:

JENNIFER: It scares me when I think that one out of two couples gets divorced. For me as a Christian, divorce is not an option. However, it will be difficult for me, because of my parents' divorce, to try and remember that divorce is not an option. I am afraid that when my husband and I have a fight I will think that the only solution is divorce. This feeling comes from seeing my father get married and divorced three times.

BRETT: Divorce is definitely wrong. When you get married, you commit. You say you'll stay together for the rest of your life when you take the vows. Plus all that it says in the Bible. I don't know if I'm really scared of being married, but it could happen to me too. But if I have kids,

ANNA:	I don't want my kids to go through what I'm going through. I'd try everything not to let it happen. 'Cause it's not fun.
ANNA:	I worry about the future. It really scares me. It scares me when I think about my marriage and whether it'll be a success. When I get married someday, I will make sure that our love is true and pure and make sure it will last forever.
ANGELA:	Someday I plan to get married and use my parents' marriage as a guideline so my marriage will turn out to be happy and fulfilling. I will be sure that there is good communication in my family.
BOB:	Someday in the near future I'll get very close to a girl. When I get married I will have a good *loving relationship*.
SARAH:	I pray about my marriage now. It's something I didn't do before. But I pray about it now—that God will give me the right person to live with and spend the rest of my life with.
CAROL:	I think divorce is the most emotionally painful situation a child can go through. I will never put my kids through a divorce if I can help it. When I get married someday I want it to be the perfect marriage—full of love, honesty, and trust.

As they begin to contemplate marriage, many older teens would be happy to see their parents remarry. Unlike younger children, they are concerned about how their parents will cope financially in the future and how they will handle the loneliness of growing old without a spouse. They may even contemplate the role they themselves will play in years to come in caring for their parents. To many, a stepparent represents companionship and a source of both emotional and economic help for the parents, and many are eager for Mom or Dad to find another spouse. Said seventeen-year-old Angela, "My mother needs to understand that there is nothing wrong with building another relationship and starting life over." Like most teenagers, Angela would like to put the divorce experience behind her and get on with life. She'd like her parents to do the same.

SUGGESTIONS FOR HELPING TEENAGERS

1. Teenagers need reassurance that their parents at one time did love and care for each other and that the child of their union was wanted and loved by both of them. Photographs depicting the child with both parents are tangible evidence that this was so. These keepsakes can help the teenager build confidence that his future holds the promise of a happy marriage and family. When circumstances surrounding the parents' marriage were less than optimal, such as a wedding forced by pregnancy, tell the child the truth, but temper it with tact and discretion, perhaps focusing on the single parent's love for him and God's purposes for his life.

2. Parents of teens should work hard to be around during this final phase of childhood, realizing the importance of home and family at this time in their lives. Lines of communication should be kept open, but the parents should refrain from pouring out their own problems and frustrations to the teens. Adults need to find other adults in whom they can confide. Teenagers, however, should be encouraged to talk their concerns over with the parents or with other concerned adults. As with younger children, listening in an accepting and nonjudgmental way is one of the most important means of support an adult can give a teenager.

3. Parents should try to change as little as possible following divorce in an effort to help teenagers feel more secure. Moving out of the family home, changing churches, beginning to date, and even redecorating the house should be approached slowly so the teenagers are not confronted with too many changes at one time. Involving the teens in the decisions surrounding these choices will help them understand the reasons why the changes are necessary.

4. Spending time with happily married couples can give teenagers positive examples and hope for their future

marriages. Couples can encourage teenagers from divorced homes by inviting them to dinner with or without a parent, or to an outing. If a teenager is comfortable enough to open up and share some of his concerns and frustrations, the couple can meet his needs by listening, sympathizing, and supporting him. Praying for him and with him and encouraging him to turn his worries over to Christ can help him realize that his "help comes from the Lord, who made heaven and earth" (Psalm 121:2). Letting him know that his door is always open whenever he would like to talk can be a tremendous encouragement, especially if he feels unable to count on support at home.

5. Phone calls to say "we're thinking about you," cards, notes of encouragement, and other gestures of friendship can boost teenagers in the midst of parental divorce. Words of praise for accomplishments of any sort or for no reason at all can inspire self-confidence.

PART THREE

TELL ME WHERE IT HURTS

8 Mirror, Mirror: Divorce and Self-Esteem

It was really bad for a while because I was always down. Always! I can't remember being happy at all. No, I don't remember being happy in the last two years.

—Sarah, age 15

Society teaches us to measure our worth basically in three ways: What we look like, what we achieve, and what we possess. Early in life children absorb the notion that physical beauty, making touchdowns or straight A's, and accumulating wealth are the things that really matter. As a result, their sense of personal worth revolves around things over which they have little control—their appearance, their talents and abilities, and the financial posture of their parents. These criteria for measuring self-worth are not only unfair, but unbiblical.

God's primary concern lies not in how we look or in what we possess or achieve, but in who we are on the inside. First Samuel 16:7 says, "God sees not as man sees, for man looks at the outward appearance, but the LORD looks at the heart." Furthermore, every person is of such value in the sight of God that the very hairs on his head are numbered (Matthew 10:30). Christ's death on the cross is the final, irrefutable proof of the significance with which God regards each of us. But even those who wholeheartedly embrace these truths may still struggle with self-esteem. Why?

The ability or inability to esteem ourselves as God does may be related to our very earliest experiences in life. The roots of healthy self-esteem can be traced to the first three years of life. These are the years during which a child's general outlook on life is formed: he learns trust and self-confidence and forms a basic concept of himself. According to Dr. Craig W. Ellison, early parent-child interaction takes place "at the point of greatest language inability. It is therefore received emotionally and in simplified form. The child reads evaluations in 'all or none' terms. . . . The result is that we feel fundamentally good or bad about ourselves according to that early parental input."[1]

Until about the age of fifteen, children are basically behaviorally oriented rather than verbally oriented like adults. This means that they perceive love more in terms of what a parent does than of what he says. Dr. Ross Campbell has suggested that many children do not feel valued by their parents because of this basic difference between adults and children. Parents may verbally affirm that they love their children, but if they do not spend time with them, play with them, make positive eye contact with them, and exercise loving discipline, children may not feel that they are loved; therefore they are more likely to have lower self-esteem.[2]

Children from either intact and divorced homes may suffer feelings of low self-esteem. In their Loneliness Research Project, however, psychologists Phillip Shaver and Carin Rubenstein discovered that children of divorce often have lower self-esteem than other children. They also found that the younger the child was at the time of the divorce, the lower his self-esteem was as an adult, and the lonelier he was apt to be.[3] Similarly, Wallerstein and Kelly found that the three-and-four-year-olds in their study were especially prone to feelings of low self-esteem.

MIRRORS

Many factors can contribute to a child's loss of self-esteem after divorce. First, when a parent physically leaves the home, a child loses one of the two people who provided him with a constant mirror of himself, his ideas, and his behavior. Opportunities for evaluating himself through that parent's eyes are dramatically reduced once he leaves the household. In addition, the remaining parent is now busier and probably more stressed and anxious than before, so the child's other constant mirror is also somewhat changed on account of divorce.

Much of what we believe about ourselves is born as we comprehend what others think about us, and this is particularly true as a child pieces together verbal and nonverbal cues from his parents. A missing parent cannot give feedback or opinion. He is not there to ask a question or give a hug. He cannot provide a buffer for the harsh words or unkindnesses the child may have encountered outside the home that day. A super-busy custodial parent may not have time to listen. Thus many of the child's day-to-day mistakes, failures, and discouragements may have to be interpreted by the child alone, apart from the maturity and objectivity of concerned adults. In this way he may gain false notions about who he really is and what abilities he has.

Feelings of being rejected or abandoned by a parent are hardly boosts to self-esteem. A child who perceives the divorce not as something between mother and father but as something between one parent and the rest of the family will undoubtedly experience great emotional pain.

If the parent who leaves the home fails to maintain contact with him, the child may see this as proof of being rejected. Since a parent—who is *supposed* to love you!—has expressed what the child interprets as rejection, feeling confident and secure with other people becomes more difficult. Sporadic visitation or planned visitations that are not kept can multiply self-doubt too.

Adopted children may especially struggle with feelings of rejection. Kids who have always secretly wondered why their biological parents gave them up for adoption may now experience the awful sensation that history is repeating itself. Now it seems that one or both of his *adoptive* parents aren't sure they want him either. One adopted teenager shared with me what she believes to be the primary reason for her parents' divorce: "Basically, my father wanted a child of his own, of his own flesh and blood, and he didn't want adopted children. He felt that only a child could give him something he didn't have. So he went off and had an affair with this lady. She became pregnant. After a year of separation my parents divorced."

Psychologists tell us that the closer we come to our ideals about how we feel we ought to be or really want to be, the greater our self-esteem. This is why Christian children of divorce may have an especially rough time with self-esteem. They know what the Bible says about divorce. They also know how people in their churches feel about what their parents are doing. And they themselves probably do not want their parents to divorce. Thus, divorcing parents fall far short of the child's ideals. He may have been from a "good Christian family" last year, but now he and his family are a "bad example." He used to feel loved and accepted by people at his church, but now he may feel shunned and avoided, or regarded with suspicion, embarrassment, or pity. The reflections he now sees mirrored in the eyes of those outside his home have been changed by divorce.

One fifteen-year-old said, "I just don't like being isolated, especially when you know something like a divorce is happening. Acting like we're freaks or we're weird, that we're different now and not normal—I don't like people doing that to me. They just don't know how to handle it. They're scared, I think."

Carol, whose parents have been divorced for nine years, said, "I wish people wouldn't be so shocked when I tell them about my family but would just accept it."

According to Christian psychologist Archibald Hart, it is not so much the divorce itself that damages self-esteem as the way people begin to treat children on account of it.[4] On all sides children are confronting frustration for something that is not their fault: parents who are changing, fellow believers who do not comfort but perhaps look down their noses at them, a legal system that is insensitive to their desires and needs, and teachers and friends who do not understand. When others do not seem to value them or support them during divorce, children may begin to devalue themselves. Said my fifteen-year-old friend, "I think I'm more open than some people are, but I know some kids who won't admit they need anything. But deep down inside they do need support from other people. And whether they admit it or not I think nine out of ten times they really welcome it."

The financial hardship that often accompanies divorce is a major cause for lowered self-esteem. A child who always viewed himself as well off or middle class may suddenly see himself as poor. Even when basic needs for food, clothing, and shelter are met, he may feel impoverished compared with the way life used to be, or compared with the way those around him live. Self-esteem is lowered because of the cultural weight put on possessions and economic strength. "The hardest part about having divorced parents," said one thirteen-year-old, "is facing rich friends."

A child's desire to achieve scholastically or athletically may be temporarily lowered due to depression. This removes some of the achievements that he could have pointed to as successes, full of potential for raising self-esteem. He may withdraw socially, cutting off friends as a source of positive input.

In addition, spontaneous expressions of love from parents are apt to be fewer during the critical months surrounding divorce. Hugs, smiles, expressions of affection and appreciation, and other kinds of nurturing from parents play a part in the child's self-esteem. These kindnesses, given for no reason other than the fact that the child is loved—what psychologists call "non-contingent reinforcement"—may virtually dry up while parents cope with their own crisis. Family may thus be temporarily removed as a source for bolstering self-esteem.

IDENTITY AND SELF-ESTEEM

Closely linked to self-esteem is the concept of identity. "Who am I?" is one of the most important questions a child must answer. The way he responds to that question is closely linked to his sense of family. Divorce can alter a family's identity in significant and lasting ways.

Benjamin, a fifth grader, described what he feels happened when his parents got divorced: "It was like our family blew up and three people went one way and one went the other. Our family was destroyed by the divorce." Sixteen-year-old Angela recalled, "I remember how empty I felt inside and how I hated my dad for taking my brother away from me. I cry when I remember the day my dad and brother left, how I felt a part of me was taken away when my brother was gone."

There may be an identity crisis even when divorce occurs after a child is grown. Bruce Yoder was finishing college when his parents divorced. He asked, "Had I come from a happy family or not? I used to think so. So too did everyone who knew me as I was growing up. But if the family was happy, why was there a divorce to contend with? What was real?"[5]

Twenty-nine-year-old Terry feels that his parents' divorce, which happened sixteen years ago, still greatly affects his family's identity. He said, "My family to this day is still divided and lacks the closeness of a normal family. We are scattered and seldom see each other. I miss family life and, most of all, no family get-togethers, big dinners, Christmas." Newly married, Terry has a dream "to have the family I never had."

Divorce can do some rather awkward things to one's identity. To illustrate, let's consider a hypothetical little girl named Molly Jones. Let's say that Molly's parents get divorced. Her mother then marries another man, John Stone. Molly will still be Molly Jones even though her mother is now Mrs. Stone. If Mr. Stone adopts Molly, she would become Molly Stone. Let's assume that Molly's mother and Mr. Stone then get a divorce. Molly's mother gets custody of Molly and goes into a third marriage to Mr. Jeffries. Mr. Jeffries does not adopt Molly. If this marriage lasts and Mr. and Mrs. Jeffries have children, Molly will have a different last name than everyone else in her family, a name that belongs to someone not even biologically related to her.

Look at the adjustments Molly will have made. First, she will have been party to two divorces. In essence, she will have had three fathers: her biological father, her adopted father, and her new stepfather. She will have had to adjust her identity three times, first being Molly Jones, then Molly Stone, and finally an outsider named Stone in a family named Jeffries.

A child of divorce may also struggle with identity when he or she becomes part of a reconstituted family, when a mother and her children and a father and his children join in marriage to form a new family. Kids like Molly who were happy with their status as an only child or firstborn may suddenly be bumped down in rank to middle child or baby.

Several of the children who made up my panel for this book were obviously lacking self-esteem. Candace, a vivacious eight-year-old, admitted, "I feel a little ugly." She also said she felt "icky." Ben, who is ten, saw himself in an unfavorable social position. He said, "Everybody teases you about only having one parent and your feelings get hurt much easier." He complained, "I feel left out with only one parent." Kimberlee, twelve, felt that her popularity was linked to her family's meager finances: "If rich people knew what it was like, they would like me." Eighteen-year-old Carol explained, "I am a very touchy and hypersensitive person, and I think the divorce had a lot to do with it. I cry a lot."

Many of the children continued to evaluate their worthiness in terms of their noncustodial parent's attention or inattention. Anna, seventeen, said, "I feel so unhappy when Dad forgets to call, birthdays, holidays."

Jennifer, also seventeen, was defensive about being stereotyped as a "child of divorce." She asserted, "Children of divorced parents are *normal!* We once had a guest speaker at our church who told everyone that the children of divorced parents are insecure and usually turn out to be very rebellious. To all the people that think that, I would like to say that most of us turn out fine. There are probably just as many rebellious teens from two-parent families as there are from one-parent families."

Sarah, whose comment begins this chapter, feels that she has now finally come full circle regarding her self-esteem. Though her parents' divorce initially burdened her self-esteem, it ultimately stimulated growth. "I used to have a very low self-image," she said, "and through the divorce and through a lot of prayer and support from other people, I've finally reached the point where I have a good self-image. I've found a lot of people that are supportive of me: they're my age too. And maybe that helped. I just know God must really have worked."

SUGGESTIONS FOR BUILDING A CHILD'S SELF-ESTEEM

1. Emphasize character qualities rather than appearance and possessions. Memorizing and discussing Proverbs and other Bible verses is an excellent way to accomplish this.
2. Help each child find his or her special talent or ability, and do everything you can to encourage its development. Do not demand excellence in areas where the child's talents and gifts do not lie. Instead, build him up and cheer him on in whatever he does well, even if you are not especially interested in his specialty. For example, fathers who would rather see their sons become Little League stars than pianists need to work hard at developing genuine appreciation for the child's musical ability.
3. Give love and approval *unconditionally*. Don't allow the child to feel that if his grades were better, or if he had made the team or if he were better looking or if he were

Mirror, Mirror: Divorce and Self-Esteem

a she, you would love him more. Let him know that he is a unique, special, and precious person to you, and he will start to view himself that way.

4. Proverbs 18:21 says, "Death and life are in the power of the tongue." Build your child up; don't tear him down with your words. Name-calling and ridicule from a parent stings more than it would from anyone else. Conversely, sincere compliments and kind words can make a child's whole day.

5. Keep in mind that even through the early teens children read actions louder than words. First John 3:18 tells us how to let them know that they are loved: "Our love should not be just words and talk; it must be true love, which shows itself in action" (*Good News Bible*). This means spending quality time with the child, talking, and listening to his stories, questions, and concerns. It means getting to know him, enjoying him, and loving him enough to exercise discipline.

Physical touch is also important. Rocking a child to sleep, spontaneous hugs, "gimme five," arm wrestling, piggyback rides, reading to him on your lap, or putting an arm around his shoulder are all expressions appropriate to different ages, but the willingness to maintain physical touch says, "I love you" at any age. Eye contact is also important since we learn not to trust those who will not make positive eye contact with us. Your example can teach him this valuable social skill.

9 The Grandparent Connection

What most people don't understand about divorce is that it doesn't just affect children and parents, but grandparents, friends, neighbors, relatives, etc.

—Bob, age 16

Grandparents are very special people. Children enjoy a unique kind of relationship with grandparents, an immunity of sorts in which they do not have to please or perform in quite the same way that they do for their parents. Grandparents for their part enjoy their status as seasoned child-care experts but with the added pleasure of not having to take full responsibility. In a sense they can enjoy their grandchildren and then return them to the parents in time to prevent an overdose.

The grandparent-grandchild relationship is often a mutually beneficial, warm, and positive experience. Youngsters benefit from Grandma and Grandpa's wisdom and experience, and the grandparents thrive on the spontaneity, love, and companionship of their children's children. Many an older person has found renewed purpose for living because of grandchildren; in return, grandparents provide children with a special kind of boost to their self-esteem: unconditional love and acceptance.

SEVERED ROOTS

One of the most unfortunate byproducts of divorce is the way it can interfere with the grandchild-grandparent relationship. A child's sense of having roots can be dramatically affected. Family law attorney Christine Gale says, "It seems that a lot of times parents and the legal system forget that one of the impacts of divorce is that the children might be with the mother and never see the father's family anymore. So they're losing out on half of their relatives."

Because of our increased mobility, our society as a whole is losing its sense of extended family. This may be a contributing factor in many divorces. Wallerstein and Kelly found, for example, that only 10 percent of the divorcing families they observed had any extended family geographically nearby. Most were isolated nuclear families struggling with their problems without the support of sisters, brothers, parents, or in-laws close enough to sit and chat over a cup of coffee.

Many grandparent-grandchild relationships are therefore necessarily long-distance ones. These ties can still be cherished and fulfilling, with phone calls, cards, photographs, and letters filling in the gaps between visits.

Whether they live across town or across the country, many grandparents have known the heartbreak of suddenly being labeled "off-limits" due to divorce. The two generations that had nothing to do with the couple's breakup are thereby divorced from one another, often under great protest from both. When this happens, of course, children are the biggest losers. They lose a sense of their heritage and, as a result, a sense of who they are. They lose yet another mirror on their lives and often one of the friendliest ones. They also lose a relationship that could have been a significant source of comfort and perspective on the divorce itself.

A custodial mother who wishes to cut all ties with her ex-husband and his family is often responsible for closing the door between grandparent and grandchild. According to attorney Christine Gale, this is most likely to happen if the father dies. Since, says Gale, "it's usually up to the father to allow his parents to see the children when he has custody," the mother may use his death to sever contact between the paternal grandparents and the children. She said that grandparents and grandchildren also lose touch when "the noncustodial parent, who is usually the father, is not playing an active role in the children's lives, isn't exercising his right to see the kids, and therefore isn't allowing his parents to see the kids."

GRANDPARENT VISITATION

Not all grandparents are willing to stand passively by when this happens. An increasing number are willing to go to court to obtain the right to visit their grandchildren. Most states now give grandparents the legal right to do this. However, those who pursue this option may have to invest considerable time and money with no real guarantee as to the outcome. Statutes vary from state to state, and sometimes judges are not sensitive to the grandparents' pleas. Even if awarded visitation rights, grandparents may still not get to see the children as much as they would like. The custodial parent may move out of the state in which the suit was brought, making visitation more difficult and requiring changes in the court order. "Any custody order," says Christine Gale, "has to be practical. If the distance is great, then the grandparents would have to bear the expense of transportation and would have to accommodate more to the children's needs."

Gale feels that many grandparents are unaware of their legal rights. She said that in Pennsylvania, where she practices law,

> As long as they have a relationship with that child, if there's a divorce or if their child—who is the parent of the grandchild—dies, they do have a right to partial custody. It's automatic if the child has ever lived with the grandparent for any lengthy period of time, usually a year. They have a right to go into court and ask for partial custody. They're certainly not going to get as much as the natural parent would, but they're going to get something. They might get one Sunday a month. If they're a good distance away, they might get a week in the summer.

Gale feels that if maintaining a relationship with grandparents was determined to be in the child's best interests, "the court would go out of its way to come up with an order where the grandparents would be able to visit."

Determining the best interests of a child can involve many factors, including the age of the child, the degree of emotional closeness between the child and his grandparents, the degree of interest shown by the grandparents, and how active they have been in the child's life in years past. One key element is the kind of relationship that currently exists between the custodial parent and the grandparents. "If the custodial parent absolutely despises the grandparents and mere contact is going to cause a lot of tension and a lot of aggravation, the court might determine that it's just not in the best interests of the children to have that tension continue," Gale said.

Grandparents who are determined to win the right to visit with their grandchilden should be prepared to answer the common defenses against this arrangement: inconvenience because of distance, or a lack of involvement in the lives of the children before the divorce occurred.

Many legal professionals and mental health experts now agree, however, that the best interests of the child usually include the right to a relationship with both sets of grandparents. The social and emotional fulfillment that grandparents and grandchildren bring to each other should be allowed to continue after divorce.

Of course, not all grandparents are highly involved in the lives of their grandchildren. In their observations of sixty families in the process of divorce, Wallerstein and Kelly found that only half the maternal grandparents and less than half the paternal grandparents maintained regular contact with their grandchildren. These researchers felt that even when grandparents did provide solid support, it was not enough to make up for the array of problems confronting these children at home.

PROVIDING LOVE AND SUPPORT

While grandparents' love and encouragement may not be able to make up for the problems at home, many grandchildren have been tremendously lifted—even if only temporarily—by the respite provided by Grandma and Grandpa. Archibald Hart, for example, recalls,

> My grandparents were extremely loving and supportive to my brother and me during this period of divorce. If they were angry at my parents, they never showed or talked about it to us. They never interfered, except to invite us to visit them as often as we wanted. We slipped in a few weekend visits that were not a part of our regular visiting schedule, and those visits were like oases in the desert. They provided relief from the tensions at home and helped me to keep my perspective.[1]

Several single-parent families with whom I spoke named grandparents on both sides of the family as primary supports. Brett and his two sisters would go home to an empty house after school if it were not for their maternal grandmother, who keeps them until their mother comes home from work. Brett's mother said, "I have the real support of both sides—my ex-husband's and mine. I'm closer to his parents than he is, because they totally support me and the kids and they do not condone at all what he's done. His mother and I are more like mother and daughter."

Jack, age ten, and his sister Carla, twelve, are in the legal custody of their grandmother. Their father, Steve, explained that there were two reasons for this. One, he said, was "so we could get them on her insurance plan, so they would be covered medically at a reasonable amount instead of spending bunches and bunches on medical expenses." The other reason was so that Steve could pursue his undergraduate degree and then seminary. Steve said, "My wife and I were not in the best kind of financial situation, which was one of the problems in our marriage. So when we split up I could not afford to rent a place of my own. My mother said that we could move in with her, so I did that. And she helped just tremendously." Jack, Carla, and Steve have lived with Steve's mother in her Arkansas home since the children were toddlers. To them, Grandmother is a very special person, in many ways a surrogate mother.

Many grandparents have felt somewhat hemmed in when a son or daughter's divorce has essentially brought them a second family to raise. Leola Archer was a bit reluctant at first to assume this role. When her son and his two children, ages two and five, temporarily moved back home after his divorce, she found that she had to limit her activities to meet the needs of her now expanded family. She wrote, "I gave up my job of teaching creative writing at the YWCA. There just wasn't time for it. Five years later when our oldest grandson, Jimmy, came to live with us permanently, I gave up all outside activities."

It was a continuing struggle for her. "Ten years had passed and I was still in limbo."

But then something happened that made Mrs. Archer feel that all her sacrifices had been worthwhile. Standing at her kitchen sink one day, she felt a cold sleeve encircle her waist. She recalled,

> I knew without turning to look that it was Jimmy. . . .
> "Grandma," a voice muffled by a mouthful of food spoke in my ear, "You're just like Jesus."
> My hands stopped dead still in the dishwater. Actually, it seemed to me like the whole world had stopped—my heart, time, everything.
> He must have sensed that I was stunned silent. "Well," he said, "you are. I was a stranger and you took me in, naked and you clothed me, sick and you visited me, hungry and you gave me food. Isn't that like Jesus?"
> I could not move or speak. The cold sleeve tightened into a hard grip, then loosed me and he walked away.
> At the door he stopped, turned, and spoke again. "You know something else? I believe you were put here special—special just for me."[2]

SUGGESTIONS REGARDING THE GRANDPARENT-GRANDCHILD RELATIONSHIP

1. Grandparents who are aware of marital difficulties in their son or daughter's home can invite their grandchildren to spend escape time with them. This may mean having them spend a weekend every so often or maybe just taking them out for dinner, to the park, or someplace special whenever possible.

2. One of the most important functions for a grandparent is to be a listener. If the child is willing to share his feelings and frustrations about what is happening at home, let him know that you will keep what he says in confidence. Do not scold him for telling you how he feels or attempt to correct feelings. Be his friend, not his critic.

3. Grandma and Grandpa should be careful not to voice their criticisms about the divorce or either parent and should avoid the temptation to take sides in any way when the grandchildren are present.

4. Long-distance grandparenting is worth the trouble. Letters, phone calls, photos, and other forms of communication help assure children that they have roots and that their grandparents really care about them. Grandparents who can afford it may want to give their grandchildren permission to call collect when they really need to talk. This could be a real comfort for some during divorce.

5. When the natural grandparent-grandchild relationship has been severed or when grandparents live far away, parents should make a practice of inviting older neighbors or church friends into their homes. In this way children can receive many of the blessings and benefits of interacting with older people. Perhaps they will even want to adopt substitute grandparents. Older folks can seek to adopt some children who need grandparents by developing a special friendship with them.

10 Report Card Blues

I think divorces are terrible and they make me cry.
—Mary Beth, age 8

Divorce commonly affects a child's ability to perform in school. For many, there is a marked inability to concentrate and an increase in daydreaming. Two-thirds of the children in the California Children of Divorce Project showed notable changes in the way they behaved and performed in school after their parents' separation. More than half were seen by their teachers as highly anxious. One-quarter were extremely preoccupied with the problems at home, and about 20 percent were felt by teachers to be experiencing "considerable sadness and depression." This sadness, daydreaming, and difficulty in concentration caused one-fifth of the students a "significant decline in academic achievement during the several months following the separation."[1]

In general, the more chaotic the household, the more difficult it is for a child to concentrate in school. Eight-year-old Candace observed, "The hardest part about having divorced parents is *thinking* about them." What are the children thinking about? Research shows that girls spend a great deal of time trying to come up with ways to reconcile their parents. Boys tend to worry more, especially when one parent is depressed.

EMOTIONS

Some children respond to the pressures of divorce by throwing themselves into their schoolwork as if their lives depended on it. For some this may be almost literally true in terms of emotional survival. By immersing themselves in their studies they are able to insulate themselves from the pain that would otherwise preoccupy their thinking. These are the students who seem to have an innate ability to hold their grades up in spite of their gnawing emotions.

Sarah, a high school sophomore, managed to keep her grades high amid bouts of depression and sorrow over her parents' divorce. She asserted,

> You can get through it. It's not the end of the world, and it's up to you to make it not be the end of the world. It's only you that decides whether you're going to allow your grades to fall and get you down or go on and live each day in a new way. Basically, it's up to you.

Nevertheless, she freely admitted,

> You know, there's just some days still that I just get so involved in it and it hurts me so bad that I can't concentrate in school. The only reason I'm there is I know I have to go on, no matter where I am and what kind of mood I'm in. I remember a day this year when I was so bad in biology class that I said to the teacher, "Look, can I go to the bathroom? I just can't sit here any longer." And I've had several days like that this year.

During divorce a child may experience a whole barrage of emotions ranging from fear and insecurity to depression and despair. The intensity of what he feels may vary from day to day according to the way the drama at home is being played out. Add to this the possibility that he may not have shared his feelings with anyone else at all, and it is not the least bit surprising that school performance may ebb and flow with the family's ups and downs.

Dr. James Dobson has said,

> *Emotions affect the efficiency of the human brain.* Unlike a computer, our mental apparatus only functions properly when a delicate biochemical balance exists between the

neural cells. This substance makes it possible for a cell to "fire" its electrochemical charge across the gap ... to another cell. It is now known that a sudden emotional reaction can instantly change the nature of that biochemistry, blocking the impulse.[2]

This is most likely to occur, says Dobson, "when social pressure is great" or "when self-confidence is low." As we have seen, a child may experience either or both of these during divorce.

Paul, a seventh grader, has trouble handling his divorce-related anxieties. His mother said, "Paul's grades have dropped since he has been in the custody of his father. He's gained a lot of weight also. Paul feels that it is his responsibility to look after his dad and to take care of him. I think Paul is unhappy." Paul knows that his burdens follow him to school, but he doesn't know what to do about it. He confided, "It scares me when I think that my seventh grade report has very low grades."

Fifth-grader Ben feels much like Paul. Ben is still sorting things out a year after his parents' divorce. He lamented, "I have lots of pressures and it is hard to complete school work and do practically anything."

Children who must move to a new school shortly after divorce may find that their grades are additionally challenged as they try to cope with their personal problems amid new teachers, new classmates, and an unfamiliar building and curriculum. The newness of their surroundings may complicate their inner struggle by introducing a sense of loneliness or isolation.

Anger can contribute to falling grades. As noted in chapter 2, passive-aggressive anger can find its outlet in a child's schoolwork. Unable to verbalize what is bothering him, he may communicate his anger by failing in school, even though he is capable of better work.

The good news is that most children are able to resume good academic functioning after they have gone through a period of adjustment. Wallerstein and Kelly found that at the five-year mark following divorce, three-fifths of the children they observed were doing average or better-than-average work in school. The majority were excellent students. Another quarter of the children in their study were achieving below average. Only 16 percent were doing poorly. Interestingly, these low achievers included a large number of thirteen-to-sixteen-year-olds, the same group who, five years before, had been intensely angry about their parents' divorce.

Further good news, according to this same research, is that once the bulk of the crisis is past, kids start to like school again. Half of the children interviewed in the California Children of Divorce Project disliked school at the time their parents separated. One year later two-thirds again had positive feelings about school.

LINGERING EFFECTS

Even when divorce is amicably and quickly resolved, it may leave its mark on a younger child's ability to learn in certain areas. There are two reasons for this. The first relates to a child's living with only his male or female parent instead of with both. Men tend to excel in analytical, mathematical, spatial, and mechanical skills. Women tend to be most proficient in verbal ability, language, and perception of detail, such as in reading. Exposure to only one set of these sex-related skills can greatly influence the way a child learns.

Children of divorce tend to score lower as a group in math and subjects that require problem-solving abilities. This may be due to the lack of paternal influence, since nine out of ten children are in the custody of their mothers after divorce. Boys tend to be more affected academically than girls, perhaps because they lack a male model to pattern their cognitive skills after. Those who have brothers tend to be less affected than those who have sisters. However, psychologist Henry Biller found that a mother can also significantly influence her sons academically by her attitude. He wrote, "Poor school adjustment among father-absent boys was associated with their mothers' negative attitude toward their absent husbands."[3]

Girls can be affected by Dad's absence from the home in significant ways too. Biller found that "father-absent girls have often been found to perform more poorly on intelligence and achievement tests than father-present girls."[4] In addition, a positive correlation has been found between a girl's verbal ability and the amount of reading her father does at home. Daughters of divorce often cannot benefit from their father's example simply because Dad is no longer at home when he reads.

The second reason divorce may influence a child's ability to learn has to do with the disorganization that so often characterizes a postdivorce household. Divorce researcher Mavis Hetherington feels that in a highly disorganized household a young child will have difficulty developing a long attention span. Problem solving requires the ability to concentrate for long periods, and a child who does not develop this ability will suffer academically. Once again, Henry Biller links this to the absence of the father: "Academic success requires the capacity to concentrate, delay gratification, and plan ahead. These abilities are less likely to be well-developed among paternally deprived children than among well-fathered children."[5]

Children who gain a stepfather soon after divorce seem to have an advantage in their intellectual development. Biller reports one study which found that "father-absent children who had a father-surrogate in their home (i.e., stepfather) did not have intelligence test scores that were significantly different from father-present children. These findings can be interpreted in terms of a stepfather presenting a masculine model and/or increasing stability in the home."[6]

IN CLASS

Teachers have observed that for many children, Monday is often a bad day. Some are still feeling the disappointment of a visit that was promised but never materialized. Others are in the process of adjusting to a change in location, perhaps having arrived home late the night before from a weekend visit with their noncustodial parent. Similarly, Friday can be a day of confusion for those who leave directly from school for a weekend with one parent or the other. *Did I remember to pack everything? Which bus do I get on today? Or is Dad picking me up? Or, is it Mom?—I can't remember!*

Teachers who observe the following kinds of behavior in their students may be wise to interpret them as possible clues that parents may be in the process of divorce:

Nodding off to sleep in class. Sometimes children become so scared or insecure after a parent leaves the home that they sleep only fitfully or try to stay awake guarding the house. Often they force themselves to stay awake when a parent goes out for the evening, even if a sitter is present. The reason, of course, is a fear that the parent will not return.

Dropping grades or failure to do homework. Previously good students may become depressed or anxious to the point of being unable to concentrate on schoolwork, either in class or at home. Poor students may begin to do even worse. Confusion at home may also contribute to the failure to do homework.

Changes in behavior. Some may become bullies, suddenly domineering or aggressive. Some just have trouble getting along with classmates. Others may become uncharacteristically quiet, withdrawing and refusing to participate. They may daydream or become touchy or grouchy. Some may become super-good or super-organized in an attempt to put order back into their disorganized lives.

Being late to school. The disorganization in the household can cause this. Children may miss the bus or be dropped off late by harried single parents who are themselves already late for work.

Losing things. The inability to concentrate contributes to this. A child may lose his homework, his lunch box, his jacket, or his books repeatedly.

What Kids Say

I asked my panel of experts how teachers could help kids through the difficult period surrounding parental divorce.

MARY BETH, 8: Understanding why I'm upset.

ANGELA, 16: Not hollering at them for daydreaming, but giving them that little extra bit of help and care.

BENJAMIN, 10: Teaching them to handle their problems and giving them a little extra attention.

KIMBERLEE, 12: Treating them like other kids.

ANNA, 17: Listening. Kids need an objective, outside shoulder to lean on, other than family.

PAUL, 12: Giving them advice on how to keep their grades up.

TIM, 9: Telling them about divorced parents.

TERRY, 29: Being more aware of "what does Daddy do" questions.

JENNIFER, 17: Letting students know that they are available to talk about any problem.

CAROL, 18: Not always assuming that kids live with both their mother and father.

SUGGESTIONS FOR HELPING A CHILD IN SCHOOL

1. Parents should make a point of telling the child's teacher that they are in the process of divorce so that the teacher can interpret any changes in the child's behavior or grades with this in mind.

2. Parents should work hard at keeping the disorganization of the household to a minimum. Regular mealtimes, bedtimes, and times for rising in the morning are

essential. Designating certain hours for doing homework can promote its completion, especially if completed assignments are the tickets to privileges such as watching TV.

3. A checklist of things that the child needs to take to school may help those who tend to be forgetful. This should be posted where the child will be sure to see it on his way out the door in the morning. It may help to keep two separate lists, one with reminders that will be the same each week and one that contains items unique to each week. For example:

Every Week	*This Week*
Monday: Lunch money for the week	Report due on Friday
Tuesday: Clarinet	Permission slip for field trip
Wednesday: Gym Clothes	Library books due Thursday
Thursday: Newspaper for current events class	
Friday: Gym clothes and clarinet	

4. Those who are picked up from school by one parent or the other on different days, or who take different buses depending on which parent they will be staying with, may benefit from a note that they can keep with them as a reminder. It may also be a good idea to give the teacher a copy of the note.

5. A child who is falling behind in his schoolwork might benefit from counseling and/or private tutoring until he is able to regain his previous level of academic performance.

6. Specific suggestions for teachers are included in chapter 18.

11 Blaming God

How could God allow this horrible thing and say He loves me?

—Divorced mother, 30

Both adults and children ask the question "How could God allow this to happen?" when divorce divides a family. It is a serious question, opening the door to other equally serious questions: Doesn't God care about what's happening to me? He's supposed to be all-powerful, so why doesn't He answer my prayers for the reconciliation of this marriage?

Jonathan has been divorced for fourteen years. He recalls, "No one can imagine the disappointment a Christian has in the first impression that prayers are not answered because God doesn't really care." A little girl named Tapp remembers when her parents divorced: "I felt I was being punished by God for being really bad, so I tried being really good so God would change His mind."[1] Ten-year-old Paige, whose divorced parents are former missionaries, told me that it all boils down to this: "The parents have got to do what God wants them to do. If God wants them to get divorced it has to be. No matter what anybody says."

Implicit in what Jonathan, Tapp, and Paige are all saying is the idea that God could stop the divorce if He wanted to. Paige goes as far as directly attributing the divorce to God. But can this ever be the case?

The most important question to answer in this regard

is really whether or not God imposes His will on people. Will God force a spouse to return to a marriage that he or she wishes to leave—just because somebody prays this will happen? Does He ever cause a husband and wife to divorce or, for that matter, to remain together against their will?

Dr. Gary D. Chapman, my friend and pastor, addressed this issue in his book *Hope for the Separated*. To those who are separated but not yet divorced, he writes,

> Your prayer must not be: "Lord, if it is Your will bring him/her back." We already know it is God's will for marriages to be restored; however, God respects human freedom . . . your spouse may choose to respond to the work of the Holy Spirit and turn from sin. On the other hand, he or she may reject all of God's pressure and walk his own way. You must give your mate the same liberty God gives.
>
> Some people blame God for allowing their marriages to break up. Do not feel that God has not answered your prayer if your spouse refuses to return. Individuals choose to get married, choose their behavior patterns toward each other, and choose to separate or resolve problems. If God did not allow such freedom He would have to reduce man to something less than man. He would have to remove the imprint of God's image in man.[2]

Says Dr. Chapman, "The truth is that God didn't send the mate away and He will not bring him or her back. God will not *make* the husband or wife return because He has given man real freedom."[3]

Both adults and children need to understand that concept. None of us are puppets. All of us are free to make choices, right or wrong, because God has given us that freedom. The Holy Spirit will influence people for righteousness in response to our prayers (John 16:8–11; Ephesians 1:18), but the decision to respond to that influence still belongs to the individual. Therefore, God is not to blame when marriages fail.

TWO RESPONSES

Some children instinctively recognize that only their parents, not God, are responsible for divorce. As a result, divorce actually draws them closer to God. Kimberlee, a seventh grader, said, "I think divorce is something that teaches faith. I am a Christian and I praise God no matter what."

Other children become so disillusioned by their parents' behavior that they turn away from God. When fourteen-year-old Ricky's father, an ordained minister, became involved with another woman and divorced his wife, Ricky's response, according to his sister, was to shut God out of his life. "I think he was mad at God," she said. "I think he didn't understand how God could allow this to happen. I think he still is mad because he complains about having to go to church and all this, and he won't pray anymore—even just at the dinner table, saying grace."

CAUGHT IN THE CROSSFIRE

Children who live in the emotional war zone of embattled households are not much different from those who reside in military war zones in the way they perceive God's hand in their circumstances. *Time* magazine visited and interviewed children in five war zones around the world and found that no matter what kind of tragedy befell their families, some responded by blaming God while others wisely discerned where the blame really belongs.

Elizabeth is a sixteen-year-old Irish girl whose mother, brother, and grandfather have all been killed in the ongoing violence between Protestants and Catholics in Belfast. She told her interviewer, "When we were younger we couldn't understand it. We didn't know where to turn or who to blame. We asked adults, and the adults, they all had different views of it. I kept askin', 'Why is all this happenin' to *us*?'" Her interviewer responded, "Did it shake your belief in God?" Elizabeth replied, "Not in God. In man."

Following a devastating explosion, Ahmed, a fifteen-year-old Palestinian boy, was asked, "Do you think: How could God allow such a thing to happen?" Ahmed answered, "No. There is no relationship between God and the people who do such things. Man does his work, God his."

But an Israeli girl named Hadara felt differently about the tragedy surrounding her. After the terrorist killing of an entire family whose children, ages two and five, she served as a baby-sitter, Hadara was devastated and cynical. She wrote:

> *If there's a God*
> *and yes, many claim there is,*
> *then how does it happen*
> *that little kids get killed?*[4]

Whether there is verbal crossfire within the walls of one's own home, or a real exchange of bullets and bombs within the borders of one's city, there will always be children who interpret it the way Kimberlee, Elizabeth, and Ahmed do. And there will always be those who doubt and blame God, as Ricky and Hadara do.

HIGH-RISK KIDS

Children who see no silver lining in the cloud of divorce are thought to be high-risk cases, spiritually speaking. This is especially true if their parents are professing Christians. Psychologist Archibald Hart has written,

> In addition to all the problems that a child has to face in adjusting to the breakup of one home and the possible creation of another, the child of Christian parents has to confront the failure of their religious system to resolve the problem of conflict in the home. . . . In the process, the child can become disillusioned with Christianity, and may seriously question whether spiritual values are helpful or important.[5]

Because of this, it is Dr. Hart's opinion that when Christian parents divorce, their children are actually worse off than children from unbelieving homes. Certainly this is true for Ricky, whose mother says he now regards his ex-pastor father as "hypocritcal, untrustworthy and selfish." Ricky's walk with the Lord appears at present to have come to a standstill.

In a kind of real-life paraphrase of 1 John 4:20, children like Ricky seem to reason, "If I can't trust my parents, whom I have seen, how can I trust God, whom I have not seen?" The irony is that it is often the *parent* who has taught the child the very values and morality that he may now oppose by his lifestyle.

DAD AND GOD

Dr. James Dobson has said, "It is a well-known fact that a child identifies his parents with God, whether or not the adults want that role."[6] We call God "Father," not "Mom" or "Grandpa," and it is the father in particular whom the child is likely to associate with God. Biblically the father is the head of the family unit just as Christ is the head of the church. The father is the final authority on what is and what is not proper behavior within the home, just as the heavenly Father is the final authority on the behavior of His children. Earthly fathers work to provide food, clothing, and shelter for their families, and they do so under God's instruction and enabling. Dads provide discipline and instruction, and our heavenly Father does the same. Thus, the tendency to equate God and Dad is not at all illogical.

When it is the father who leaves the family, the child is not unreasonable in wondering whether God has similarly abandoned him when his prayers do not seem to bring answers. He may even wonder if Dad took God with him when he left. Like it or not, parents—especially fathers—represent God in the eyes of a child.

The whole issue of earthly fathers representing the

heavenly Father became clear to me when I met a little guy named Torrey. I was assisting with a class of first graders in my church's Vacation Bible School. Torrey and I became fast friends the first day. He was a dark-haired charmer, and I was flattered by his childish affection. He would squirm ahead of the others in line and beg to hold my hand as the class made its way from one activity to another. He wanted my approval for his artistic accomplishments and his memorization of the required Bible verses. He tried to sit next to me when we went to the auditorium or to the church library.

It wasn't long, however, before I realized that Torrey not only wanted my attention, but desperately needed it. If I were busy with another child or intentionally trying not to favor him over the other children, he would run to the nearest other adult for special attention. As I observed this, I came to realize that emotionally Torrey felt very insecure and tentative about himself and about almost everything he did. I began to probe my little friend gently with questions about his family. He confirmed what I had suspected: Mom and Dad were divorced. His father, it seemed, lived far away in California and Torrey missed him acutely.

One morning the class trooped into the auditorium and assembled in the choir loft for music. Torrey was in the row in front of me and several seats to my left. The music instructor began to teach the simple praise song, "Father, I Adore You." The children sang, "Father, I adore You, lay my life before You. How I love you!"

As the words soaked in, Torrey came unglued. An emotional nerve had been touched. He swung around in his seat, visibly upset. "Why are we singing this?" he sputtered. "What do they mean, *father* I adore you?" As a teacher leaned forward and explained that the song was meant for our *heavenly* Father, he calmed considerably. As I watched, my heart ached for my little friend. Clearly, the words to the song had released his feelings for his dad.

Separating God's representatives from God is not easy for a child to do. The younger the child, the more Mom and

Dad appear like God: omnipotent, infinitely wise, all-loving, and good. In the normal course of growing up, a child slowly comes to the realization that his parents are fallible and have some very human frailties and faults. They make mistakes, they sin, and they fail, just as he does.

Divorce can knock a parent from a child's pedestal almost overnight, however. The knowledge that parents are not all-powerful comes as a shock, and divorce may be perceived as a terrible event that no one can stop: not the child, not his parents, not even God. There is no one else to turn to. Disillusionment can be the result.

SORTING IT OUT

As we have seen, children who lose faith in their parents do not necessarily lose faith in God. Yet divorce may pose a child's stiffest spiritual challenge. Tim LaHaye has said,

> The most mixed-up children do not come from excessively strict homes, but those where teaching and example live in conflict. . . . What turns young people against Christ and His church is to hear the parents give lip service to Bible standards of morality but practice the reverse in the home.[7]

The proverbial expression that "actions speak louder than words" is true when it comes to parental modeling. A child will usually internalize the parent's behavior before he internalizes any of his verbal assertions about right and wrong. When these are in opposition, the child must struggle to sort truth from error.

Twenty-seven-year-old Brandon expressed concern over the sorting-out process he feels sure his children will face. He said, "Later on in their lives they'll look back on the fact that we broke up and that the Bible says it's wrong. I think they'll have trouble with that: 'If this is wrong, why did you do it?' I think it's definitely going to stay with them for the rest of their lives."

Other single parents are burdened by the way they have already seen divorce affect their children's spiritual lives. Glenn, age thirty, was not awarded custody of his daughters, ages eight and eleven. He said, "I think my children are not getting as good a training as they would have under my care. Spiritually my children are zero. No one can imagine the heartache I have for my children's lives."

Jonathan said of his nineteen-year-old son and twenty-year-old daughter, "My children are following in the footsteps of their other parent, who does not attend church often nor practice Christian patterns in the home. Although they believe in God, they don't understand how He can be important to them. After all, hadn't their earthly father relied on Him?"

Others, like Kathy, are optimistic. She said, "Spiritually, my child is not lacking. God has given me grace to persevere and purpose to lead her spiritually." Sandy believes her children have been spiritually strengthened by her divorce. She said, "I think they will be real lights in the world because of what they've been through."

Most of the children with whom I talked while writing this book felt that divorce had actually drawn them closer to God and to the family members they lived with. These were typical comments:

> God loves me very much.
>
> I wasn't mad at God. That was where I went to. I guess you could say I ran to Him.
>
> God knows all, so He's my only true friend.
>
> It's a comfort to say a prayer at night to God. He's really one person who listens to me and helps take the burden away.
>
> Divorce is rough, and most kids turn to drugs; not me, I turn to God.

I believe that any child who turns to God in the face of parental divorce will be much better off than one who does not—even if that turning is just the barest starting point of a relationship with God. In Christ there is hope and a source of help and healing that transcends the best human efforts to comfort a child of divorce.

Consider Anita, who was twelve when her parents divorced. According to her brother,

> Six months before the separation that caught us all off guard, Anita had had recurring dreams that her parents were divorced. She believes that it was God, reaching out to her, strengthening her, helping her become familiar with unknown and painful territory. Healing was taking place before any of us were conscious of the wounds. That is a testimony both to God's grace and to Anita's deep sensitivity to others and to God.[8]

I asked Kimberlee about her experience as a Christian child of divorce. She told me, "When I got old enough to understand what Christianity was, I prayed about everything that I didn't understand, and most of the time God gave me an answer to every question I had. Most of the time He did."

"That's neat," I remarked.

"It sure is!" Kim smiled. "It's a *relief!*"

SUGGESTIONS FOR HELPING A CHILD SPIRITUALLY

1. Children must understand that their parents, not God, willed the divorce to happen. It may comfort them to hear that God would like the relationship to be reconciled as much as they would. Help them understand, however, that God lets everyone—parents and boys and girls—make choices. If parents choose to divorce, God will not stop them even though divorce makes Him sad.

2. Encourage the child to tell God of all his feelings, fears, and anxieties. Pray with him and for him about each of his concerns.

3. Parents should seek to establish or enhance their own relationships with God by becoming active in a Bible-

believing church that welcomes single-parent families. Most pastors would be happy to meet with those who have questions either about their church fellowship or about how to establish a personal relationship with God through Christ. Don't give up the search for a church home until you find a place where both parent and child can be spiritually nourished and emotionally encouraged. (See appendix B if you are unsure how to establish a personal relationship with God.)

4. Make up a promise box of encouraging verses from a children's Bible or from a modern version such as the Living Bible or the New International Version. Write verses on separate slips of paper, fold them, and place them in a box or coffee can. Allow the child to draw out one promise to claim each day, perhaps during breakfast. Discuss the meaning of the verse and how it applies to the child's life. Here are some verses you might want to include.

John 14:27	James 4:8a	Proverbs 16:20
Romans 8:28	Romans 5:3-4	Proverbs 1:33
James 1:2-4	Philippians 4:6-7	Hebrew 13:5
Isaiah 26:3	1 Peter 5:7	Psalm 34:19
Psalm 18:32	Isaiah 55:8-9	Luke 12:7

5. Involve the child in Sunday school, children's church, Vacation Bible School, church camp, or other church-related activities designed for children. Neighbors and relatives of children whose parents do not attend church can offer to take the children and introduce them to peers and teachers.

6. Custodial parents can make a practice of holding regular family worship times with their children. These should be short enough that they do not outlast a child's attention span and should include some form of prayer and Bible reading. With very young children, prayers can be mere sentences and Bible reading should be very short, either a few verses or a story from a child's Bible story book. Singing, holding hands, and creative activi-

ties can make this a warm, enjoyable time for both parent and child.

7. Make a prayer-request journal. On the lefthand pages of a notebook list the things you and the child are praying about. On the opposite pages record how and when God answers these requests.

12 Money Matters

People at church don't understand what it's like to be poor.

—Kimberlee, age 12

Divorce always entails financial adjustment. In most cases, those who divorce step down financially, not up. According to recent research, "In most divorces the couples and their children will suffer a period of economic chaos and will be forced to downgrade the quality of their lives because of reduced income."[1] Experts feel that it costs a full 25 percent more when the same number of people go from maintaining one residence to maintaining two. This is particularly ironic since financial problems are often part of the reason why many couples seek divorce.

One way divorce affects a child is by introducing financial and material changes into his lifestyle. In our culture, material needs and emotional needs are strongly intertwined, and as we have already noted, we tend to link financial strength to self-worth.

The period immediately after divorce is likely to be painful both financially and emotionally. Family members are dealing with what sociologist Susan Anderson-Khlief calls a "strong sense of downward mobility."[2] The family home may have been sold, forcing family members into smaller dwellings, sometimes in housing or neighborhoods that was previously considered unacceptable. A mother who has not worked outside the home before the divorce may suddenly find herself on the job market, newly burdened with the responsibility of supporting a family. Child-support payments and other financial help from the noncustodial parent may be inconsistent or minimal. For a time, finances may be so tight that going out for dinner, movies, or the like become extravagances beyond consideration. While these are certainly not essentials, their sudden lack contributes to the family members' feeling that "something terrible has happened to us." They are now poor in their own eyes, and they may feel tremendously embarrassed by this.

Sometimes, however, the period of economic chaos is only temporary. If adequate child-support arrangements can be agreed upon and if the custodial parent already has found or is able to find a good job, the family's financial state may soon approximate the predivorce conditions.

More affluent families may experience only minimal financial adjustment in divorce. Spencer and Suzanne are one couple whose financial adjustment was relatively smooth. Spencer is an ophthalmologist who earns between $70,000 and $78,000 a year; Suzanne is a registered nurse who earns about $18,000. Thus, their combined annual income was between $88,000 and $96,000. After they separated, Spencer agreed to give Suzanne about $400 a week to supplement her earnings, since they planned to share custody of their four children. The children will undoubtedly face many adjustments as a result of their parents' divorce, but material want is not likely to be one of their problems.

Unlike Spencer and Suzanne, most divorced couples do face period of financial readjustment. The Children of Divorce Project disclosed that virtually *every* parent in the study was preoccupied with the financial changes created by divorce.

SINGLE MOTHERS ARE AFFECTED MOST

While both single-father and single-mother families commonly experience financial difficulties after divorce, the women typically struggle harder and longer. Research by Susan Anderson-Khlief reveals that the average divorced woman's income declines by an astonishing 43 percent from her married income level. Other findings show that some women experience as much as a 70 percent drop.

Wallerstein and Kelly found that at both the eighteen-month and five-year marks after divorce the women in their study fared worse than the men. At eighteen months they observed, "Slightly more than a third of the women lived with an extremely erratic financial situation. They were unsure of continued support, anxious over mounting expenses, and frustrated that their own employment did not adequately contribute to any increased sense of financial security."[3] At five years after separation, half the men who were studied "continued to be solidly upper and upper-middle class" while "with few exceptions the women were poorer than they had been during their first marriage and appeared likely to remain so. One-third of the women were enmeshed in a daily struggle for financial survival."[4]

Amazingly, single-mother families account for half of all American families living below the poverty level. According to ABC-TV, of the four million single mothers who should be receiving child support, 53 percent get nothing at all. ABC calls these single-mother families the "fastest growing poverty group in the country."[5] The 1980 census indicated that mothers who do receive child-support payments get an average of only $150 a month. Since 90 percent of all children of divorce reside with their mothers, most of them are well acquainted with the economic hardships that divorce imposes.

Brandon, a single father of two, acknowledged that women have an especially difficult time.

> In a lot of cases, it's a lot tougher for a mother to raise her kids than it is for a father. The financial pressure on a mother is almost unbelievable. If the mother hasn't been trained and hasn't been on the job market, it's hard to get back into it and make enough money to be able to support herself alone, even without kids.

Before the divorce, Brandon's wife did not work outside the home. Brandon said, "I was making all the money to begin with, so there was no adjustment for me following divorce except the added cost of day-care." As vice-president of a small tool and machine company, Brandon's income is adequate for the needs of his family. Even so, he is glad for the small amount of child support that he receives from the children's mother. "It takes an awful lot of money to raise kids," he concluded, "especially when you're on your own."

Because men tend to be better off financially after divorce, custodial mothers often feel angry about the inequities they see when they compare their circumstances with their ex-husbands'. Both mothers and children may struggle with feelings of deprivation, anger toward the father, and a sense that life is grossly unfair. In addition, many remember the higher standard of living the whole family shared before the divorce.

Sandy is a thirty-seven-year-old mother of three who typifies the single mother hardest hit by divorce. Her income, which she earns as a typist for an insurance company, combined with the child support she receives from her former husband, provides barely enough for her to raise her family.

Sandy and her children believe that the key to their economic survival has been their faith in Christ and in His purposes for their lives. Their financial difficulties are pervasive and ongoing, yet they cope remarkably well with little, very much aware, Sandy says, "of how God takes care of us." She spoke candidly when I interviewed her.

> We have suffered, and we still are suffering terribly, financially. I am very frank with the kids. I tell them, "You see this bill right here? I can't pay this. There's not enough money. I gave the landlord a check for the rent, but there's not enough money in the bank. And my car insurance is due in three days!" And they know that, and we pray about it. The kids have seen how God provides for us—those kids' faith is as deep as mine.
>
> Because of our economic situation I do not buy clothes. The clothes that we wear are given to us, and we take what

we get. It's been hard, especially for the girls, as far as the peer attitude. My older daughter is getting to be a teenager and she is more clothes conscious. I can't just go out and buy the latest fashions. It's hard in a single-parent situation. Most of the kids my children run around with have both parents and lots of money, everything they need. And here's my daughter with her meager clothes.

I'm not saying I don't take help, because there are times when people help us along the way and I couldn't make it without them. I've had less help financially this year than I've ever had and I guess that's why it's so hard right now. I got one card in the mail this Christmas that said, "From a Christian Friend," and it had a hundred dollars in it. That's the only help I had at Christmas this year. Usually there will be several people who will help us.

When my son is grown and he is successful at whatever God has for his life, he's going to look back and say, "I appreciate my mom who raised me in the hard circumstances I was raised in." It will make my children stronger, better people.

The children have had some opportunities to do some things that are high on my priority list as far as how the money is spent, not only for their basic needs but for their emotional needs. I forked out eighty-five dollars in the middle of December so my son could go on a trip with the youth group, and I didn't have it. I still don't. But to me that eighty-five dollars was important. There are a lot of things I do for them that I don't really have the money for, because they have to be well-balanced emotionally.

There's nothing worse than a kid who grows up and says, "Well, my parents were divorced when I was little and we never got to go anywhere or do anything." And they're miserable and unhappy because they had a miserable childhood. When my kids grow up they're going to remember poverty, but they're going to remember a good, happy, fulfilled childhood. Sometimes people do not understand my priorities, but I'm the one raising those kids, and I have peace with God that I've done the right thing.

Keenly aware of the need to pinch pennies, children in single-mother families often become very sensitive to the financial stresses Mom faces. Seventeen-year-old Jennifer said, "Sometimes I worry about how my mom will survive when my dad's alimony runs out next year."

One positive by-product of economic hardship can be

an enhanced appreciation for both the parent and the things in life that don't come with a price tag. Paige told me, "I don't have a lot of clothes, but I have toys and stuff. But my mom gives to us more than she gives to herself." Kimberlee said, "When people try to show their love, they spend time with children, just doing things with them. They don't have to spend money—just take them to the park, cook them lunch, or do anything that makes them feel good, feel loved."

In his book *Father, Child and Sex Role,* Henry Biller notes,

> Paternal absence or inadequacy is often associated with a lack of material resources. Economic deprivation can make it much more difficult for the father-absent child to avail himself of experiences which might positively affect his development. Consistent economic deprivation makes it easy to develop a defeatist attitude about one's potential impact on the environment.[6]

Many single parents wisely recognize that meeting their children's emotional and social needs is as important as meeting material needs. Sandy, quoted earlier, is a good example: "There are a lot of things I do for them that I don't really have the money for, because they have to be well-balanced emotionally." Unfortunately, not all single parents are this sensitive.

Many children of divorce in long-term tight-money situations must routinely forfeit opportunities for personal growth and enrichment. Tickets to the symphony, a play, or a sporting event are rare. Lessons of any sort, whether ballet, piano, gymnastics, or tennis, can be afforded only with deliberate sacrifice. Similarly, cosmetic luxuries such as orthodontic braces or contact lenses rather than eyeglasses may be low among the parent's financial priorities. Purchasing clothes in the current fashions may be out of the question. Little or no spending money may be available for the child to use in recreational activities with friends at the roller rink, movies, or community pool.

All these restraints impinge on a child's self-image and how he views himself in relationship to his peer group.

Boys may be more sensitive than girls to the effects of family economic woes. Interviewers for the Children of Divorce Project detected "a significant link between depression in younger boys and the reduced social and economic circumstances in the postdivorce family."[7]

MOM'S ATTITUDE IS KEY

Henry Biller notes, "The mother's attitudes are related to her social and economic opportunities and are readily transmitted to the child."[8] Wallerstein and Kelly found similarly, "The children's response to the economic pressures in the family was mediated through the mother-child relationship. Their adjustment was not directly affected by the economic circumstances alone."[9]

The most important factor, then, in a child's adjustment to reduced income after divorce may well be his mother's attitude. The way she feels about her financial circumstances—and her more financially stable ex-husband—has a significant impact on the way her children will cope with their economic circumstances and respond to their father.

CAN MONEY TALK?

The typical financial advantage of fathers over mothers after divorce can be particularly destructive when used to sway a child's loyalties. In such cases the child is tempted materially and forced to choose between a "have" and a "have-not" parent. Since any child is likely to have needs and wishes that his financially poorer parent probably cannot fulfill, such a temptation coming from the father may be especially alluring. The real issue here, of course, is that the child is used as a pawn in the ongoing parental dispute. That is, if having the child's affection and loyalty is a source of pleasure, then not having it is a source of pain; and the objective of the "have" parent is often to inflict pain on the "have-not" parent, even if it means putting the child in an unhappy tug-of-war.

Brenda, a forty-four-year-old divorced mother of two, is familiar with the problem. Her daughter Angela, age sixteen, lives with her in their home outside a large northeastern city. Her son Paul, twelve, lives with his father not far away. Angela holds a part-time job and uses her earnings to provide for many of her own needs. Her brother, however, is too young to hold a job and seems caught in the struggle between the "have" and the "have-not" parent. Brenda is the "have-not" parent and has anxiously watched her son turn first one way and then the other.

When Brenda and I first talked, she was pursuing custody of Paul.

> I feel very sorry for him, and this is one reason I'm fighting for him—because I feel he would be in a better environment should he be with me, even though I have to work to support the children and my ex-husband can buy Paul everything he wants.
>
> I told Paul, "If you come to live with me, I cannot give you all these material things. The only thing I can give you is love and understanding." He's very torn. He said, "If I go with you, Mom, Dad will be mad. If I go with Dad, you'll be mad." And I told him, "Paul that's not so. I will always love you." I really don't feel that he has that assurance from his dad.

Karen, a twelve-year-old from a mid-sized southern city, has the reverse of Paul's problem. The "have-not" parent, her mother, is the one applying the pressure. Karen's father has had very little contact with her over the past several years and that hurts her very much. Yet Karen's mother has told her clearly what to expect if Karen should ever be swayed by her father's financial advantage. Karen explained,

> See, my father is rich now. He could offer me anything. He could buy me a car right now. My mom said, "I don't care what he offers you. If he offers you three or four cars when you grow up, don't accept. And don't go with him. If you do, I could probably never forgive you, because I've stayed with you this whole time."

Kids like Paul and Karen have been placed in a difficult and uncomfortable position by their parents. The desire to know and relate in a positive way to both parents is a normal, God-given desire. When money is used as a weapon in the ongoing parental war, the best interests of the child are laid aside. In fact, whether money is an issue or not, any time a parent demands that a child renounce his relationship with his other parent, that child is likely to become depressed, anxious, and preoccupied with his frustrating and unresolved dilemma. Many feel caught in the middle. Seventeen-year-old Anna lamented, "My mother needs to understand that I need to have a relationship with my dad. I need him in my life right now."

Research has shown that the children who cope best with divorce are those who maintain stable, close relationships with both their custodial and their noncustodial parents. In other words, kids need good relationships with both parents to make the best adjustment after divorce. A parent who attempts to buy a child's loyalty, or threatens to withdraw his love if the child sells out to the other parent, diminishes the chances for the child's good recovery.

POOR BABIES

A more benevolent version of the "money talks" idea is "poor babies." This is basically an attempt on the part of adults to compensate children materially for the unhappiness divorce brings into their lives. Anyone can participate in this tactic—parents, grandparents, aunts and uncles, boyfriends and girlfriends of the parents, and anybody else who can be made to feel sorry for the children.

To a point, this extra compensation is a very good idea. To some children a gift from an adult says "I love you" more clearly than anything else can. Children of divorce need reassurance that they are loved and cared about. Sometimes a gift or a special outing or treat is an excellent way to help ward off any insecurity or loneliness that may be cropping up. There are a multitude of genuine practical needs that can legitimately be met by nonparents: school clothes, haircuts, lunch money, or tuition, for example.

The "poor babies" attitude does not become a problem until adults express love in this way too often. When the child survivors of a divorce war are routinely indulged with an inordinate amount of goods, they quickly join the ranks of those our grandparents would have considered "spoiled." Showered with gifts, toys, money, and treats from sympathetic adults, these children are quick to learn that with little effort they can obtain almost anything they want. A little pouting or crying goes a long way: someone always seems to come through with the desired item. "Well, after all, his parents are divorced, poor baby."

These pampered children can easily grow up feeling superior to others and develop a distorted perception of love. Worse, they may subscribe to the notion that they should be catered to in a similar fashion by teachers, employers, and future spouses—not exactly a prescription for success!

Only a portion of the children of divorce experience this kind of treatment, of course, but they can be found in almost any postdivorce setting, whether affluent or financially struggling. This is because it is the economic posture of those outside the single-parent family—usually generous relatives—who make it possible. Certainly much depends on the children themselves. Those already bent toward feelings of greed, deprivation, or manipulation are prime "poor babies" candidates.

David Martin, a Christian counselor, told me,

> I think it's typical. I think what I've seen most in the children that I've counseled is that all of a sudden they start getting a whole lot more gifts. Grandparents start supplying them with things that they could never have had when they were with the parents. Boyfriends or girlfriends of the parent bring them gifts to try to win their affection, and they become spoiled. This is especially the case with single

children. They become spoiled to the point where they expect gifts. And if the parent marries this boyfriend or girlfriend and the gifts stop coming, that's usually when I start seeing the children.

Noncustodial fathers are often the greatest indulgers of "poor babies." Even in normal, intact families the father is traditionally the parent "from whom all blessings flow," as Biller and Meredith put it in their book *Father Power*. They comment, "The father may ... give gifts to his children to gain a feeling of control, of adequacy, or of being needed in the family. He may feel that he is an outsider, a walking wallet. Thus, he may use the only power he feels he has, the power of money, to ingratiate himself into his child's life."[10]

If this is true of fathers who are still married to the mothers of their children, it can be more sadly true for fathers who are separated from their children after divorce. Divorced fathers may feel even more compelled to play Santa Claus in an attempt to appease their consciences regarding the divorce or to make up for a lack of time spent with their children. In the Wallerstein-Kelly sampling, "at least one-third of the men were unusually generous to their children, plying them with special treats or money.... This role strained the fathers financially and emotionally and ... often angered their divorcing wives."[11]

Mothers and stepmothers can be guilty of playing Santa too. In fact, when both sides of the family are "haves," the whole "poor babies" issue gets even stickier. One thirteen-year-old girl said,

> My mom bought me a sweater. I wore it to my dad's, and my stepmother went right out and bought me a windbreaker. I wore the windbreaker home and my mom went right out and bought me a down vest. I didn't dare wear that back to my dad's in case they felt they had to buy me a fur coat.[12]

Children, of course, enjoy material things and will seldom refuse adult generosity. However, no amount of material gratification will ever provide more than a superficial sort of nurture for a child. His greatest needs are more emotional than material, and even the most extravagant gifts will do little to make him feel more secure or less afraid after divorce. He needs a competent, involved parent far more than he needs anything that parent could purchase for him.

"Attempts at bribery do not escape the child," write Biller and Meredith. "He knows when he is being bought, when material things are being used in place of true nurturance."[13]

A girl named Andrea, who helped write *The Kids' Book of Divorce,* saw the real motive behind her parents' generosity. She related,

> Once my dad gave me a pair of sneakers and I wore them to my mom's house for the weekend. My mom saw them and right away took me out and bought me a more expensive pair of sneakers. When I went back to my dad's house he took me out and bought me a pair of running shoes. Before I knew it I had five pairs of sneakers and track shoes. I liked having so much footwear, but I hated the fact that my parents were trying to prove they were better than each other by the sneakers they bought me.[14]

Sometimes children in Andrea's situation learn to manipulate and take advantage of generous parents by playing them against one another. One crafty college freshman confessed, "I wrote two letters at the beginning of the term to my father and stepfather. I told Dad that my stepfather hadn't come through with the allowance he'd promised, and I told my stepfather the same thing about Dad. Bam. Two checks arrived and I was good until Christmas."[15]

THE OTHER EXTREME

Many fathers who would like to play Santa cannot. They can barely pay their own bills, let alone meet their legal child-support obligations. In response to the crushing financial burdens that are inherent in supporting two households, many fathers moonlight on second jobs to make ends meet. In the already stress-filled aftermath of divorce, this can prove to be intensely draining, both mentally and physically. Besides wearing the father out, working two jobs severely limits his time for recreation, socializing, or visiting with his children.

Middle- and upper-income fathers tend to be more regular in their child-support payments and in their visitation than men in the lower income brackets. These two issues—child support and visitation—appear to be separate aspects of fathering after divorce, and they are treated that way by the legal system, but in reality they are closely linked.

Men who can afford to make their child-support payments sometimes deliberately withhold them as a protest when their former wives refuse to allow them to visit their children. At the other end of the scale, men who must choose between paying their rent and making child-support payments often let the child support slide. Payments may be sporadic at best. Not only does this make them feel more sheepish about visiting, but it ensures that their former wives will be less happy to have them do so. Either way, the children lose twice. They miss out on much-needed time with their fathers and they miss out on much-needed financial support. Resolving this kind of impasse quickly is vital to the well-being of the father-child relationship. Research has shown that the pattern of visitation shaped during the first eighteen months after divorce is likely to continue through the years.

Women find it easier to take legal recourse regarding child support than men do regarding visitation. The reason for this, according to family law attorney Christine Gale, is that "child support is not considered the mother's right. It's the child's right." She says, "Even if the mother absolutely refuses to let the father see the child, the father can be brought into court to pay child support, and if he doesn't comply they can get a wage attachment and it'll be taken right out of his pay."

Fathers face a much tougher battle if they wish to see their kids when the mothers are against it. Often it means repeated court appearances, legal fees, and lots of hassle, especially if the mother and child reside in a different city or state, since the litigation usually takes place where they live. Only rarely are fathers willing to go through the long and drawn-out procedure that may be necessary to obtain their rights. It doesn't happen very often, says attorney Gale, "unless the father *really* wants to see those kids and doesn't care about the time that he spends or the inconvenience."

Gale notes that mothers who feel stronger about the father's not seeing the children than they do about receiving child support may be saying in effect, "'If you just drop everything about visitation I won't sue you for child support' and it's kind of a silent agreement that neither one of them is going to pursue their legal rights and obligations."

By contrast, mothers who really want the father to visit are sometimes frustrated by the resistance they meet. Christine Gale said,

> There are a lot of cases that I've had where the father doesn't care about visitation and doesn't pursue it and just wants out altogether. When the divorce takes place he divorces the kids just as much as the parent. So visitation is something the mother can't force the father to do. It's the father's right, but it's not considered the father's legal obligation. You can get a court order forcing the father to pay support, but you can't get a court order forcing the father to visit the child. And the child needs both. The child needs the father's input in his life just as much as the father's financial support. But one is easy to enforce and the other's not. It doesn't take much to get a wage attachment to force the father to pay child support. It would be a little bit difficult to force the father to visit the child—how would you go about it? You can't force a parent to care; you *can* force a parent to pay.

Suggestions for helping single-parent families financially are included in chapter 18.

PART FOUR

FAMILY TIES

13 Woe Is One

It's not really fun not having two parents. Sometimes it's a lot of hassle.

—Paige, age 10

God seems to accomplish a lot of important things by using two people instead of one. When Jesus sent His disciples out to witness, they went two by two (Mark 6:7). Instructing them concerning prayer, He told them that if two of them agreed in prayer about anything, God would do what they asked. He also promised to be in their midst whenever two or more gathered in His name (Matthew 18:19–20). When it was time for Him to make His triumphal entry into Jerusalem, Jesus sent two disciples to bring the colt upon which He would ride (Mathew 21:1–2).

In every case it seems that Jesus paired the disciples off, not for His sake but for theirs. Anyone who has ever gone out witnessing knows the value of having a partner to lean on. Prayer, too, is often more faithfully accomplished with a partner's support and encouragement. Even an errand is somehow easier to run when there is a friend along for companionship—as when Jesus sent disciples for the donkey's colt.

PARENTING: A TASK FOR TWO

It is not surprising, in light of these things, that God sees parenting as a task to be shared by a team of two. This becomes especially evident when we consider the life of Jesus Himself. Since Jesus was born of a virgin, technically God didn't need Joseph. All He needed was Mary. Yet God knew that Mary needed Joseph. She needed physical and emotional support and help, which Joseph no doubt ably supplied throughout the long journey to Bethlehem and perhaps during Mary's labor and delivery as well.

After the baby was born, it was Joseph to whom the angel gave instructions for the family's safety: "Flee to Egypt, and remain there until I tell you; for Herod is going to search for the Child to destroy Him" (Matthew 2:13). God wanted Mary to have the companionship, protection, and support of a husband, and He wanted Jesus to grow up in the context of a family—father and mother, brothers and sisters. Based on Mark 6:3 we can assume that Jesus had four brothers and at least two sisters. God also knew that Jesus needed two earthly parents to grow up properly prepared for all that God had sent Him into the world to accomplish.

If the very Son of God needed two earthly parents, how much more must the rest of God's children need both a mother and a father! And if Mary needed a partner to help parent the only sinless child ever born, how much more do the rest of us need a co-parent! Since the Garden of Eden, parenting has always been a job big enough to require the combined strength and energy of two people. To a large degree, it is the positive synergism of the marriage relationship that enables a man and a woman together to become stronger and better parents than either could become alone. Ecclesiates 4:9–12 is a good illustration of synergism.

> Two are better than one because they have a good return for their labor. For if either of them falls, the one will lift up his companion. But woe to the one who falls when there is not another to lift him up. Furthermore, if two lie down together they keep warm, but how can one be warm alone? And if one can overpower him who is alone, two can resist him.

When a marriage weakens and dies, synergism ceases between the parents, often leaving one of them with the major portion of responsibility and far less motivation to keep going. With no other adult at home to rely on and consult with, single parents must often stretch their own strength, wisdom, and time to encompass the roles of both father and mother. Kathy, a thirty-year-old single mother, feels the frustration that is typical:

> Once you're used to functioning as two people in two roles and all of a sudden you're one person but still two roles—how do you handle it? I struggle with having to work all day, having to pay for everything, having to do everything in the house, take care of the car, pay medical bills, do all the shopping, try to have a social life, try to find babysitters, and then feel guilty because I don't see Katie as often as I want to! The point is, there's never enough time or energy to be mom and dad both and it's very difficult not to feel guilty.

Kathy's frustration stems in part from her inability to be something she was never meant to be: both a mother and a father to her child. She is, in a sense, trying to become androgynous—male and female at the same time. Because of her love for her daughter and her sense of responsibility, she has been able with great effort to succeed to a measurable degree in giving her child both masculine and feminine nurture and in filling both male and female roles in her household. But while God created some androgynous members of the plant kingdom, He did not create any androgynous people. He created us male and female.

No woman, no matter how firmly and consistently she disciplines or how successful she may be in the workplace, can ever communicate to a child what it means to be masculine. No man, no matter how warm or gentle or how emotionally supportive he may be, can ever adequately demonstrate to a son or a daughter what it means to be feminine. Each parent's inherent masculinity or femininity will dominate, as God intended. Only as two halves of a whole can a mother and father provide the balance that properly parents a child.

It is evident that God designed the two-parent partnership not only for the benefit of the adults but also for the benefit of the child. Researcher Marsha Weinraub has written,

> A parent whose needs for love, affection, and security are satisfied by another adult—the second parent—is better able to respond effectively to the child's needs. Several studies have demonstrated how the father may influence the mother-child relationship. Although more limited, there is also evidence of how the mother's relationship to the father affects the father-child relationship. It is becoming increasingly recognized that the quality of the relationship between the two parents will affect each parent's ability to respond effectively to the child.

Jody, whose parents divorced when she was sixteen, would agree. She said, "I expected my parents to love each other and when they didn't I felt very insecure. I really believe that the greatest thing parents can do for their children is to love each other."

Each parent models something different for the child. The father models instrumental behavior: mastery and competence, planning ahead, delaying gratification, and interacting with the world beyond the family unit. He sets limits, he disciplines, and he is generally perceived by children as the more authoritative parent. A mother is usually more expressive. She tends to be more verbal and more concerned with interpersonal relationships, modeling sensitivity, caregiving, warmth, and emotional support for the child. While a father is also expressive in many ways, and a mother is also instrumental, each tends to provide the child with a different yet complementary care style.

As noted earlier, fathers also tend to play with their children in more physical ways, while mothers tend to be more verbal. Both are important to a child's development.

Children respond to men and women in different ways. One study showed that children were significantly more responsive to an adult of their same sex when they were engaged in a collaborative task—anything that an adult and a child might do together such as washing the car, building a treehouse, or baking cookies. Children were found to be most responsive to an opposite-sex adult when the adult assumed an encouraging and praising role: "You're doing a good job!" Thus a child's sense of camaraderie was stimulated best by an adult of the same sex, while his sense of fulfillment through approval and praise was brought out best by an adult of the opposite sex.

The researchers were unable to speculate whether the dynamics of a parent-child relationship would be the same as those they observed in their experimental setting, but they did conclude, "These results indicate that adults of both sexes are crucial and complementary influences in children's socialization."[2] Based on these observations, we might assume that boys perhaps respond best to their fathers when they feel a sense of comradeship with them and to their mothers when they feel appreciated and praised by them, and vice versa for girls.

As a child observes his parents, he learns that while they are similar in many ways, they are also different from one another. He learns to become sensitive to social cues as he observes their conversations and behavior. They hold different opinions on some issues and respond in different ways to things; they also have somewhat different expectations for the child's behavior. Discriminating the subtle and not-so-subtle differences between a male and a female parent and listening to two adult points of view is thought to stimulate a child's analytic skills.

From watching their parents, children also learn patterns for relating to their future spouses. As a single parent, Sandy is aware that her children are at a disadvantage in this regard and she tries hard to compensate. She said,

> As far as preparation for marriage, boys need to know how to treat women. And they learn in two ways: in their relationship with their mother and from the relationship between husband and wife. Now in a single-parent situation you don't have that. So it's really important as a single parent to remember that your children are watching how you relate to members of the opposite sex, because they don't have the mother-father relationship to fall back on. When little girls don't have a daddy, we have to go to the

next best thing, and that is friends of Mama. So I've been really careful about who my friends are.

Children in two-parent homes have more opportunities to observe adult conversation and interaction. They can more easily compare masculinity and femininity and learn firsthand about conflict resolution, compromise, and teamwork. They also benefit from the fact that two parents can balance out each other's anger, mistakes, and miscommunications with the child. They can fill in for each other when one is sick or tired or must be out of town. There is also a better chance that a two-parent home will be financially stable.

Children in one-parent homes have none of these benefits. While they may not be able to verbalize it, they may feel a vague sense of insecurity because the supports that are built into a healthy two-parent family are missing from their own. Wallerstein and Kelly remarked, "The divorced family in which the burden falls entirely or mostly on one parent is more vulnerable to stress, has more limited economic and psychological reserves, and lacks the supporting or buffering presence of another adult for the expected and unexpected crises of life."[3] As a result, life is harder for both parent and child.

JOINT CUSTODY

The benefits of significant influence from both parents is one reason why joint custody is rapidly gaining approval and popularity. In joint custody, both parents share the legal right to make decisions regarding the child and in most cases parents also share physical custody. This is highly beneficial for the parents, because the burden is no longer overwhelming. Instead, it is shared, giving each parent an opportunity to have some free time and to feel relieved of the many inherent pressures and duties of single parenting. Fathers, who often feel useless and depressed after divorce because their children seem to be totally removed from their lives, can enjoy their children and share responsibility for them.

The benefits for the children are numerous. They are able to continue to relate to both parents in a situation that most closely approximates normal family life, especially when they spend part of each week with each parent. They can grow up knowing and relating positively to both parents, benefiting from their differing styles of parenting, their masculine and feminine nurture, and their love. They have a greater sense of roots and can more easily be in touch with both sides of their family. Instead of one home being unhappy, they now have two that presumably are easily accessible, peaceful, and relaxed. In addition, joint custody is thought to benefit children by helping them to develop flexibility as they move from one location to another. Also, waiting to spend time first with one parent and then with the other helps them learn to delay gratification.

Scott and Stacy are two teenagers for whom joint custody has worked out well. They live with their father four days a week and their mother three days a week in her nearby apartment. They appeared on a television documentary called "Divorce: Kids in the middle." Here are some of their comments:

> SCOTT: At first it really didn't suit me, how I wanted my life to be, going back and forth. I thought that it should be their life that should change, not mine. But then I realized it was a compromise: that their life was changing and my life was changing. I realized that it's for the good of everybody.
>
> STACY: Each time I go to my mom's I get a duffle bag and I pack my clothes for three days. And it's trouble, and I don't like it—bringing them back and forth—but it's worth it.
>
> SCOTT: It feels like they're still married. I mean, I know they're not and never will be—and I really don't want them to be because there'd be too much fighting—but I just feel that I'm closer to them and I feel that even when we're at my dad's I feel a ghost of my mom and at my mom's I feel a ghost of my dad."[4]

The key element in a child's successful adjustment to divorce is the continued positive involvement of both his father and his mother in his life. "It is clear from research," wrote psychologist Archibald Hart, "that those children who have the most contact with both parents are the least likely to be damaged by divorce."[5] For many, joint custody is the answer. Dr. Benjamin Spock writes, "I'm strongly in favor of joint custody for all parents who think they can summon the co-operation required."[6]

The major problem with joint custody is that it requires the same ingredients that may have been lacking in the marriage: maturity, good communication, and the ability to cooperate and compromise. For this reason, only a small number of divorced couples—some say only about 10 percent—are capable of making joint custody work. The Binuclear Family Research Project, conducted at the University of Wisconsin at Madison, found that 85 percent of the joint-custody couples they observed had conversations "either in person or on the phone at least once a month" and about a third interacted weekly. Most of these conversations pertained to the child-related issues, but half these parents also reported discussing issues totally unrelated to their children. Many said that their feelings for one another were "caring, respectful, and friendly." Twenty percent even described their post-divorce relationship as "intimate."[7]

Legal experts are beginning to recommend joint custody to people who are tempted to relinquish full custody to the other parent. The reason for this, they say, is that situations change. Finances, people, circumstances, and occupations are all subject to change. Children and parents both grow older, and no one can predict the future. A parent who surrenders all legal say-so in the lives of his children may live to regret his decision.

OTHER KINDS OF CUSTODY

Attorney Christine Gale said, "Custody is the one area in family law that means the most when you're dealing with a child's life. Support is fine—I'll battle to get the woman the greatest child-support order possible because I know that she needs it—but custody, you've got to be very sensitive and very careful with that."

One determining factor in every custody decision, of course, is the degree to which each parent is willing to be responsible for the child. Joint custody requires the most commitment from each parent and is awarded far less often than sole custody, which is most common.

Sole custody gives one parent, usually the mother, all legal rights concerning the child and places him under her care. The other parent has only the right of visitation.

Split custody is probably the most disruptive to a family that is already divided and under stress. This kind of custody gives each parent one or more children. Losing a brother or a sister in this way imposes yet another traumatic loss on a child, and many legal professionals feel that split custody is usually the least preferable solution.

Divided custody may be a workable plan for many couples who are not quite able to handle joint custody. In this arrangement the children spend part of the year with each parent, and for the period that they are in his care that parent has full responsibility concerning them.

There is a growing body of evidence that suggests that same-sex custody is best for a child. A study done at the University of Texas at Dallas found, "When parents are divorced, boys who are living with their fathers and girls who are living with their mothers seem to be warmer, more sociable, more independent, and to have higher self-esteem than children living with a parent of the opposite sex."[8]

It seems that there are two reasons for this. One is that same-sex custody removes the possibility that the parent will view the child as an emotional substitute for his or her spouse. Therefore, possible oedipal conflicts and the pressure for the child to step into an unrealistic role are eliminated. The other reason is that living with the same-sex parent enables the child to identify with and model his behavior after the parent whom he most naturally and appropriately emulates.

ALL KIDS HAVE TWO PARENTS

Children remain unshakably committed to the concept of a two-parent family after divorce. No matter what the custodial arrangements are or how frequently or infrequently a child may see his noncustodial parent, in his frame of reference there is no such thing as a single-parent family. He continues to think of himself in the context of both parents. Both continue to be important to his adjustment to divorce—even when one is no longer an active part of his life. For example, Wallerstein and Kelly found, "Paradoxically, by his absence a father continued to influence the thoughts and feelings of his children; most particularly, the disinterested father left behind a legacy of depression and damaged self-esteem."[9]

These same investigators felt that a very critical factor in a child's good adjustment was a close and nurturing relationship with the custodial parent, and they linked this to the child's success at school, social maturity, and ability to feel good about himself. When the relationship between the custodial parent and the child was not nurturing, they felt that the visiting parent was unable to play a significant enough part in the child's life to compensate for this.

A child's personal identity is inseparably linked to both his mother and his father, whether the parents are married or divorced. For the children who adjusted best, Wallerstein and Kelly suggested, "Perhaps the most crucial factor ... was a stable, loving relationship with both parents, between whom friction had largely dissipated, leaving regular, dependable visiting patterns that the parent with custody encouraged."[10]

Henry Biller reports research with intact families that helps explain why this may be so: "The child's emotional health appeared to be closely related to the quality of the emotional relationship between the parents ... and the quality of the father-mother relationship was more important than the psychological status of the individual parents."[11] Divorce, of course, often either eliminates or severely burdens any emotional relationship between a child's parents. When they remain hostile toward each other or are uninvolved in the child's life, the child's emotional health may suffer accordingly.

Psychiatrist Armand M. Nicholi has written,

> If any one factor influences the character development and emotional stability of an individual, it is the quality of the relationship he or she experiences as a child with both parents. Conversely, if people suffering from severe nonorganic emotional illness have one experience in common, it is the absence of a parent through death, divorce, a time-demanding job, or other reasons. A parent's inaccessibility, either physically, emotionally, or both, can profoundly influence a child's emotional health.[12]

WISHING FOR A STEPPARENT

Children inherently sense that they need both a male and a female model and that their single parent needs a helpmate. This is evident in the almost universal longing among children for a reconciliation between Mom and Dad. When it becomes obvious that the dreamed-about reconciliation is no longer a possibility, some begin to wish for a stepparent.

When children reside with a custodial father, they do not often lack female role models. Aunts, grandmothers, friends of Dad, and hired housekeepers are more likely to be on hand to help a divorced father than a divorced mother. But 90 percent of the time, the mother is the custodial parent and the children are often left without a competent male figure to observe and imitate. Research suggests that "stepfathers can have a facilitating effect on the father-absent child's development, particularly if the stepfather-child relationship begins before the child is 4 or 5 years old."[13]

Young children are generally more receptive to a stepparent than older children are. Those under the age of eight are often father-hungry and eager to welcome a stepfather into the family. Children between nine and fifteen are the least likely to respond to the idea with enthusiasm. Older teens may again start to view remarriage positively, primarily because they see the benefits it could bring to their single parent.

Kimberlee is hopeful about the possibilities for a stepfather. She said, "I feel like my parents were married long enough for three children to be born and raised in a Christlike way. And then God had something better for us, better than our real daddy, maybe. I guess. Maybe a better father who cares more and does more for you. I feel we'd have a better relationship with a better father."

"So you're thinking that your mom will remarry?" I asked her.

"Yeh. I hope!" she responded.

Kim's one big wish for her family would be "that my mom could get married to who she wanted to get married to, that for the rest of our lives she could have a happy marriage." She confided, "Sometimes I worry, wondering if my mom will ever have somebody else."

Children of divorce who have lived in a single-parent home for a number of years sometimes fantasize about the ways their lives would change with the addition of a stepparent. One girl said, "Sometimes when we go out somewhere my mother doesn't have anything to do and while we go out and play she sits there and reads the newspaper or something." But if she remarried, "She'd have somebody and everybody could play together. That'd be pretty nice."

Fifteen-year-old Brett said, "I don't have too many friends whose parents are divorced. I mean, everybody has both parents. My mother's always working, and she can't go out and play football or something like that." He also misses not having a father to confide in. "I mean, you can't go to your mother with some things," he added.

Paige's mother "almost got married" once. But how would Paige feel about having a stepfather? "I would like it very much because I miss my father," she said with her heart on her sleeve. "I think having a mother and father builds the family. You have more things to be happy about."

REMARRIAGE

Adults typically go through a three-year adjustment period after divorce. The first year tends to be highly disorganized, even chaotic. During this time they communicate poorly with their children and find it hard to enforce discipline. Money is tight, tempers flare, housework piles up, and parent-child conflicts, especially between mothers and sons, can become almost routine. Single parents may experience psychosomatic illnesses or depression, and for all family members it's usually a pretty rough year. So rough, in fact, that the supposedly intolerable marriage no longer seems all that bad in retrospect. Many begin to regret the decision to divorce. Those who never wanted the divorce to begin with may feel much like Kathy, who said, "Sometimes I wonder why I ever got married in the first place! And I think of how different things might have been."

The second year brings more stability at home as the single parent and the children begin to make some progress in dealing with their new lifestyle. The mother-son relationship is still likely to be conflict ridden. Boys' aggressive tendencies, while improved over the previous year, have still been found by Hetherington, Cox, and Cox to be "higher at two years [after divorce] than aggression of sons in intact families."[14]

The parent's self-worth and feelings of attractiveness may hit an all-time low during the second year. It is during this time that he or she often becomes extremely active socially in an attempt to compensate. This is also the most likely time for a divorced person to seek out sexual encounters meant to boost a sagging self-esteem. For Christians this can be a time of great sexual temptation.

By the third year the majority of adults have restabilized psychologically. People who are still intensely angry, coping with financial hardship, or involved in litigation are exceptions. In most cases both parent and child have regained much of their equilibrium in most areas and have lost much of their anxiety. Good parenting is likely to resume at this point along with order at home. Adults, disillusioned that the anticipated glories and freedoms of single life have not materialized, begin to long intensely for the commitment of marriage once again. As a result, the remarriage rate during the third year is high. By the fifth year after divorce four out of five people will have remarried.

The odds for a lasting second marriage seem to depend on who marries whom. Domestic-relations lawyer Herbert A. Glieberman has said,

> If a divorced person marries a widow or widower, there's a greater probability that the second marriage will be successful because, generally speaking, the widow or widower came from a happy relationship—or at least one that they learned to live with and are attempting to duplicate. But when you have two divorced people remarrying, they generally have not learned the reason why they got their first divorce, and so chances are great—probably better than 50 percent—that they're going to make another mistake very quickly.
>
> However, if a man who was abandoned by his first wife marries a woman who had the same thing happen to her . . . there's a good chance the marriage will work, since both are looking for security.[15]

Overall, about 60 percent of second marriages fail. And many children are put through the ordeal of divorce all over again.

SUGGESTIONS FOR HELPING SINGLE-PARENT FAMILIES

1. Children need to collaborate on tasks with adults of their same sex and to receive praise and encouragement from adults of the opposite sex. Relatives, friends of the family, children's Sunday school workers, and others can encourage children of both sexes in these ways. Parents should be sure that their children of the opposite sex have plenty of positive input and happy times with other adults of the children's same sex.

Single mothers whose sons have all female school teachers and Sunday school teachers, for example, may want to consider enrolling their sons in programs such as Cub Scouts or Boy Scouts.

2. A single parent's friendships with both men and women can have a positive influence on her children by exposing them to adult conversation and male-female differences. Frequently inviting couples or single friends of both sexes for dinner and family fellowship can be one way to expose children to the complementary yet contrasting differences in men and women. Couples who want to reach out to singles should recognize that their friendship can benefit a single person's children as much as it can the single adult.

3. Parents who are able to maintain a postdivorce friendship should seriously consider the possibility of joint custody because of its many benefits to children. Older children are best suited to this arrangement; the constant upheaval of moving from one parent's home to the other's may prove too stressful for a younger child.

4. When children in a divorced family are all girls or all boys, it may be wise to consider same-sex custody, providing that the parent-child relationship is a loving and nurturing one.

5. Parents, children, and all others concerned should be aware that the typical family faces a three-year period of adjustment following divorce. Knowing that this is common and that many stresses are inherent in this time period may help them prepare for what lies ahead.

14 The Case of the Missing Father (Single-Mother Families)

Many things have made me cry but the divorce made me cry the most.

—Ben, age 10

Kathy's divorce took place three years ago, but she vividly recalls how she felt:

> It was like an amputation. There's a part missing that should have never been removed. I felt so like a failure and was so confused and depressed and angry that I began resenting my daughter. It's not hard to take things out on kids when you're that hurt and they're the only ones there. Divorce is one of the most devastating experiences anyone could ever go through. It is the destruction of a "permanent" union and makes you feel like you've been ripped in half! My divorce was one-sided, unexpected, and devastating. I thought I'd never know joy again.

Marian had been divorced just five months. Like Kathy's, her divorce was one-sided, and the reality of her loss was still incredibly painful as she talked with me:

> Divorce is devastating to your self-image, your security, your ego, really your total being. It leaves a void within and causes a *real* pain that hurts from the top of your head to the bottom of your feet, but you know you have nothing physically wrong. No one can imagine how much you hurt from the rejection and the void within. Someday I will be in heaven and won't remember this sinful, black, terrible ordeal.

Kathy and Marian have only begun to describe what life is like for many divorced mothers. Besides coping with their own pain, rejection, and anger, they must think about their children: what *they* are feeling, how to provide for them financially, how to concentrate on meeting their needs while shouldering the full responsibility for running a household.

According to the 1985 U.S. Statistical Abstract, at last count this country had 5,718,000 single-mother households with children under the age of eighteen.[1] In Forsyth County, North Carolina, where I live, one in every six families has a female head of household.[2] Here and elsewhere, single-mother families are a reflection of the spiraling rate of divorce.

One of the toughest problems faced by single mothers, as has already been mentioned, is trying to eke out a living. In my county, where women make up 46 percent of the labor force, single-mother families comprise 55 percent of the families living below the poverty level. Some 3,100 single-mother families live in federally subsidized housing. For many, life is just one financial crisis after another. Those who have reasonably adequate incomes by comparison struggle too. Patty, a schoolteacher, said with frustration, "My kids think I am a superwoman and that I have a money tree at the bank."

There is some evidence that having a working mother is quite beneficial for a child whose father has left the family. It is thought that working mothers provide children with a model for competence and independence in the absence of a male figure in the home. In low-income single-mother families, according to one study, children may get better grades in school if their mothers work outside the home.[3] There are indications of a relationship between a single mother's positive feelings about her job and feelings of high self-esteem in her children. What matters most is that the mother feels secure in her feminine role and is also happy with her job. When this is the case, a working mother can have a very positive influence on a child of divorce.

The biggest problem that a single working mother is likely to have aside from low wages is the way a job can cut into her time—time for relaxing, socializing, interacting in a meaningful way with her children, and tending to the myriad details of running a household alone. She has little time to develop meaningful friendships, little time to serve her church, and little time to develop her own talents and gifts. Life is often reduced to a balancing act that never quite feels balanced. Buy the groceries, take the car for repairs, pay the bills, mow the lawn, do the laundry, vacuum the carpet, paint the porch—it's all up to her, and she may feel as though she lives in a lonely pressure cooker much of the time.

One single mother said, "I look at all those other full-time mothers and I hate them. I call them 'the cozies,' the ones with the cozy marriages. I can't go to any of the things they go to. I can't relate to them in any way, shape or form. I couldn't care less about the pattern of their china. It just doesn't relate. Life is much more serious for me now. It's a full-time job."[4] Said Kathy, "My child gets angry because I'm too tired after working all day and too frustrated with feeling inadequate to relax with her and spend quiet time with her."

Sometimes the emotional burden is worse than the actual tasks at hand. Kathy related, "No one can imagine, except another single mother, how difficult it can be to accept the fact that you alone are responsible for training and providing for your child, while as a mother all you want to do is stay home and be Mom—not Mom and Dad both!" Said Marian, "Emotionally, I get very lonely at times and feel a tremendous weight of responsibility upon my shoulders with the girls."

Every single mother seems to have a pet worry. For Patty, it is financial problems. Marian's is her retirement years. Kathy worries about "the possibility of being solely responsible for my daughter for the next fifteen years and not being able to provide the overall well-balanced training I want for her."

LIFE WITH MOM

Nine times out of ten, mothers receive custody of their children after divorce. There are probably as many reasons for this as there are divorces, but with very young children, the presumption that children belong with their mother has a factual basis. Dr. Ner Littner, who specializes in psychoanalysis, has served as a court-appointed psychiatrist in hundreds of cases. In an interview published in *Chicago Lawyer* he said,

> The best kept secret in divorce court . . . is that young children who have been brought up by their mother can be severely damaged when they are separated from their mother. . . . present law sort of treats mothers and fathers equally, as though the harm done in separating the child from the father is equivalent to the harm done in separating the child from the mother.

The reason for his concern, of course, is that separation breaks the mother-baby bond. "The breaking of that bond is extremely damaging to a young child and can result in a variety of disturbances," Dr. Littner said. At what point does breaking the bond cease to cause problems? He replied,

> I artificially divided children this way: The first five years of age the separation trauma is extremely great, and can drastically scar the child for the rest of his life. It can influence the way he treats his own children. So I think that separating children under the age of six from their mothers should only occur in situations where mothering is so bad that it is worse than the separation trauma. In children from six until puberty the separation trauma is still strong, but much less than under the age of six, so here one is less hesitant to separate the child from the mother if it is clear that the father is the better parent. The third group would be where the children are adolescent, where probably the separation trauma would have little effect. And then one looks at the other factors.[5]

It appears that three attitudes of a mother can significantly influence the way mother and child adjust to the single-parent situation and to each other after divorce.

The first is the mother's perceptions of her own ability to make it without a husband. In a 1960 study of single mothers who were coping well after the deaths of their husbands, Biller reports that the researchers found that

> mothers who could utilize their own and outside resources and assume some of the dual functions of mother and father with little conflict appeared to be able to deal constructively with the problems of raising a fatherless family. . . . It is important to emphasize that the mother's ego strength rather than her warmth or tenderness seemed to be [the] essential variable in her child's adjustment.[6]

Sometimes divorce evokes strength a woman never knew she had or forces her to become stronger than she knew she could become. Marian is a good example of this. She said, "My divorce has brought out my strengths and I have become a more determined person. I had to, to survive. I'm happy that I have changed in positive ways instead of negative ways."

The second and third factors that influence mother-child adjustment are the way a mother feels toward her former husband and toward her children. Mothers who feel abandoned by their husbands and angry that they are "stuck" with the children are apt to both view life and treat their children differently from mothers who are determined to grow from the divorce and approach single parenting with a positive attitude.

Kathy's outlook is a good one. She says, "I think my child is beyond a doubt my greatest joy and blessing. I'm greatful to have had her—it would have been worse to go through my divorce without her." Mothers like Kathy who are psychologically healthy, personally mature, secure, and able to relate well to others are the most likely to promote good adjustment in their children. Again, divorce may be the catalyst for personal growth. Kathy said, "Through counseling and faithful friends I have been able to achieve a better balance emotionally than I probably had before."

But even when a mother is approaching single parenting with a positive attitude and doing her very best in every respect, there are still likely to be rough spots in the parent-child relationship. The most common problem for single mothers is usually difficulty in disciplining their children. Hetherington, Cox, and Cox found that children—especially boys—tend to behave more poorly with mothers than with fathers. Their research showed that during the difficult first year in particular, "Children in divorced families were more dependent, disobedient, aggressive, whining, demanding and unaffectionate than children in intact families."[7]

At the same time, the mother is under more emotional stress than previously, is busier than ever, and is less apt to be patient. She is likely to be oriented more toward making her children comply with her immediate requests than toward using discipline as a means to develop long-term character goals. She is usually less affectionate following discipline and less inclined to give verbal explanations concerning what is wrong with the child's behavior than a mother in an intact family. Mary Beth, who is eight, complained, "My mother is always in a bad mood and spanks me."

Mary Beth might be surprised to hear it, but many mothers tend to be more affectionate toward their daughters than toward their sons at this time, perhaps because they are directing toward the son the resentment they feel toward the father. The mothers tend to expect better behavior and more independence from boys, and they give them less support than they give their girls.

The truth is that boys generally take divorce harder than girls and really need to feel that they can count on Mom at this time. As a result, a boy's response is usually to become more demanding, asking more than his emotionally stressed mother is capable of giving him. When he senses that he cannot depend on his mother, he becomes fearful, argumentative, and resentful. The result is often a serious long-running, nose-to-nose conflict between mother and son. Mothers in the Hetherington, Cox, and Cox study described it as "a fight to the finish," "a battle for survival," and "like being bitten to death by ducks." Said the principals of the study, "Each is under stress and they devour each other." [8] Ten-year-old Ben knows the feeling. "My mother seems terrible and mean because we are around each other so much. I wish my mother would work on her temper," he said.

What's missing from the home is the father's authority. Before the divorce, the mother may have left most of the discipline up to him. Even if she didn't, children whose fathers are living at home are still likelier to obey. One study showed that even if fathers said and did *nothing,* their presence alone was sufficient to make a child more likely to comply with the mother's requests for discipline. Many mothers experience a great deal of anguish when they are suddenly in the position of having to discipline their children without a husband's support.

Fifteen-year-old Sarah has noticed her mother's difficulty in this matter. "I think she has more trouble being the disciplinarian, showing authority over us, and she's having to take on a lot of the role that my dad used to have. And it's still hard on her; I can see it. It stresses her so much that after she has to do something to either one of us she'll just go into her bedroom and cry."

Sandy, who has been divorced for several years, appears to have been able to resolve the issue of discipline in her home. She asserted, "I set standards high as far as expecting right behavior from them. I've never been slack: 'Well, *you know,* their daddy's left them and you can understand their poor behavior.' Some people use a single-parent situation as an excuse for rotten behavior. I've kept my standards as far as my children's behavior, and it's made them stronger."

Anger may contribute to a child's misbehavior. When Dad leaves, children may be angry that he has left and angry that Mom let him go. Ideally, since the father is the one they are angry with, he should take time to talk with them about their feelings and help them deal with their emotions. Although sons are more prone to get angry than daughters, both would benefit from a father's model of how to handle these potentially destructive feelings. Talking them out is best, but helping a child to find harmless physical outlets like jogging or pillow punching might be an acceptable alternative. Many fathers, however, are feeling guilty about having left and are by nature uncomfortable talking about feelings. They may be unable or unwilling to help the child deal with his anger. That leaves it up to Mom.

Mother can spend extra time with the angry child, encouraging him to talk about his anger and to transfer the energy it generates into socially acceptable channels. One danger, however, may be that in hearing the child express his anger, her own may be rekindled. When this happens, she should refrain from adding fuel to the child's fire, striving to be only an understanding listener.

When fathers are unable or unwilling to help their children through their anger, a mature Christian man who relates well to children and whom the children respect may be able to serve as a partial substitute. A few sessions with a professional counselor may also be beneficial for an angry child.

TIME WITH DAD

Children of divorce experience a wide variety of relationships with their noncustodial fathers. Some fortunate children grow closer to them as a result of spending regular time together, something that may not have occurred before the divorce. At the other end of the spectrum are those who rarely if ever see their fathers. These children are paternally deprived and may lack for a male figure in their lives until their mothers remarry or until other adult males step in to fill the void. Between the two extremes lies a middle group of children who see their fathers either regularly or irregularly but the relationship is not especially close. For some it is strained, awkward, and uncomfortable. Both parent and child put in the time, but neither touches the other emotionally in more than a superficial way. To varying degrees, these children may also experience paternal deprivation.

This is what makes the mother-child relationship so vitally important. In many cases she is the only full-time, involved parent the child has. And she essentially mediates the relationship between father and child.

When fathers do visit their children on a regular basis, it is usually because the mother has encouraged them in their efforts to do so. Wallerstein and Kelly found that a friendly relationship between the parents, along with the mother's interest in the father's visiting, helped encourage the men to be regular and continuous in visitation. Children whose dads spend regular time with them are often the envy of their friends—whether their parents are divorced or not. One little girl even asked her mother if her parents could get a divorce so that she could spend all day Saturday with her father as her friends got to do!

Many children expect to see at least as much of their fathers after divorce and are even promised that this will be the case. Often this is true at the outset, but the time spent with Dad may dwindle over the long haul. Hetherington, Cox, and Cox found that divorced fathers in their study "became less nurturant and more detached from their children with time" and "ignored their children more and showed less affection."[9]

In an article called "My Turning Point," a girl named Kris Beckvall expressed her bitter disappointment over her father's lack of attention. Kris wrote,

> It's a big joke when your parents get divorced and promise you you'll see them more now than you did when they were living together. That's the biggest lie I ever heard from either one of my parents. I haven't seen my father since a couple of weekends ago when he came over to bring something to my mom. The last time I spent any time with him was on Christmas Day over at my grandparents' house.
>
> I used to think it couldn't happen to me. Now I know better. I'm not going to take so many things for granted any more, like my parents are always going to be there when I need them.[10]

Ironically, it is often the father who cares the most about his children who visits them the least. Fathers who

The Case of the Missing Father

were previously very involved in the lives of their children, sometimes as a substitute for what was lacking between husband and wife, feel intense pain at being separated from them. To the great frustration of their children, they often cope with their pain by deliberately seeing them very little.

This seems to be the case with Brett's father, and Brett is understandably confused and angry. "I don't understand," he said. "He says he does it because he loves us, but to me, I think he should—it would help if he did—come around instead of staying away. Staying away from us makes it worse!" Brett has concluded logically that "he doesn't care enough to come to see us."

Many single mothers like Brett's must help their children cope with inattention from Dad. When both the quantity and quality of visits is poor, there is no getting around the fact that this spells pain for a child of any age. "I cry at the thought of living without my father," said seventeen-year-old Anna. "I love him so much. We were so close. But since I live with Mom, I don't see him." With this kind of profound loss, it is especially important that the child feels loved by Mom and that Mom is sensitive to what the child is experiencing. Suggesting that the child is better off without his father anyway is to deny his pain; insisting that the father *does* love the child is pointless. Actions from Dad, not second-hand assurances from Mom, are what will convince him.

Author Gary Chapman has suggested that a mother might want to gently probe the child for clues as to what specifically makes him feel that Dad no longer cares. He may mention the fact that Dad doesn't call as much as he used to or that he hasn't come to any basketball games since his son made the team. The mother can then relate these things to the father and offer a few suggestions about how he might communicate his love for the child.[11] Since the father may feel guilty about the lack of time he has been spending with the child, it is very important that the mother do this gently, being careful only to make *suggestions* and not demands.

One of the hardest tasks for any single mother is

coping with her own feelings regarding an uninvolved father's behavior and her fears about the way it may affect the children. She may, like Kathy, feel heartbroken that he pays little or no attention to the children: "I still get upset realizing that my daughter doesn't know her dad or even what a daddy is. I wish my child could simply know the love and discipline and protection of a *father*."

Marian worries about the lack of a male figure in her daughters' lives. "My children need opportunities to have meals and fellowship with families where men are present," she said. Brenda fears that her ex-husband's bad example will be followed by her son. "He needs exposure to other men so that he realizes that his father isn't the only type of man in the world," she said. "Men *do* grow up and they *are* good and they treat their families right and they treat their wives right."

Mom may have trouble keeping her opinions to herself, which can be particularly upsetting to some children. What may simply be self-expression for her can spell real distress for a child. Brenda, for example, says, "My son thinks I should not express my hurt emotions." But her son, Paul, sees it as more of an attack on Dad: "I wish my mother would not talk about my dad the way she does." Carol, a college freshman whose parents divorced when she was nine, says, "My mother constantly criticizes my father and stepmother." Since her father is also constantly trying to undermine Carol's relationship with her mother, Carol has grown up feeling caught between them and quite miserable about the whole thing. She'd like her father to understand that "my mother's faults don't make her unlovable to me," and she wishes that her mother would "care a little more about my sister's and my feelings."

Studies have shown that mothers who disparage their former husbands in the eyes of their children teach them negative attitudes about men. For boys, this can be very detrimental to their masculine self-images. Conversely, a mother's positive attitude helps a boy to learn to appreciate and value his maleness.

Although it has not always been easy, Sandy has worked hard to teach her children to love their father. "I have always taught my kids to love him," she says, "no matter what he does, no matter how many months go by that he does not come to see them. The first year after he left he saw them about six hours. And during that whole time I taught them to love him—not to love what he's *done,* but the person himself. He is part of them, no matter what. You can't respect his behavior, but you have to respect who he is—he's their father."

TO NONCUSTODIAL FATHERS ONLY: A PLEA

Carol Nelson's book for children, *Dear Angie, Your Family's Getting a Divorce,* contains a chapter called "Ostriches." In an unforgettable scene, Angie's grandfather tells his son—Angie's father—what he thinks about her father's decision to leave his wife and children.

> "I have come 2,300 miles to tell you this. It's about ostriches, Lewis. I came to tell you about female ostriches."
> My father was looking at grandpa now. It was like he couldn't help it.
> "The Bible says that ostriches leave their eggs in the earth and warm them in dust, forgetting that feet may crush them or wild beasts may break them. It says that ostriches are hardened against their young ones, as though they didn't belong to them. . . .
> "You know what I'd do if I were a female ostrich, Lewis?" grandpa asked.
> My father cleared his throat. "No, sir."
> "Oh, I beg your pardon," grandpa said. His eyes were like blazing, piercing lights looking at my dad. "I thought you did know. Yes, sir, I thought you knew. Well, sir, if I were a female ostrich I would do what the jackass does. I would get myself a little room with a bath in town, and I would leave my young ones out in the dust of the earth, as though they didn't belong to me, where they could be crushed or broken."[12]

Angie's grandpa is referring to Job 39:13–17. In his aged wisdom, he has pointed out a truth that Lewis, like a great many fathers, would rather not hear. In the United States the "ostrich" problem has reached epidemic proportions. Millions of children have been abandoned by their fathers after divorce—emotionally, financially, or both.

If you are a noncustodial father, remember that even though you and your children's mother are divorced, you are still vitally important to their well-being and happiness, both now and in the future. Your ex-wife may be doing an excellent job of single parenting, but as a father there are ways that only you can influence your children.

Your parenting role is unique and important. To you, not to your ex-wife, God has entrusted the primary responsibility for your children's material provision (1 Timothy 5:8) and moral and spiritual upbringing (Ephesians 6:4; Deuteronomy 11:19). The children's mother may remarry and they may gain a stepfather, but you are the only "real" father they will ever have. Don't abandon them! You don't have to be married to their mother to be a good dad. Research strongly suggests that your continued positive involvement in their lives can significantly influence them in many important areas, including these:

GIRLS	BOYS
• Acceptance of the roles of wife and mother	• Formation of mathematical and analytical abilities and aptitudes
• Feminine self-concept	• Ability to delay gratification
• Ability to achieve sexual fulfillment in marriage	• Control of aggressive tendencies
• Ability to restrain aggressive impulses	• Ability to refrain from trying to prove masculinity with antisocial behavior
• Formation of positive attitudes toward men	• Masculine self-concept
• Control of aggressive tendencies in relating to men	• Level of anxiety

- Positive self-esteem
- Ability to make long-term commitments, both vocationally and interpersonally
- Concept of God
- Level of anxiety
- Ability to get along with peers
- Choice of vocation
- Intellectual development
- Academic achievement
- Heterosexual orientation
- Motivation to achieve

- Positive self-esteem
- Ability to make long-term commitments, both vocationally and interpersonally
- Concept of God
- Sensitivity to moral issues
- Ability to take responsibility for own actions
- Ability to be creative, flexible, and imaginative
- Vulnerability to peer pressure
- Motivation to achieve
- Ability to get along with peers
- Academic achievement
- Attitudes about fatherhood and marriage
- Heterosexual orientation
- Ability to display leadership and take responsibility
- Choice of vocation*

Suggestions for helping single-mother families are included in chapter 18.

*Lists compiled from *Father, Child and Sex Role: Paternal Determinants of Personality Development*, 55–81, 106–112, 115–18; *The Role of the Father in Child Development*, 364–66; *Father Absence, Divorce and Personality Development*, 502–524; *Paternal Deprivation*, 53–71, 75–114, 121–52; *mother/child father/child Relationships*, 111; *Dr. Dobson Answers Your Questions*, 43.

15 When Mom Bails Out (Single-Father Families)

The hardest part about having divorced parents is feeling like you caused all the unhappiness and are in the middle of two feuding parents.
—Carol, age 18

In the 1800s and early 1900s fathers had the absolute right of custody after divorce. The prevailing view in society was that the father was better equipped than the mother to provide for his children financially and educationally. Until early in this century, in the rare event that custody went to the mother, the father then had no legal responsibility to provide support for the child.[1]

As the role of women in American life gained more status and respect, the pendulum began to swing in the other direction. By the 1920s motherhood had become so revered and elevated in the popular consciousness that maternal rather than paternal custody became the rule and even the law. But over the past twenty-five years, society's growing concern for equality of the sexes has opened the door once again to father custody.[2]

Although women are still awarded sole custody 90 percent of the time, this is usually because the father does not challenge the decision. When he does, statistics reveal that he has a 64 percent chance of winning custody, especially if his children are all boys or if his ex-wife has already remarried.[3] According to the 1981 census figures, there are now at least 666,000 single-father families in the U.S., up 50 percent from just ten years before.

Single fathering is becoming increasingly popular,

having been spurred on by films like *Kramer Vs. Kramer* and other media spotlighting of what is still largely a social anomaly in this generation. Many divorced fathers are beginning to wonder if they too might have what it takes to raise their children alone. Those who try are usually surprised and pleased to discover that they do and that people applaud their efforts at solo parenting. "I get a lot of support from my friends and from people in the church, too," said Brandon, a twenty-seven-year-old single father. "People encourage me a lot. They say things to me that make me feel like I'm doing something special almost. People say this is really great, here I am taking care of the kids and we seem to be doing OK."

The same people who strongly support a single father often regard his former wife with contempt: How could a mother leave her children? Why would she do such a thing? One study showed that women who commit the day-to-day care of their children into the hands of their ex-husbands rarely do so for the feminist reasons that many people assume. Relatively few throw off the yoke of child rearing in order to fulfill their own goals or to run off with another man. The majority do so because they are struggling financially and feel they are less capable of providing well for their children than their more financially stable ex-husbands.

For many mothers this is an agonizing decision that they keep carefully hidden from co-workers and others, for fear of being labeled as some sort of modern-day monster. Many of these women are angry about society's prevailing double standard: women are quickly seen as having abandoned their children, while men who allow their wives to have custody are generally viewed with more acceptance and understanding. Many mothers feel quite guilty and miserable about the father-custody arrangement; yet from a dollar and cents perspective, both they and the fathers have usually agreed that this was best for the children. These are women who visit their children on weekends and struggle to make a living during the week.

Of course, there are both mothers and fathers who

abandon their children in pursuit of the "better life." Women who bail out of their marriages may, for completely selfish reasons, uncaringly bail out of their children's lives as well, leaving their total care and upbringing to the father. Some start a postdivorce relationship with the children and then seemingly have a change of heart.

This is the case with Steve's former spouse. He related, "When I went back to my undergraduate work, my ex-wife stopped seeing the children for some reason. I don't know why. She never discussed it with me; she never said that she was not going to see them again. She just stopped, cold turkey." As a result, says Steve, his son and daughter "don't have any relationship with her at all. She doesn't call or ask to see them or anything. The only time she does see them is by chance."

A NEW ROLE

There seems to be plenty of evidence that children in single-father families usually fare just as well as those in single-mother families. One study found no differences at all but emphasized that the critical factor in a child's good adjustment remains, as always, whether or not the child has access to his noncustodial parent. Another study found that, at least for six-to-eleven-year-old boys, father-custody may even be preferable. These children were rated higher in warmth, self-esteem, maturity, sociability, and independence than boys who lived in intact homes with *both* parents.

Researcher Marsha Weinraub commented, "With the exception of the initial pregnancy and delivery process, fathers appear equally competent—both biologically and psychologically—to fulfill the parenting role.[4] Canadian sociologist Bob Knight said, "There is a paternal instinct just as much as maternal and there is probably no difference in their makeup. It's the unconditional love for a child, the sense to provide security and protection."[5] Further debunking the myth of a father's parenting handicap, researchers James C. Young and Muriel E. Hamilton wrote, "Parenting skills, like most other skills, are basically learned behaviors, not biological endowments."[6]

Giving a father custody may be the most sensible thing to do in many cases, especially if he was actually more involved in the children's lives before the divorce than the mother was. Some men are simply more nurturing and temperamentally better suited for the parenting role than the women they married.

Being basically nurturing and temperamentally well-suited for parenting, however, does not guarantee that a man will find single parenting an easy task. Many find it to be one of the toughest challenges of their lives for one big reason: men are not socialized to fill the mothering role. Even in the most egalitarian marriages, most men function only as mother's helpers in caring for their children. Consequently, when divorce occurs, very few approach single fathering prepared to assume full responsibility for meeting all their children's physical and emotional needs.

To many fathers, a child's physical development may be something of an enigma: What is normal and what is not? Should my son be talking by now? Is he too heavy for his height and age? Is my child old enough to be potty trained? When will my daughter have her first period? There may be other baffling questions too: What do you do for diaper rash? How can I help my son stop wetting the bed? What can I give my daughter for cramps? How do you bring down a fever? Many single fathers have never had to confront these kinds of problems before.

With the feminine half of the parenting team missing, fathers often find themselves in unfamiliar and uncomfortable territory when it comes to meeting a child's emotional needs. Many feel that this is actually the toughest part of being a single father. One father said, "I felt unprepared for dealing with the children's emotional needs and being open to what they were feeling. I was very inadequate in that I couldn't deal with my own feelings very well. I was afraid, I didn't know how to listen or respond to them."[7] Another said, "Dealing with feelings openly or expressing them, especially negative feelings, like grief or anger . . . those were the areas where I felt totally handicapped."[8]

Some men feel awkward giving their children the expressions of affection they crave, especially in the wake of divorce when feelings of anger, grief, and insecurity may abound. Very young children who have the most trouble talking about what is bothering them make the challenge to single dads all the greater. Some fathers, like Jonathan, seem unusually well-equipped to deal with both their own and their children's feelings. He reflected,

> Emotionally I considered myself an extremely weak person during and after the divorce, but I have since realized that I was much stronger than many in similar circumstances. I am a person who feels deeply, who allows emotions to surface without difficulty. I believe this is good, because my spouse kept such emotions under too much seclusion.

Beyond learning to deal with their children's physical and emotional needs, single fathers, like single mothers, must cope with the mammoth task of running a household without the support of a spouse. For men this may be further complicated by having to learn how to do things they may not have attempted before–sewing on buttons, roasting a chicken, buying children's clothing. Like custodial mothers, they may live a perpetual balancing act. They work all day, do housework in the evenings, try to be both mom and dad to their children, shop for groceries on Saturday, and try to regain their sanity on Sunday!

Brandon said,

> I realize that by choosing to keep the kids in my custody it is an awful lot of work, an awful lot more responsibility than I had before. It's not shared any longer; it's all mine. When you're the only one doing it, you have to go to work all day and come home and work all night. You finally get to sit down around ten o'clock at night and unwind. It's not that terrible; don't take it wrong. It's just that by the time you make supper and clean up, it's seven or eight o'clock; then you've got to get the kids ready for bed and read them a story. You don't even have that much time to spend with them, the time you'd like to have. Then when they're in bed you've got more to do: keeping after the house, keeping the wash caught up, keeping the bills paid. There's so much.

California disc jockey Ralph McCarthy, a single father, told *Time* magazine, "I was surprised at how much time the kids needed, how much I didn't know. Even now, the kids still miss the bus, and I've got to take them to school. There's never enough clean clothes. There's just too much for one person to do."[9]

Full-time child rearing can put a real strain on one of a man's primary sources of personal identity, his job. Like single mothers, single dads may have to take time off when their children are sick. But they are even less likely to meet with understanding from superiors and co-workers. School vacations pose a similar problem. Overtime may be ruled out by day-care centers that close at the end of a normal workday. Moonlighting at a second job is impossible for most single fathers.

Single parenting often limits a man in his upward job mobility. If a promotion means having to travel, he may have to turn it down. If it means transferring to a new community, it may be out of the question, particularly if relatives who now live close by are an important source of support and child care. Thus, while the financial problems of a single father are not apt to be as crushing as those of a single mother, they may still exist alongside an inability to make career advancements.

Even though a single father may struggle to make ends meet, he probably can afford to hire baby-sitters or occasional household help—something many single mothers only dream about. This gives men an advantage in pursuing a social life and recreational activities that can provide them with a breather to meet some of their emotional needs.

ATTITUDES

Single parenting often changes a man in some positive and unexpected ways. A Brandeis University study found that single fathering generally makes a man "more people oriented" and less focused on his job.[10] Most men become very close to their children, and most wouldn't trade their newfound relationships for anything. "I feel inside as if it's pretty neat to be a father and to be able to do all this—to kind of be a mother," said Brandon. "I feel as if I'm closer to them now than I would be if I were still married." Another single father put it this way: "If anything positive has come out of this, it is day-to-day intimacy. I was too busy to spend this kind of time with my children before. There's no other way in the world that I would have sat down with my kids to fold the laundry."[11]

Another benefit is likely to be increased self-esteem for Dad. Meeting the challenge of going it alone and being able to master a whole new role and its related tasks causes self-confidence to soar. A study done in Greensboro, North Carolina, with twenty single-father families concluded,

> These fathers felt quite capable and successful regarding their ability to be the primary parent of their children and . . . the confidence they expressed and the satisfaction they seemed to derive in fatherhood was very difficult to deny. The sense of pride in being able to cope with the challenge of parenthood and of seeing their children mature under their guidance was a major compensating force.[12]

However, both a sufficient income and a cooperative relationship with their children were found to be important factors in the lives of fathers who felt this way.

Many single fathers also experience emotional growth. Dealing with children's feelings and problems on a much closer level than before may help develop an interpersonal sensitivity hitherto lacking. Many become more conscious of the needs of others and more responsive toward people in general. The many needs and questions that a single father is likely to have concerning his new role may also force him to communicate with other adults in a deeper way. Motivated out of need, he may begin to discuss his real fears and feelings with others, both men and women, perhaps for the first time. This carryover into relationships with other adults of both sexes can result in more satisfying personal relationships and thus a happier father. One father called single parenting "a very humanizing experience." Another described it as "a great equalizer." Both seemed pleased at their increased sensitivity and growth.

WHAT ABOUT MOM?

Like single mothers, single fathers may struggle to keep the other parent in a positive perspective before their children. Brandon admits, "Knowing what I know about the situation, it's hard for me to think a lot of her myself, so it makes it a little bit harder—it's as if you're tempted to tell them that she doesn't love them." Brandon has managed to handle those feelings, however. "I think it's bad to break the image of the other one, to break the image that they have of their mother," he said. "I try—I think it's better—to encourage them. I don't want them to hate their mother."

Jonathan, a part-time single father, agrees. He said, "My kids think their other parent made a great mistake in allowing the marriage to end in failure and that she made a bigger mistake in marrying a man who broke up their home. But they also think their mother is a wonderful person and a terrific parent. I would not deny them that thought." Steve's rule is, "I don't discuss her in front of them. I don't really want to diminish their view of her. I want their view of her to be very positive."

SUPPORT

Because single fathers are so few in number, many do not know even one other man in a similar situation. Most have no one with whom to compare notes, no other man who really knows what it's like to be both a mother and father to a child. As a result, spending time with "the other single mothers" becomes almost a necessity for many single dads, and most must rely on female friends and relatives for advice and help in fulfilling aspects of the mothering role at times.

Some of Steve's most difficult times have come on occasions when mothers are expected to participate with their children in special functions. "The hardest part," he said, "is when they have a mother-daughter banquet at church and Carla doesn't have a mother. And when they ask for the mothers to come in and help out at school, the kids don't have a mother. I would say that's the hardest part: not having the other half of your family there to be what they're supposed to be." Steve's mother, the children's grandmother, often fills in, but this isn't always possible. Steve recalls that on the evening of his church's mother-daughter banquet, "Mama was tied up and couldn't go, so I went. I was the only man there. There wasn't even a boy there, but I enjoyed it. I knew most of the people there and they knew the situation and they understood why I was with Carla."

Right after his separation, Brandon did something that turned out to be a vital source of support. After his wife left, he hired his cousin Sally to baby-sit his two preschoolers and to help with the housework temporarily. He remembers, "Sally, whom they knew very well, came into the house to take care of them. I have to say I was amazed. I expected them to cry and cry their little eyes out and they really didn't do that at all. But I think it's because I didn't have to take them out somewhere. I was able to have someone whom they were very familiar with come here to the house. Todd made the comment to his grandpa, 'Guess what? I've got two mommies!' It wasn't like they had lost one; they still had her. They had gained another one."

Having Sally's help did a lot for Brandon, too. "The first few months—because you're going through so much mentally—if you can at all find somebody to help you with the housework, it's just a necessity. Sally came in and kept my house clean, did my wash, folded it, put it away. She always had supper on the table when I came home. That was better than I had it when I was married! Seriously, that did so much for me because it had been a very hard time. You're making an adjustment inside to a broken relationship. It was really great to be able to have that help for those three months."

After that period of time, Brandon placed his children in day-care and began to take responsibility for all the household duties. He feels that having Sally's initial help enabled him and his children to make a smoother transition. "What was really good," he said, "was that it was a step. It wasn't everything all at once to have to adjust to. It was one little thing at a time."

For many single fathers, singles groups have been lifesavers, especially during the time when they were adjusting to their new roles as divorced person and single parent. Steve's group was in his church. He said,

> When a couple are divorced, there is a period of time in which you have trouble identifying who you are. There is no set amount of time for this crisis. It may be a month or two or it may be several years.
>
> The local church can and must help during this time in order for the divorced person to gain self-respect and confidence. For me, well, I was fortunate enough—or better, divinely guided—to a group of adults who were enough attuned to God to care about me and others like me. My friend who encouraged me to come was dating a divorcee with one child. So I got to spend some time with her, through him, and we talked. There were a few people there who had gone through divorce, but I was the only man in the group who had children.

Brandon found a group that was led by a Christian counselor. He said,

> The group was *very* important. It gave me outside friends, people that understood what I was going through. I could talk until I was blue in the face with my family and my close friends about the situation. They were very receptive, but let's face it: they didn't know what I was going through. But these people knew what I was going through and there's something really special about that.
>
> Yet, what did me the most good was that *I was able to help them*. That did a lot to give my self-esteem back. It's very important to have a good feeling about yourself, and the fact that I was able to contribute to someone else really helped me. I highly recommend a group like that, especially a Christian group. It was important for me to be in that group where almost everyone was either separated or divorced. Either way, you're separated. And these were the

ones who didn't want to be. I don't know how I ever would have made it without this group.

WORTH THE TROUBLE

One study showed that a majority of single fathers feel that their social lives would be much different if they did not have custody of their children. Many could advance in their careers and most would lead less harried lifestyles if their children were not constantly in their care. Obviously, it takes a special man to be a single dad. But given the many problems and complexities of raising children without a wife, is single fathering really worth it?

"Definitely," said Brandon. "There's nothing in the world that's more worth it than your own kids."

Suggestions for helping single-father families are included in chapter 18.

16 Family Heirlooms

> *My grandfather had been married about six times; my parents have been divorced. I think about it all the time. It's scary. It could happen to me, too. Because after my dad and his dad, I think it runs in the family.*
>
> —Brett, age 15

When two people marry, they take the first step in a lifelong series of events. From the wedding day forward they are married, and this fact is reflected in a hundred different ways that touch every subsequent day of their lives. Similarly, divorce is not just a single event that happens one day in the life of a child and is forgotten the next. The severing begins a chain of events that colors a child's life in a multitude of ways from the point of divorce onward.

FIRST, THE BAD NEWS

The *Winston-Salem Journal* invited children of divorce to write in, answering two questions: "Has divorce affected you?" and "What would you tell a friend whose parents were getting a divorce?" A young woman named Debbi responded this way:

> My parents were divorced when I was 3. I've had no family life to speak of. There were custody fights, suicide attempted, two stepfathers, not to mention being tossed from relative to relative. It was not unusual to change schools three times in one year.

To top it all off, my parents could not stand to be in the same room. You can see that my graduation and wedding were lacking in loved ones. It has been as if I had to choose between them all my life.

I am now almost 26, happily married and have two children. You would think I made it pretty well to have come from a broken home. However, I find that my problems are just starting.

I found it very difficult fitting into my role as mother. My mother worked all the time and dated. That left very little time for the kids. I don't recall her ever playing with me or reading a story.

My responsibilities at home were many, including keeping my sister and later stepbrother and stepsister. That carried over into my motherhood, giving me problems with feeling trapped. Sometimes I feel I've kept kids all my life. I believe my husband is a good father—or at least my idea of one. I don't really know much about fathers; mine was never around.

The real pain came when I realized my children were going through the same thing. Three sets of grandparents is hard enough to explain, without the complication of two of them being so immature that they can't be in the same room. The children began to think the missing grandparent doesn't love them. Boy, does that ever sound familiar! I feel my children have become a little unsure of our own home life because of this.

There is no good way to handle it because divorce isn't good. It does help to have parents who don't shut you out and do communicate with each other. My faith has been a great comfort.

My message to all parents who are thinking of divorce, is not to. At least try everything before you do. (That should take you a couple of years!) . . . If you feel you can't make it, keep in mind you are divorcing each other, not your children.

You owe it to them to at least be civil to each other. Divorce affects not just the two of you, but your children and their children and their children.[1]

Like Debbi, many children of divorce grow up, marry, and have children, hoping to establish a happy home and leave the past behind. What they often find, however, is that their problems, in Debbi's words, "are just beginning."

Unhappy Memories

No person can alter his personal history, preserved in the form of memories. As time and maturity put things into perspective for us, an unhappy childhood can be forgiven, understood, or reinterpreted from an adult point of view, but it can never be forgotten. Childhood memories, whether happy or unhappy, accompany us throughout life.

The period of time surrounding parental divorce is almost always remembered as unhappy. For the more fortunate, it is the only dark spot in an otherwise carefree and happy childhood. For others, like Debbi, the memories of childhood may blur into one long, unhappy stretch of time that seems like an endless night: "... custody fights, suicide attempted, two stepfathers, not to mention being tossed from relative to relative."

Twenty-nine-year-old Jody, whose parents divorced when she was sixteen, remembers,

> I thought divorce was a welcome event. My parents had a loveless marriage leading nowhere. My dad could do nothing right, according to my mother. She had a lot of problems and expected my dad to fulfill all her needs. She eventually became an alcoholic. She locked us out of the house often and I remember some days never getting lunch. I remember sometimes my mom would pack her clothes and leave and as she walked out the door she would make me decide if I would stay with her or dad. I always picked my dad and then she would call me names. I hated her then.

Terry, also twenty-nine, recalls a montage of scenes:

> My mother—always busy working and trying to support the family. She had no time for self or children. When self-interest overcame interest in children, the children were left after school many extra hours. We practically raised ourselves and got into trouble—there was no one to say no. My mother was not able to control my brother. I remember other parents coming out to see their children play ball and wondering where my father was. No interest shown from my father in my life. I know no one from my father's family. I remember my grandmother working past her years to help support us. Growing up alone, not enjoying childhood. I think divorce is a crying shame.

Barbie, age thirty, said,

> My parents didn't divorce until after I was married, but sometimes I wonder if we all wouldn't have been better off if they had done it sooner. My childhood was definitely the worst time in my life. I remember my father slamming doors and shouting, my mother crying and being depressed, and lots of family arguments. Holidays were always uncomfortable times for me because that was the only time my father spent time with the family. It felt so fake—unnatural and strained.
>
> My father never showed much interest in me, and my mother was often too depressed to think about anyone but herself. I feel like I grew up alone. I never shared my life with them because they never shared their lives with me—or with each other. I think I was depressed for most of my childhood. I know I didn't do as well as I could have done in school, and I know the insecurity I felt at home carried over into my relationships with other kids.

Ongoing Hurts

A poor relationship between former spouses is not likely to improve just because their children grow into adults who have families of their own. Even some children of divorce who have now grown up find that they are still in the center of the conflict. Terry, for example, said, "They always blame the other and try to trap me in the middle." He admits, "I cry when my father or mother uses the other as an excuse not to participate in an activity with me."

Terry is very frustrated about his continuing poor relationship with his father. "In his youth," Terry said, "he had no interest in seeing me play ball or having any part in my life. Now that he is old he expects my time and wants me to come and visit but still refrains from visiting me." Terry's mother, burdened with guilt about the past, is now trying hard to make up for it. Terry said, "I don't harbor bad feelings because of neglect in my childhood—past is past and all we have is the future. You can't repay the damage of neglect with money and gifts but only with true love. I wish my mother would stop trying to overcompensate for the past and live for the future."

Carol's parents' divorce happened almost a decade

ago, but to this day, she says, "they hate each other." For Carol this "causes hurt and pain that always seems to be there."

Melodie, thirty-one, is bothered in two ways by her parents' divorce, which occurred when she was twenty. The first, she says, is

> knowing that our family would never be the same again. I knew the younger children would never know their dad the way I had. I also realized that the dad I knew had changed, so in a sense I had lost him too. Because of what he did to our family, our relationship can never be quite the same. Oh, I still love him and have forgiven him, but there is a loss of respect that I'm not sure can be regained. The scars of pain and sorrows will always remain. The pain goes on *forever*, not only for the couple but the entire family.
>
> But worse than that is Christmas. My husband and children and I always try to spend a week with mom. There are six other children in my family and we always try to be at mom's the same week and spend time together as a family. But we brothers and sisters also try to spend one evening at my dad and stepmother's to exchange gifts. The hardest thing is leaving mom there at home alone. I always feel like a traitor. It just doesn't seem fair that at a time when families are reuniting in a special way, ours has to be pulled apart and old hurts rekindled.

Jody also greets the Christmas season with mixed emotions. She said, "The hardest part about having divorced parents is what to do on holidays. Any tradition is dissolved when parents divorce. You have to give each parent equal time during holidays, and according to your parents, it is never enough."

Milestones

Debbi's lament that "my graduation and wedding were lacking in loved ones" would draw sympathy from many other children of divorce. Milestones of any sort can be a mixture of pleasure and pain if the chemistry between Mom and Dad is still volatile.

The sense of satisfaction and accomplishment that should be felt upon graduation from high school or college may be dimmed by the pain of an absent parent, or by two parents who attend but sit in separate sections of the auditorium as though they were strangers. The joy that should typify every wedding may be dampened by the same problem. If both parents attend the wedding, how should they be seated? What about stepparents? What about photographs?

Weddings are especially difficult because they bring the now-divorced couple back to the altar where they pledged their lives to one another "till death do us part." The recollection of this may stimulate some erratic emotions for the parents and add to the insecurities and questions of the prospective bride and groom, who may already be wondering if their marriage can weather the storms that lie ahead.

Melodie recalls,

> I remember wondering on my wedding day if our marriage would end up the way my parents' did, wondering if we had what it takes to make the marriage a good one. Was I sure Bobby was the right man? Could I handle it if I ever had to go through what my mother did? I had seen something that had been so stable in my life, my parents' marriage, crumble. Was I in love deep enough to make it last? I guess, in short, I was really insecure.

Even the birth of a baby—certainly one of the most joyous occasions of all—can be diminished by the awareness that two phone calls, rather than one, must be made just to inform one set of grandparents. Having to make four phone calls can be even more disheartening. The realization that the newborn will never know his grandparents as a couple may also be discouraging.

Crises

When divorce forces a mother to work outside the home for the very first time or for the first time since her single days, her trauma can be a heartbreaking experience for her older children. For the woman herself, this is a time of unprecedented personal crisis. For her children, it is a time of great anxiety, complicated by the fact that they cannot look to their other parent for any sort of assistance or support. Leslie Williams put her feelings into words:

What on earth is mother going to do? She has spent her lifetime raising us, like most of the women in her generation, and she has no marketable skills at all. She's never worked in her life, and how on earth is she going to find a job that will support her, when she's nearly fifty years old? It seems grossly unfair.[2]

Like Leslie, we who have watched our mothers struggle through the difficulties of postdivorce adjustment time know the push and pull of many different emotions. Feelings of outrage and chagrin that a fifty-or-sixty-year-old woman should be forced to compete with high school seniors for low-paying, menial work may be just the beginning. There may also be anger toward Dad, who by comparison lives in luxury, seemingly unconcerned about his ex-wife's plight.

During this time most women need to lean heavily on the remaining members of their families, namely their children. And the children are likely to respond, brokenheartedly, by beginning to parent their parent. Mothers may look to their children and their children-in-law for advice on putting together a resume, filing income tax forms, making out a will, moving into a new apartment, selling a car or other possessions, doing bank statements, making major purchases such as appliances, and doing a vast array of other things that she may once have looked to her husband for. The children feel constrained to help—to not let her down in any way, lest her pain be compounded. At the same time, they know that if Mom is to survive on her own, she cannot become too dependent. Discovering how much to do for her and how much to insist that she do on her own can cause some real internal struggles.

Children also worry about their newly single parent regarding her emotional, social, and spiritual well-being. How will she adjust to living alone? Will she make new friends? What about her safety? Will this be a time of spiritual growth or falling away? There is increased emotional stress for all concerned and often a sense of helplessness and frustration for the children, since their most earnest and deliberate efforts to help sometimes seem like Band-Aids on a gushing wound.

When a serious physical or mental illness or the death of a parent occurs after divorce, the children are often required to face it without the slightest bit of emotional support, financial help, or physical assistance from their other parent. This may be because the other parent in fact does not care, but it may also be because the parent who is ill does not want to involve the ex-spouse. Or it may be a decision made by the children to spare themselves and their parent needless additional conflict and stress at the time of crisis. Regardless of the reason, seeing one parent through a major crisis without the support of the other parent can be one of the most difficult and trying times any child of divorce will face. Those who are only-children with no siblings to help shoulder the load may face the hardest time of all.

Pass-along Problems

As I read Debbi's letter in the *Winston-Salem Journal*, her last sentence in particular stood out to me: "Divorce affects not just the two of you, *but your children and their children and their children.*" Her words reminded me of Exodus 34:7: "He will by no means leave the guilty unpunished, visiting the iniquity of fathers on the children and on the grandchildren to the third and fourth generations." If I understand this verse correctly, it does not mean that God punishes children and grandchildren and great-grandchildren for the sins committed by their predecessors. Rather, it means that God allows some of the natural consequences of their actions to take their course as they filter down through the generations. Children inevitably reap many things that their parents and grandparents have sown. This is true whether the seed sown has been positive or negative. Psalm 103:17–18 illustrates the positive side of the same principle. "But the lovingkindness of the LORD is from everlasting to everlasting on those who fear Him, and His righteousness to children's children, to those who keep His covenant."

The sort of things these verses refer to are not passed on in the same way that one might receive Grandma's antique clock or her silver tea set after her will is read. Instead, these are intangibles that are absorbed by a child over a period of many years. They are silently instilled rather than deliberately bequeathed. Values, attitudes, ways of treating others, feelings about how husbands and wives should carry out their roles, ideas about how parents should raise their children, expectations of marriage and of a marriage partner, family traditions—these and many other things are passed from one generation to next in this way. Most of these are internalized so unthinkingly and so deeply that we may have difficulty recognizing why we hold certain opinions or how it is that we have come to expect certain things.

Every family passes on both positive and negative ways of behaving and thinking to children. Those whose families have been splintered by divorce, however, often inherit some of the least desirable "heirlooms."

Fear of Marital Commitment. Eighteen-year-old Carol said of her parents, "It scares me when I think that two people who thought they were in love enough to marry now hate each other." In the same way, Melodie expressed bewilderment "that after twenty-six years of marriage and bringing seven children into the world a marriage could go bad." Observing the dissolution of something that once seemed permanent and secure can at the very least cause a child to become more hesitant and thoughtful about making commitments of his own.

This may prove to be a positive consequence except for those children who have witnessed the dissolution of several marriages. A child who has been party to a series of breakups may be extremely disillusioned. After experiencing repeated pain and grief at losing people in whom he had emotional investments, he may decide to protect himself from additional loss by putting less at stake in his relationships. This can also be true for the child who has developed close relationships with mother and father surrogates who happen to be boyfriends or girlfriends of Mom or Dad. When the relationship ends, the child experiences another loss. Either way, the child may learn in effect that commitment ultimately results in being hurt and that it is better not to set oneself up for it. For reasons of his own, nine-year-old Tim has already decided, "I am not going to get married."

Those who marry may consciously or unconsciously refrain from making a full emotional commitment, to the obvious hurt of the family. Ironically, in so doing they may sow the seeds that will eventually result in their own divorce.

The only thing worse than a fear of marital commitment may be having too light a regard for it. Actress Jodie Foster probably represented thousands of other children of divorce when, while she was a teenager, Parade magazine asked her, "What about marriage?" She replied,

> I do think about it. . . . But not for a long time. I'm too young. I haven't finished having fun. But I'm sure I will. I'm sure I'll get divorced too. Why not? You've got to do it once. Everyone seems to.[3]

Choosing the Wrong Mate. The desire to marry a man who is "just like Daddy" or "a girl just like the girl who married dear old dad" is not unusual. After all, parents are a child's primary sources for obtaining information about what a husband is, what a wife is, and what marriage means. That children grow up and apply what they have learned firsthand when they select their own mates is hardly surprising. Children of divorce, however, may find themselves caught up in patterns that confuse their mate selection and virtually guarantee their unhappiness, since they may still be dealing with many unresolved issues from their childhood.

Dr. Robert S. Weiss, a professor of sociology at the University of Massachusetts and a lecturer at Harvard Medical School, feels that children of divorce have a tendency to commit themselves to unpromising relationships that may mirror their parents' breakup. He believes that even in the most promising relationships, children focus not on the present happy times or dream about a future together but on the breakup they feel sure is to come.[4]

Daughters of divorce sometimes grow up thinking of themselves as co-victims along with their mothers when Dad leaves home. It is the speculation of some that having "lost" in an emotional sense as children, these women continue to view themselves as losers and they expect to lose in their other emotional relationships. As a result, they are automatically attracted to men who are unable to meet their emotional needs and who will abandon them or treat them as their fathers did.[5]

Men and women alike will sometimes marry people with the same kind of personality traits that they abhorred in their parents. One reason for this may be what mental health professionals refer to as the "rescue fantasy"—a spouse's attempt (either conscious or unconscious) to change his mate into a parent figure with the qualities for which he longs. This rarely if ever works. The result is usually hostility on the part of the one who is being pressured to change. Often the hurt of not being loved and accepted for who he or she is eventually drives the spouse away.

One prominent way in which parental divorce contributes to a child's choice in a mate is an unplanned pregnancy. As we have already noted, teenagers from divorced homes are more likely to be sexually active and to have more partners than other teens. Whether they are simply seeking comfort following a family breakup or trying to substitute sex for a missing parent's love, many are caught unprepared by a pregnancy. The result is often a marriage that was never meant to be and one that may easily result in divorce within a few years. One-third of the divorcing couples studied by Wallerstein and Kelly had rushed into marriage because of an unplanned pregnancy. On the average, these marriages lasted eight years.

Excess Baggage. Children of divorce and those who grow up in intact homes where there is a great deal of discord and unhappiness tend to develop a certain outlook on home and family. Serious parental conflict that endures over time tends to alter the meanings of terms like "father," "mother," "family," "marriage," and "husband-wife relationship." Children define these words on the basis of their own experiences, which may be vastly incongruous with the experiences of other children.

Christian children of divorce know *two* definitions for each of these words. They know the way things are supposed to be, as defined by the Bible and the Christian subculture of which they are a part, and they know the way things have turned out to be in their own particular corner of the real world. Trying to reconcile both definitions can be confusing and painful. A sermon on "the Christian home" can be hard to bear because the child knows he *had* a Christian home—but something wasn't right. Sorting through what was and what ought to have been is necessary to establish what kind of a marriage, a spouse, and a parent he himself will become. It is a sticky task that may occupy his thoughts for many years before his wounds heal and his perspective clears.

When a young person marries before that sorting and healing process is completed, it is likely that he will carry some excess baggage into the marital relationship. In that baggage there is bound to be a "how-to" book with specific instructions for handling conflict and resolving the problems that are typical to any marriage.

Most newlyweds seldom need to consult the text, however, because the movie version was shown so many times at home. They may literally have the lines memorized! If the bride's parents dealt with the conflict that led to their divorce by throwing plates and slamming doors, she will no doubt have a good idea of how to behave at the first sign of disagreement. If the groom's parents were in the habit of sweeping the problems that led to their divorce under the rug, it is highly probable that somewhere in his baggage there is a broom of the same make and model.

All of us tend to reproduce the kind of family environment in which we grew up. Children of divorce, however, are likely to have internalized patterns of communication and conflict resolution that will probably be as counterproductive as they were for their parents.

Young adults from divorced homes may also carry in their baggage an inordinate number of emotional needs that they unrealistically expect their spouses to be able to meet. They may view their spouses more as surrogate parents than partners, expecting them to pick up where negligent parents may have left off. Their need for security, nurture, and attention may be far more than the spouses are able or willing to supply, thus burdening the marriages from the outset.

Parenting Patterns. "Most people do what they do out of habit, not because of rational considerations. Parents behave toward their children by and large in the same way their parents behaved toward them," write researchers Young and Hamilton.[6] Studies have proven rather conclusively over the years that this tends to be the case, and this is precisely why children of divorce sometimes grow up confused about how to parent their own children.

As Debbi put it, "I found it very difficult fitting into my role as mother. My mother worked all the time and dated." How, she seems to be asking, can you model yourself after someone who is seldom around? Young mothers from divorced backgrounds, like Debbi, often feel that they have been handed a blank slate on which they are somehow expected to know how to write a mother's job description. Yet, according to psychologist Carin Rubenstein, these women cope very well and "tend to be strongly involved" in their marriage role, "perhaps unconsciously anticipating their own possible status as single parents."[7]

Curiously, the opposite tends to be true for men whose parents were divorced. They are more often uninvolved as fathers, perhaps closely imitating the pattern set by their own dads. Boys whose fathers leave all child care to their wives after divorce may grow up perceiving parenting as "women's work." Because of a fear of seeming feminine, they may refrain from participating in the care and rearing of their own children. Their sons, of course, may one day repeat the pattern in their own families.

A child who suffers inattention from an overly busy or unconcerned parent naturally has trouble learning to express love and care for others, including his own children when he becomes a parent himself. This can be true even when the parent is a Christian. Dr. James Mallory writes, "When we take genetics and environment into consideration, it is not surprising that there are atheists who are more loving than Christians. A person's theological position is not the only variable related to love."[8]

Parental divorce can affect not only a person's perceptions of the parenting role also his expectations toward his marriage partner. Twelve-year-old Kimberlee remarked, "Most of the time, with divorced parents, the mother gets the children because the father is the one fooling around and doing all that other stuff. So, if the father gets the children, most of the time it's an unhappy place." Her experience? "The way my dad acted, they almost put him in jail because he wouldn't pay the child support." Kimberlee has already formed some pretty definite opinions about fathers, which she has generalized, of course, from her own father's behavior: Mothers are responsible and fathers aren't. Mothers care; fathers don't. Kim's future husband may have quite an uphill climb before he can defuse his wife's negative expectations about his ability to be a good father to their children.

People who, like Debbi, have had little or no contact with their fathers may have fewer notions about what the partner's role should be: "I believe my husband is a good father—or at least my idea of one. I don't really know much about fathers; mine was never around."

Thus, depending on when and how it occurred, parental divorce can greatly affect the way a child will someday parent his own children. Henry Biller stated, "Perhaps the best way to develop the abilities of being a good father is the experience of having had one."[9] Obviously the same goes for mothers.

The experience of parental divorce may be a determining factor in the decision not to become a parent at all.

Those who approach adulthood still feeling great emotional neediness may choose to forgo child rearing completely. Those suffering from acute parental neglect have not had parents they could imitate, and they fear they will bequeath the pain of their childhoods to children of their own. Biller reported, "Women who rejected the feminine role of wife and mother were more likely to come from broken homes than were women who accepted these roles."[10]

Divorce as an Option

E. Mavis Hetherington has made the unsavory prediction that three out of four children of divorce will one day get divorced themselves.[11] The irony in her prediction lies in the fact that those who have experienced parental divorce as children are usually the most determined to keep their own marriages together. Several adults in the Wallerstein and Kelly study who were in the midst of their own divorce proceedings spoke of traumatic childhood memories surrounding their own parents' divorces. They had resolved never to put their children through the same kind of misery. Nevertheless, they found themselves repeating the cycle and subjecting their children to the very dilemma they had vowed to avoid.

A few of the single parents I encountered in my research were themselves children of divorce or from unhappy homes, but none as adults initiated their own divorces. One told me,

> My folks were divorced. Then they were married again; then they divorced again. The circumstances in which my folks had split up I don't feel had any influence in my divorce. I really don't, because when I married, I married once and for all. I had no idea of divorce. Divorce was nothing in my realm. We even talked about it beforehand. Both of us had this idea that you work out your problems; you don't go run to the divorce court at the first little sign of trouble.

Another shared,

> My divorce was unique for me because I had married "for life" and had not anticipated a marriage failure. It was

especially hurtful for me because as a child, I had been deprived of a normal family relationship and my goal in life was to be a good husband and father. Sometimes I wonder why it was that I waited so long to get married—because I wanted a lasting relationship—only to have it dissolve with so much pain and bitterness.

Most of the children who shared their thoughts about marrying one day were resolute in their determination never to divorce. Benjamin, ten, vowed, "I will try and work everything out with my wife and try to stay together 'till death do we part.'" Candace, eight, asserts that when she marries, "It's going to work out." Twelve-year-old Paul was typical of many when he said, "I would not want my family to go through what I went through." Eight-year-old Mary Beth stated, "When I get married someday I will stay married." Brett, fifteen, said, "I'd try everything not to let it happen."

Teenagers like Brett often feel just as strongly as younger children about not divorcing, but they have an inkling, perhaps, that having experienced parental divorce places them at a disadvantage. Jennifer, seventeen (who is quoted in chapter 7 in the same regard), said, "For me, as a Christian, divorce is not an option. However, it will be difficult for me, because of my parents' divorce, to try and remember that divorce is not an option. I am afraid that when my husband and I have a fight I will think that the only solution is divorce. This feeling comes from seeing my father get married and divorced three times." Jody, who has already been married for several years, said, "Divorce is out of the question—*we will make our marriage work.*"

Despite such sincere determination, experts say that it is likely that some of these children will experience divorce again as adults. Why should this be so? According to Christian counselor David Martin, children of divorce are

> looking to make their marriages better than their parents' was and they are determined not to do what their parents did, and in doing so, they end up doing so!
> What we are teaching our children is: "If you get into a relationship that is not good, one of your alternatives is to

get out of it. But marriages and relationships are still good. And so you go into another one. And we set a precedent for them: And we teach them through our actions that if the first one doesn't work, go find another one. If that doesn't work, go find another one. And in that way [statistics] show that children who have been the product of a divorced marriage in many cases will use divorce as an alternative for their own marriages, because they've been exposed to it so long and they've seen their parents go through it. In a lot of ways it's like history repeating itself. We feel as if we can do better the second time around.

God intended the family unit as a school and the parents as private tutors for their children. Social scientists have long been aware of the fact that children who are physically or emotionally abused often grow up to abuse their own children. They know no other parenting patterns, and without professional help they seem destined to repeat them. Similarly, it now appears that many children from divorced homes may repeat the pattern of divorce unless they receive help in establishing new patterns for relating to and communicating with their mates.

Personal Legacy

Studies that follow the children of divorce into adulthood are still relatively few. At this point there are more questions than answers concerning the long-term impact of parental divorce on a child's life. The studies that have been done, however, seem to indicate that many of the effects that linger over the years are not consistent with good adjustment or conducive to personal happiness.

Richard Kulka and Helen Weingarten, social psychologists at the Survey Research Center at the University of Michigan, did two studies—one in 1957 and one in 1976—designed to determine whether children of different generations might respond differently to parental divorce. They concluded that while society has changed and divorce has increased, the way that children respond to it remains the same. Some of their findings:

- Between the ages of twenty-one and thirty-four, adults from divorced homes were less likely to be "very happy"

and more likely to report symptoms of poor physical health
- At all ages, people from divorced homes were likely to
  — recall their childhoods as the unhappiest time in their lives
  — say they've been on the verge of a nervous breakdown
  — feel that bad things often happen to them
  — have troubled marriages
  — have a different outlook on the marital role than other people
- Men, especially, were more apt to experience feelings of anxiety[12]

Phillip Shaver and Carin Rubenstein, who conducted a Loneliness Research Project at New York University, found that adults from divorced homes were:

- Lonelier than other adults
- Lower in self-esteem than other adults
- More likely to have crying spells, insomnia, constant worry, feelings of worthlessness, guilt, and despair
- More likely to feel afraid, anxious and angry when they were alone, similar to the separation anxiety young children feel when separated from the person to whom they are most closely attached[13]

Other studies show that people from divorced homes have shorter life expectancies, are likelier to have dropped out of school, and are likelier to have run away from home or been cast off by parents too wrapped up in their own lives and problems to care any longer about their children. According to "The Children Nobody Wants," from *Reader's Digest,* "The majority of homeless kids at runaway houses come from broken homes."[14]

NOW, THE GOOD NEWS!

Determinism is a school of thought which says that who we are and what we are capable of accomplishing in life hinges solely on the experiences that befall us.

According to this doctrine, our environment, experiences, and upbringing pretty much determine how our lives will turn out.

Those who subscribe heavily to this line of thinking have a difficult time believing that the children of divorce have much of a chance to climb out of the rubble. While it is true that many of the observations and predictions of researchers do not in fact paint an optimistic picture, the time has come to balance their findings with some additional truths.

The major flaw in the doctrine of determinism is that it ignores both God and the God-given human capacity for exercising the will. Thus determinism is at best only a partial truth. The fact that we are influenced and molded by the things we experience coexists with the truth that we can choose to regard our misfortunes as steppingstones rather than stumbling blocks. We can decide to rise above hurtful experiences and to grow from them. Beyond that, we can choose to follow Jesus Christ as Savior and thereby become heir to all His promises, provision, and healing. If there is good news about children and divorce it is found in the light of these two hope-filled truths.

In responding to divorce, as with almost anything else, a person's attitude is often the most critical factor. He alone determines how he will regard his situation. His attitude can either free him to solve his problems or keep him imprisoned behind them, bemoaning his fate.

There is a pearl of wisdom in the little rhyme, "Two men looked out from prison bars. One saw mud, the other, stars." Here are two people facing identical circumstances, yet responding in opposite ways. Both options were available to each man. Why did one choose to look up and the other choose to look down? Perhaps the man who chose to look at the stars had a team of encouragers made up of friends and family who helped him view his situation in a positive perspective. Maybe they had succeeded in showing him that this potentially lonely and unhappy time of confinement could also be a time of great personal growth and development. Maybe their love helped him see the silver lining in his cloud of isolation and gave him something to hope for. Maybe they had helped him place his trust in our faithful and unfailing heavenly Father.

The challenge of helping children of divorce is a lot like that. No knowledgeable person would deny that divorce is very hard on a child. The facts certainly indicate otherwise. Even so, no thinking person would be foolish enough to assert that when parents divorce, a child's course in life is set. Nothing could be further from the truth.

Leslie Williams wrote, "My sisters and I realized one thing quickly: We could either face the experience [of parental divorce], learn from it, grow from it, and increase our faith from it; or we could let it make our lives bitter and unhappy, never resolving our problems and repeating the mistakes of our parents."[15] These girls realized that they were free to make the choices that would color their lives and determine their growth. Like many others, they chose to focus on the stars rather than the mud.

Initially most children can see only mud when their parents break up. Their world comes crashing down. The rug has been pulled out from under them. They are miserable, insecure, depressed, and afraid. They experience grief over their many losses. Only after the period of mourning and mending can they begin to consider the possibility that stars exist. They have been afraid to look up for fear of being wounded again through trusting. As I see it, part of our job as those who wish to help is to provide gentle assurance, not only that the stars do indeed exist, but that they exist for *them*. We need to help them see that there is purpose in what they have suffered and that part of that purpose may be to ready them for some very special tasks in life.

Seeds for Success

Surprisingly, perhaps, some children whose parents divorce will grow up to be more successful and more creative, coming closer to realizing their full potential than they would have been able to do if their parents had remained together.

Christian counselor David Martin has observed,

> Divorce does some times strengthen [children]. It makes them develop coping skills that a lot of children never develop until they're adults. I think we have a concept of the 'ideal' marriage and family, and that ideal is sometimes more dangerous than it is helpful: . . . a family where the children are protected from everything, the father goes out and does his job, the mother stays home and protects the children . . . the "Father Knows Best" type of family—we're not in the 1950's anymore. We can't live there. And the children that I see who are becoming our leaders, that are taking on responsibility, are these children of divorce, because they've had to go through so much. They take on the challenge.

For some children, as Martin has described, the heirlooms of divorce may include a special motivation to succeed. An uncommon desire to excel apparently arises out of the profound losses they feel they have sustained. Why this characterizes some children and not others is not easily understood, but it is clear that such inner drive cannot be instilled by others. Instead, the child himself, in an almost mysterious sort of personal quest, embraces something he finds deep inside that propels him toward achievement. This special kind of drive toward excellence has been observed in the lives of many people who have achieved extraordinary things in life—scientists, inventors, statesmen, and others who have gained worldwide recognition for their outstanding accomplishments and creative genius.

J. Marvin Eisenstadt of East Plains Mental Health Center in Hicksville, New York, studied the lives of 573 of the greatest men and women throughout history and concluded that "a key ingredient of greatness may evolve from surviving some tremendous loss—like the death of one or both parents at an early age."[16] One-quarter of the people he studied had lost at least one parent by age fifteen. By age twenty-five more than half had lost one or both parents.

Addressing this same phenomenon, Henry Biller referred to Eisenstadt's work and noted that he "put forth the argument that the bereavement process can be worked through in a very constructive manner by some children so that they become particularly motivated and energized toward creative accomplishment."[17]

In another study, Victor and Mildred Goertzel probed the lives of four hundred unusually successful people and discovered that fully three-quarters of them had experienced some sort of childhood trauma, ranging from poverty, parental divorce, or poor parent-child relationships to physical handicaps or academic failures.[18] Dr. James Dobson has pointed out that of the eighty-five fiction or drama writers included in this study, seventy-four came from homes where "they saw tense psychological dramas played out by their parents." With regard to all four hundred subjects, Dobson commented, "It seems very apparent that the need to compensate for their disadvantages was a major factor in their struggle for personal achievement. It may even have been *the* determining factor."[19]

"God Meant It for Good"

One of the most exciting paradoxes in the Bible is that God can take a negative or even terrible situation and from it bring results that are good. The story of Joseph in the Book of Genesis illustrates this principle.

At the age of seventeen, Joseph was sold into slavery by his brothers, who were jealous of their father's great love for him. He ended up in Egypt as the personal servant of the Pharaoh's commanding officer, Potiphar. While he was there, Potiphar's wife tried to seduce Joseph; when he resisted, she turned the tables, claiming that Joseph had made advances toward her. Falsely accused, Joseph was thrown into prison and remained there until God orchestrated a chain of events that led not just to his release, but eventually to his becoming prime minister to the Pharaoh. Years later when a famine in Caanan forced Joseph's brothers to journey to Egypt in search of food, the family was reunited. Instead of being bitter about all he had suffered, Joseph told his brothers, "You meant evil against me, but God meant it for good" (Genesis 50:20), or, as the Good News Bible phrases it, "God turned it into good."

Times have changed, but God has not. There is nothing from which He cannot bring ultimate good, and divorce is no exception. On the one hand, children whose parents divorce often experience more emotional pain and suffering than their peers. Childhood may be an unhappy, stress-filled time, and they may even appear to be handicapped in some ways as they approach adulthood. But on the other hand, these same children may enter adulthood better prepared to face other difficult times, with stronger character, greater maturity, and a solid recognition of their need to depend upon God. Certainly that would be God's desire for them. He would not have them crushed under the load, but rather strengthened and prepared by it for greater things in life.

Children who do not know Christ as Savior at the time their parents break up may be jolted to a new awareness of things spiritual. For those who discover their need of Christ and yield their lives to Him, divorce will have been a blessing in disguise. Children who already belong to Christ may experience a tremendous spiritual growth spurt as they come to depend upon Him in deeper ways. Greek scholar Kenneth Wuest has written:

> Christian suffering, whether it be in the form of persecution because of a Christlike life, or whether it comes to us in the form of trials and testing which are the natural accompaniment of a Christlike life, such as illness, sorrow, or financial losses, is always used by a God of love to refine our lives. It burns out the dross, makes for humility, purifies and increases our faith, and enriches our lives. And like the goldsmith of old, God keeps us in the smelting furnace until He can see the reflection of the face of the Lord Jesus in our lives.[20]

Divorce is not good in and of itself. It was never in God's plan. Yet, God uses it for good, and because He does so, the hardships divorce may bring into a child's life are not meaningless or purposeless. They are incorporated into God's plans for making us more like Jesus, and those plans are always good. " 'For I know the plans that I have for you,' declares the Lord, 'plans for welfare and not for calamity to give you a future and a hope' " (Jeremiah 29:11). Thus divorce can actually be a key ingredient in the development of Christlike character, an eternal heirloom that will not fade with age or time.

PART FIVE

HEALING PROPOSITIONS

17 A Modern Ministry

People at church have really not helped at all.
—Paul, age 12

"Then the King will say to those on His right, 'Come, you who are blessed of My Father, inherit the kingdom prepared for you from the foundation of the world. For I was hungry, and you gave Me something to eat; I was thirsty, and you gave Me drink; I was a stranger, and you invited Me in; naked, and you clothed Me; I was sick, and you visited Me; I was in prison, and you came to Me.'

"Then the righteous will answer Him, saying, 'Lord, when did we see You hungry, and feed You, or thirsty, and give You drink? And when did we see You a stranger, and invite You in, or naked, and clothe You? And when did we see You sick, or in prison, and come to You?'

"And the King will answer and say to them, 'Truly I say to you, to the extent that you did it to one of these brothers of Mine, even the least of them, you did it to Me.'

"Then He will also say to those on His left, 'Depart from Me, accursed ones, into the eternal fire which has been prepared for the devil and his angels; for I was hungry, and you gave Me nothing to eat; I was thirsty, and you gave Me nothing to drink; I was a stranger, and you did not invite Me in; naked, and you did not clothe Me; sick, and in prison, and you did not visit Me.'

"Then they themselves also will answer, saying 'Lord, when did we see you hungry, or thirsty, or a stranger, or naked, or sick, or in prison, and did not take care of You?'

"Then He will answer them, saying, 'Truly, I say to you, to the extent that you did not do it to one of the least of these, you did not do it to Me' " (Matthew 25:34–45).

TWO KINDS OF NEEDS

In this passage of Scripture Jesus expresses compassion regarding two kinds of human needs: physical and emotional. Both are equally legitimate needs and both are equally characteristic of the human experience. Jesus was concerned that both kinds of needs be met. When He says, "I was hungry . . . thirsty . . . naked," He is recognizing the most basic of all our needs: the needs of the body. Without food and water people eventually sicken and die. Without proper clothing we are at the mercy of the elements—sun, wind, snow, extremes of temperature.

When Jesus said, "I was a stranger and you invited Me in . . . sick and you visited Me . . . in prison and you came to Me," He is addressing emotional needs. Our emotional sensitivity distinguishes us from the rest of God's creation.

Made in His image, we can feel the warmth of companionship or the ache of loneliness, the security of knowing someone cares or the despondency of bearing our burdens alone. Like our Creator, we are endowed with the capacity to experience emotionally whatever realities characterize our circumstances.

When He was on earth Jesus experienced both physical and emotional needs because they are inherent in the human condition. As God in human flesh, He grew hungry, thirsty, and tired the way we do. He knew physical agony as He hung on the cross, hands and feet pierced through with nails. Emotionally He experienced the pain of rejection by supposed friends and felt fear as He faced crucifixion. He knew the ultimate loneliness: not only did He go to the cross alone, but He hung there undeservedly for the sin of the world—even God the Father turned His back.

Because He has been there Himself, He understands physical and emotional neediness. Hebrews 4:15 says, "We do not have a high priest who cannot sympathize with our weaknesses." Rather, we have a brother who cares deeply for those whose needs are unmet.

Matthew 25 is clear about the role we are to take in meeting the physical and emotional needs of others. We are responsible for meeting them. We are responsible because it is Christ Himself whose needs we are responding to, so deeply does He align Himself with humanity. He views our meeting such needs as one and the same as meeting His own needs: "To the extent that you did it to one of these brothers of mine, even the least of them, you did it to Me . . . to the extent you did not do it to one of the least of these, you did not do it to Me" (vv. 40, 45).

Divorce commonly creates great material and emotional needs in the lives of those whom it touches. It sometimes backs them into corners where desperate forces can be brought to bear. As we have seen, tremendous financial burdens can arise when one paycheck must be stretched to support two households, or when a mother must enter the job market without the skills to command sufficient income to adequately support her children and herself.

Simultaneously both parent and child may be sinking under overwhelming feelings of rejection, depression, loneliness, anger, and loss, often without any encouragement or support from people outside the family unit.

In his third epistle the apostle John wrote, "Beloved, I pray that in all respects you may prosper and be in good health, just as your soul prospers" (v. 2). This kind of prosperity involves the well-being of the whole person, inwardly and outwardly, and encompasses every level of human need: material, physical, emotional, and spiritual. John was saying, in effect, that he was praying for God to provide a measure of wholesome prosperity for his readers in each of these aspects of life.

Research done decades ago by A. H. Maslow suggests that such prosperity is in fact necessary if we are to make the most of our lives. Maslow suggested a hierarchy of human needs that looks like this:

1. Basic physiological needs, such as food and water
2. Safety needs, like security and stability

3. The need to feel that we belong and are loved through receiving affection from others and identifying with a group such as our family
4. Self-esteem needs such as prestige and self-respect.
5. Self-actualization, the highly personalized need to make one's dreams, ambitions, and personal potential into reality

Maslow believed that only as a more basic need is adequately met can a person move on to the next higher level toward self-actualization.[1] Notice again how physical and emotional needs each play important roles affecting our achievement of our potential. A third need, not mentioned by Maslow, is spiritual. Without Christ as Savior no one can truly be "self-actualized" or fulfilled.

It would appear that in a general way, Maslow's list parallels the stages of a child's development. As an infant matures from a state of total dependence (the first level) toward a state of total independence (the last level), the influence of his home and family is highly significant. the way that his physical and material needs are met, the way he develops emotionally, and what he achieves have much to do with the stability or instability of his parents' relationship. Divorce threatens a child's progression through Maslow's hierarchy and in fact has the potential to impede him at every level to some degree.

THEN AND NOW

In Matthew 19:3 the Pharisees asked Jesus, "Is it lawful for a man to divorce his wife for any cause at all?" Dr. John MacArthur has pointed out that this was no whimsical question, but one designed to discredit Jesus in the eyes of the people and make Him unpopular. MacArthur comments,

> Divorce was very, very common. Women were treated as if they had no rights at all, and the Pharisees were leaders in this, not only by what they taught, but by the example of their lives. They were constantly and continuously divorc-

ing their wives. And they were also teaching that you *could* divorce your wife for any reason.[2]

In those days, only the husband had the right to initiate divorce. In the agricultural society of the Jews, a woman simply did not pack up her possessions and children and launch out on her own. Survival would have been very difficult. By contrast, today a woman can exercise the option of divorce because our economic system provides opportunities for her to support herself independent of a husband and because our legal system gives her the right to divorce.

Scripture gives no clues as to how a divorced woman who did not remarry got along financially in biblical times. Nor does it specifically address the issue of children and divorce. However, that is not to say we are without biblical guidelines for responding to today's survivors of divorce.

In many ways, single parents and the children of divorce are modern-day equivalents to the widows and orphans about whom the Bible has much to say. The words of Lamentations 5:1–3 could well be the cry of many modern children of divorce:

> *"Remember, O Lord, what has befallen us;*
> *Look, and see our reproach!*
> *Our inheritance has been turned over to strangers,*
> *Our houses to aliens.*
> *We have become orphans without a father,*
> *Our mothers are like widows."*

Some children of divorce have been crushed by the rejection of a father whose remarriage includes other children. His own children then feel replaced. Their material and emotional "inheritance has been turned over to strangers." Others have watched as the family home is sold due to economic strain. As they go into apartments or smaller houses in new locations, they cling wistfully to childhood memories as they relinquish their "houses to aliens." Some children never see their fathers again once the marriage bond is severed. Those whose mothers do not remarry can easily grow up as "orphans without a father" whose "mothers are like widows."

The word for *orphan* in Lamentations is *yāthōm*. In Hebrew it means, literally, "lonely" and "one deprived of one or both parents." Our modern use of the word is similar. Although we typically think of orphans as having no parents, Webster's New World Dictionary says the word *orphan* is "sometimes applied to a child who has lost only one parent by death."

Children of divorce are deprived of one parent most of the time. When they are with their custodial parent they are deprived of their noncustodial one; when they are with the noncustodial one, the other is absent. They are rarely in the company of both parents at the same time. In some cases these children are orphaned almost literally. The noncustodial parent pays so little attention that for the children it is almost no different than if the parent were actually deceased.

Meeting the needs of widows and orphans has always been characteristic of God's people. Elisha cared for them in 2 Kings 4:1–7. The apostles arranged for their care in Acts 6:1–3. Paul commanded it in 1 Timothy 5. We continue to provide for them through a multitude of organizations today. The time has come, however, to expand our definitions of *widow* and *orphan*. When we do, many applications can be drawn from the Word of God that are entirely appropriate and relevant to those touched by divorce. If we think of single parents and their children as widows, orphans, or fatherless, the following Scriptures abound with modern applications. Notice how we are commanded to address both physical and emotional needs.

> This is pure and undefiled religion in the sight of our God and Father, to visit [single parents and their children] in their distress (James 1:27).
>
> "He executes justice for [single parents and their children], and shows His love for the alien by giving him food and clothing" (Deuteronomy 10:18).
>
> "Every third year you are to use your entire tithe for local welfare programs: Give it to the Levites who have no inheritance among you, or to foreigners, or to [single parents and their children] within your city, so that they can

eat and be satisfied; and then Jehovah your God will bless you and your work" (Deuteronomy 14:28-29 LIVING BIBLE).

Defend the poor and the [child of divorce]; do justice to the afflicted and needy (Psalm 82:3 KJV).

"I delivered the poor who cried for help, And the [child of divorce] who had no helper. The blessing of the one ready to perish came upon me, and I made the [single parent's] heart sing for joy" (Job 29:12).

"When you reap your harvest in your field and have forgotten a sheaf in the field, you shall not go back to get it; it shall be for the alien, for the [child of divorce and the single parent], in order that the LORD your God may bless you in all the work of your hands" (Deuteronomy 24:19).

In the same way, the promises that God makes to the widow and the orphan can rightfully be claimed by single parents and the children of divorce:

But I will preserve your [children of divorce] who remain, and let your [single parents] depend upon Me (Jeremiah 49:11 LIVING BIBLE).

"For in Thee the [child of divorce] finds mercy" (Hosea 14:3).

"The unfortunate commits himself to Thee; Thou hast been the helper of the [child of divorce]" (Psalm 10:14).

He is a father to the [child of divorce]; he gives justice to the [single parent], for he is holy (Psalm 68:5 LIVING BIBLE).

"The Lord protects the strangers; He supports the [child of divorce and the single parent]" (Psalm 146:9).

RESPONDING IN LOVE

Divorce has a profound effect on literally millions of people. When they ache, Christ aches with them. Their needs present us with tremendous opportunities to demonstrate God's love—not necessarily toward hundreds or even dozens of people, but toward the two or three or four whom God has already placed in our paths.

It is to our shame that our Christian response to those wounded by divorce, both adults and children, has often been to turn our backs. One of the biggest reasons why we do is because we possess stereotypical, self-righteous, and even Pharisaic attitudes that keep us from ministering to our own wounded and the wounded that knock at the door of the church. Laying aside these attitudes and cultivating compassion is one of our greatest challenges.

When divorce happens, especially to a Christian, there is already a heavy burden of guilt, regret, and self-condemnation. The very last thing any divorced people or children of divorce need is condemnation from others. What they do need is encouragement, relief, and understanding. Many churches are doing an excellent job of providing this, while others still have a long way to go. And this means that individually, Christian by Christian, the same is true.

Kristine Miller Tomasik, a divorcee, writes that many divorced Christians have

> known the hurt of rejection from God's people—the very people they thought would understand most. Like me, they had felt that sharp sting of spoken and unspoken judgment: "Well, if only you hadn't been so (check one) weak, immature, unspiritual, emotional, etc., etc., you'd still be married." Like me, they had wanted to retort in kind, but instead, some of them quietly shrugged their shoulders and walked away from the church.

She added,

> ... experiencing a divorce de-Pharisaized me. I used to be the first to point a finger and say, "Tsk, tsk" when a fellow Christian fell short. Now I know what it feels like to be on the other end of the finger. I hope I am now more understanding and tolerant.[3]

The children and single parents whose comments appear in this book represent a variety of churches, some tremendously encouraging and supportive and some that have done little or nothing to help people cope with the personal tragedy of divorce. Sandy was one whose experience was positive. She said,

> It was really hard to say, "My husband left." But when I finally could, my children and I started coming back to church. The hardest thing I have ever done, just about in

my life, was to say, "Hey gang, I'm separated." Once I did, I got an awful lot of support. Immediately there was support and understanding in that Sunday school class. My church is super as far as their support of the singles department, and not all churches have that, I know.

Jonathan, too, experienced support during and after his marital crisis. Those at his church, he said,

> although stunned over news of the separation and divorce, nevertheless openly showed their love and support. Many of them, including my pastor, encouraged me to seek God's will in what was happening to me and my children. And they always let the children know they were loved and appreciated.

Brenda's experience was quite different:

> People at church have been very unresponsive in offering understanding about the divorce situation. Spiritually, I have strengthened my faith in God, but I've lost faith in what I considered Christian church-going people. Christians have proven to be the least helpful in a crisis such as divorce.

Kathy also felt unsupported by her church and has since changed churches:

> People where I attended during the divorce were so uncomfortable and unfamiliar with how to deal with divorce that they never talked about it, never asked how I was, or if I needed help—it was awful! Christian people would do well to concentrate on God and His character and grace and less on the shortcomings of the divorcee. It's never necessary to make the person going through divorce feel like they failed or they should have tried harder—they already feel it more than anyone could ever know!

Marian said that her Christian friends "gave a tremendous amount of support" to her, but added "my children did not feel much of this support from the church." It seems that even in those churches such as Marian's where much love and encouragement are extended to the adults of divorce, children are often overlooked. Several of them told me that in their churches, people . . .

MARY BETH: . . . do not care about it.

ANGELA:	... never said anything about it or offered to help in any way.
BEN:	... haven't talked about it to me.
ANNA:	... know the problems, but no one really understands.
CAROL:	... have been helpful at times, but condemning also.

Like the adults, though, some have had warm, positive encouragement from their churches. Paige said, "They really show that they care. They're nice people." Those at Jennifer's church "have let me know that they would be there if I needed to talk." Bob described his church family as "close to me."

THE BOTTOM LINE

"I know now that no matter how drastically our lives may be shattered—by divorce or other difficulties—God is able to put the pieces together again," writes Kristine Tomasik. "I only wish that more of us would be willing to become channels of God's healing, restoring love to our hurting brothers and sisters."[4] As her words suggest, we—God's people—are the channels that He eagerly desires to use to communicate His love to those who have been broken and discouraged by divorce. Yet it all hinges on our willingness to be used.

Why are we so hesitant to say yes? When a woman is widowed or a child orphaned due to the death of a spouse or a parent, we instinctively respond according to the law of love. That is, we demonstrate compassion by reaching out to help meet both material and emotional needs. When a spouse or parent is lost through divorce, should we do any less?

18 A Pound of Cure

If it hadn't been for my Christian friends I probably would have done something stupid like try to commit suicide.
—Sarah, age 15

When divorce splinters a family, the most important functions for those outside become listening, encouraging, and offering practical help to both parent and child. Such kindnesses are often most helpful during the first year-and-a-half after divorce when the family is likely to be experiencing the most upheaval and stress.

FIRST AID

Reaching out to children following divorce is not vastly different from reaching out to adults. It is important to keep in mind that divorce is a crisis situation in the life of a child, and the most significant aspect of helping anyone in a crisis is listening. Simply listening, however, may be more involved than we might at first imagine. It may require repeated investments of time, and it requires patience and an understanding of what the child is likely to be feeling and needing when he confides in you. His basic needs are threefold.

He Needs to Talk

If a child has demonstrated the willingness to open up to you with his feelings and fears and anxieties, it goes without saying that he feels the need to express what's going on inside. His grief is not unlike the grief he would be feeling if one of his parents had literally died. One of the reasons he may need to talk has to do with the depth of the emotional hurt he has suffered.

Even when he has obtained all the "right answers" to his questions and intellectually grasps what has happened between his parents, he may still feel unsatisfied. Explanations can only satisfy the intellectual side of a person. His deepest emotional needs do not respond to facts and logic. This is why he needs a sympathetic listener rather than someone with answers. An adult who will give him the respect of listening without correcting his wording, urging him to cheer up, or interrupting him with pearls of wisdom and advice stands a good chance of winning the opportunity to continue to play an important ongoing role in his life.

As time distances a child from divorce, his need to talk may actually become greater. He may be searching for a clearer understanding of what really happened and may have many unsettling thoughts and feelings as his focus sharpens. Weeks, months, and even years after divorce he may feel a need to talk about it, as time changes his perceptions and contributes to his growth and healing. Bringing his thoughts out into the light of day where he can examine them with the help of a good listener may be precisely what he needs to do.

Adults from intact, happy homes may have the least tolerance for this verbal sorting-out process. They can't understand why the child cannot just put it all behind him and forget it. People sometimes respond to those who are mourning the death of a loved one in the same way. "Five weeks after the funeral," wrote Gloria Ichikawa, "as I kept jabbering on about Nora, another person said I 'shouldn't keep dwelling on it.' It frustrated me to try to convince people that I needed to talk about this person I loved."[1] In a similar way, children may need to talk about the beloved family that has been changed by divorce.

He Needs to Feel Your Concern

Because kids tend to be more tuned in to what adults do than what they say, it is important that a child be able to feel your concern as well as receive verbal assurances of it. At every age, the following will help communicate that you care:

Eye Contact. When you look a child in the eyes, he is assured of your full attention, which is the biggest compliment you can give him. He may also like you and trust you more if you make good eye contact with him.

Be a Friend. Counselor David Martin suggests that when they are conversing with a child, adults should position themselves so that they are on the same eye level as the child. The idea is to avoid literally talking down to the child.

"When I'm talking to a child," says Martin, "if the child is sitting in a chair, I might get out of my chair and sit on the floor, because that way, we're buddies." He feels that it is also important for the child to sense that his adult friend is nonjudgmental. This gives him the freedom to express his feelings and thoughts even if they are negative.

Touch. A hug, an arm about the shoulders, a gentle touch or pat can do more to say "I really care" than a great many words. Some studies have shown that when counselors utilize touch in their therapy their adult clients tend to be more responsive. And children, who are less verbally oriented than adults, are even more likely to read a loving touch loud and clear.

"What" Questions. Counselors suggest asking the child "what" questions instead of "why" questions. A child cannot usually answer "why" questions because they imply things like "Why are you the way you are?" A child normally cannot fathom the reasons behind his feelings and behavior and will typically respond to a "why" question with "I don't know." "What" questions are much more profitable. When asked, "What is happening at home?" or

"What do you like to do after school?" the child can tell you, and you've begun a dialogue.

He Needs to Know He Can Trust You

Trust is a key element in any relationship where people share their innermost thoughts and feelings. A child needs to be secure in the knowledge that what he says will not be reported back to Mom and Dad. Martin says, "When I feel that something the child has said needs to be shared with the parent, I ask the child first if that would be all right. After all, I'm dealing with confidential material here." The final decision belongs to the child. To overrule him is to violate his trust and risk damaging your relationship with him.

INTENSIVE CARE

No two children respond to divorce in exactly the same way, even when the two are siblings. Each child is unique; so is each divorce. Yet certain children are more likely than others to take divorce very hard. These are the children who stand to gain the most from loving, positive concern from adults outside the family.

- Boys. In general, boys feel the affects of divorce more severely than girls, especially at ages three to five and nine to ten.
- Only children. Children who have no brothers or sisters with whom to share the often scary, lonely time of divorce may be overwhelmed more easily than others.
- Those who have been abandoned by a parent.
- Those whose parents rely on them for the emotional support that ought to be coming from other adults.
- Those who have experienced many significant changes and upheavals in their lives in addition to divorce.
- Those who receive very little attention from the custodial parent.
- Those who are employed as messengers or spies in an ongoing parental conflict.

- Those whose parents continue to display hostility in their dealings with one another.
- Those who are being fought over in a custody battle or being pressured to reject one parent in favor of the other.

HOW ADULTS HINDER A CHILD'S ADJUSTMENT

Well-meaning adults sometimes say and do things that get in the way of a child's recovery from divorce. Often this happens because a child's unhappiness makes us uncomfortable, and in an effort to ease our own discomfort we toss out pat answers or assert what we see as our adult wisdom over him and his problems. Many times these responses are thoughtless, without concern for the child and the burden he bears. The following are guaranteed *not* to help:

- Insisting that big boys don't cry or that the child should grow up or "stop being such a baby." The truth is that the losses of divorce are profound, and children need to express their grief.
- Suggesting that if the child's behavior has always been as bad as it is now, it's no wonder that daddy left home. This essentially lays the blame for the divorce at his feet, creating a terrible weight of guilt.
- Placing blame on one parent or the other, or speaking unkindly about either parent in front of the child. His emotional attachment to both parents is tremendous. He knows what his parents have done—you don't have to remind him.
- Pretending nothing has happened and offering no expression of concern, perhaps avoiding the child altogether. Simply saying, "I'm sorry to hear about your parents' divorce; if you ever want to talk, I'm available" is enough to let him know that you know, and that you care.
- Feeding his reconciliation fantasy with false hopes. Helping him to accept what has happened is kinder and more realistic in almost every case.

- Encouraging him to reject or take sides against one parent. No matter what the circumstances, choosing sides will never benefit the child.
- Focusing exclusively on the needs of the parents, forgetting that virtually every child is hurting after divorce too.
- Telling the child that he hasn't lost anything of significance, and that he is better off this way. This communicates that you don't understand what he's going through.
- Focusing on how terrible the present situation is instead of stimulating trust in God's faithfulness and nearness during difficult times.
- Reaching out to the child or to his family with a condescending attitude. It might actually be better to do nothing at all than to give the impression that you think you are doing them a favor.

HOW FRIENDS AND RELATIVES CAN HELP

There are countless ways in which friends and relatives can help a child adjust after divorce. The age of the child, the kind of relationship we have with him and with the parent or parents, and the amount of time we have are the major determinants in what we can do. As friends or family members we can leave a lasting and valuable imprint on a child's life by providing emotional support, sincere compliments, financial or material help, spiritual counsel, and just-for-fun times of recreation.

I asked several single parents how they felt friends and family could help their children adjust to life after divorce.

SANDY: Just love them. That's the most you can do for kids is to just love them. And do things with them. Find out what the child likes or wants to do. Go to the movies; you know, that's a *big* treat: 'me and so-and-so are going to the movies!' My kids love to be hugged. If it's from someone that they're close to, they'll take a hug anytime. Little girls need to be hugged by male friends if they have a comfortable relationship where they can do that. And tell them how pretty they are.

BRANDON: Support them and understand them. And be a little more patient with them. I think they probably need to be encouraged a little bit more when they do something good. Taking an interest in them, going out of your way to say "Hi" to them and other little things like that will make them feel accepted.

PATTY: Take them out to eat or to the movies; be supportive in verbal ways.

MARIAN: Telling them, "I know you hurt. I'm here to help if I can, and you will make it."

STEVE: People who have never been married and haven't been around kids much need to be very, very tolerant of these kids and accept them and talk with them and hug them and do something other than say, "Won't you please be quiet?" or "How can you ever hear when these kids are around?" They've got to be almost as positive as the parents toward the kids.

KATHY: Spending time with them, letting them know that Mom isn't the only adult who loves them. This applies particularly to male friends. I've had people act as though my daughter were more of a bother than anything and that causes real problems. Often I have found myself beginning to treat her badly and to resent her because someone else thinks she's too much trouble.

Further Suggestions

1. Nourish self-esteem by being generous with smiles, compliments, and expressions of appreciation and approval for what the child accomplishes in the way of housekeeping tasks, good test grades, athletic achievement, and displays of good judgment, kindness, or generosity in dealing with others.

2. Invite him to your house or apartment to provide distraction from problems at home. Involve him in some project such as raking the yard, baking cookies, painting a room, or washing and waxing the car. In this informal and comfortable setting he may feel like talking about what's on his mind. Be ready to be a good listener if he opens up.

3. Mark your calendar ahead of time with reminders about his birthday, football schedule, piano recital, school play, and so on, and make plans to be on hand to provide encouragement and support.
4. Send cards or gifts on special occasions such as his birthday, Valentine's Day, and Christmas. Phone calls, visits, and notes are sometimes just as good or even better.
5. Invite him to come along on family outings or errands or shopping.
6. Welcome him to spend time at your house after school if he is alone until Mom finishes work.
7. Pray for him and ask him to share his prayer requests with you. Check with him periodically to see how things are progressing. Give him the privilege of praying for you too.
8. Surprise him with a spur-of-the-moment expedition to the ice cream shop, to the movies, to play miniature golf, or to go sledding. Or invite him over to join your family for an evening of popcorn and board games.
9. Ask for a lesson in something the child does well that you would enjoy knowing more about.
10. Ask him to pet-sit or plant-sit when you are away. This shows that you consider him responsible and competent. Be sure to pay if you can.
11. Try to foster any mutual interest you have with the child by sharing magazine articles, inviting him over to work on your interest together, swapping tips and equipment.
12. Initiate discussions that will allow him to talk about himself, his interests, his friends, and school activities.
13. If finances are a problem in the single-parent family, be creative in finding ways to enrich his life—but avoid the "poor baby" syndrome. Ideas: Give him a scholar-

ship to camp, buy him a new Bible, arrange to pay for lessons that will develop his particular talent or give a gift that will help him to use his talent—ballet shoes, baseball glove, art supplies, sheet music. Take him shopping for school clothes, give him a magazine subscription, or buy him extras like designer jeans, a tape, or a longed-for toy or game.

Always ask the parent's permission first, however. Ask, too, if there are any particular pressing needs you might be able to meet instead of buying a gift. School supplies or fees, dental work, new glasses, or the like may fill a felt need for both parent and child.

14. Spend a day together designed for cultural or educational enrichment. Museums, planetariums, petting zoos, and nature trails are ideal and inexpensive choices.

15. Invite him to spend the weekend with your family. Not only will this give you extended time with the child, but it will be a welcome vacation for his parent.

16. Children who are old enough to bathe and exercise pets, baby-sit, run errands, or do yardwork or housework can be given opportunities to earn spending money while helping you out at the same time.

17. If you enjoy doing woodcraft or needlecraft, consider making the child either a name plaque for his room or some other personalized gift that says, "You're special."

18. Offer to help him with his homework.

19. If there is more than one child in the family, be careful not to play favorites in gift giving or special activities. Be sure too that the parent is in full agreement with anything you want to do with or for the children.

Helping Single Parents

It is important to remember that a child's adjustment is primarily mediated through his relationship with his custodial parent. His adjustment is inseparably intertwined with the parent's adjustment. Thus, any ministry to the parent is automatically a ministry to the child as well. A single parent whose emotional needs are met and who senses the support and encouragement of friends and family finds it easier to meet the needs of his child. As Sandy put it, "The faster I know who I am and where I'm going the faster I can concentrate on my kids."

Many things can be done to provide encouragement and practical help for single parents, which in turn can help them in their parenting role. Kathy says, "My close friends have never condemned, and the most helpful things I remember are invitations to dinner, notes in the mail with Scripture verses just to let me know I was loved, small gifts for no reason, offers to baby-sit so I could have time out. Those meant so much."

Sandy suggests, "Sit with them in church. The first year we sat by ourselves."

Steve, Sandy, and Brandon all pointed to the singles group they were involved in as a major source of support. Encouraging a single parent to get involved in a singles group or singles Sunday school class could be one of the most helpful things of all. Steve recalls, "I really didn't feel in place with them at the time, since my divorce was still pending, but one of my friends that I grew up with encouraged me to come, and I went and enjoyed it. I've been active in that group ever since." Sandy asserts,

> It's so important, even though you're separated or freshly divorced, to go to the singles socials. For two years I would go to every function they had even though I died through the whole thing. I hated it. I was so unhappy and I hurt so deeply inside at every social I went to, but I knew that I had to go because it was a part of the mending and growing and healing process.

Here are some other ideas for helping and encouraging single parents and their families:

1. Find out on which evenings the family eats dinner together and call ahead to say, "I'm bringing your

dinner." Then show up with the kind of meal they probably would not fix for themselves. Since so many single-parent families have more than their share of frozen dinners, hotdogs, and macaroni and cheese from a box, this can be a real treat and lots of fun too. Why not make plenty so that you can stay for dinner and enjoy their fellowship?

2. Call for no reason just to let them know you are thinking of them and keeping them in your prayers. A cheery card in the mail fulfills the same purpose.

3. If you are at home during the day, make yourself available as an emergency babysitter. When a child is sick it's often difficult for a single parent to take time off from work to stay home to care for him.

4. When the single parent is sick, offer to provide transportation for children to lessons, appointments, or church. Offer to keep the children at your home for a while to give the parent time to rest. Let the parent know you're available to go to the drugstore to fill a prescription or to buy groceries if necessary.

5. Sit and talk with a single parent over a leisurely cup of coffee, offering your companionship and a listening ear.

6. Invite a single-parent family to join yours on a family outing such as a picnic or trip to the pool or the roller rink.

7. On gift-giving occasions consider luxury items that a parent on a tight budget probably would not buy for himself. Here are some ideas:
   - A subscription to a Christian magazine or special-interest publication
   - A record, tape, or book
   - An I.O.U. for a specified amount of baby-sitting to be done by you for free or by someone you have prepaid
   - Tickets to a concert, ballet, play, or movie

- Money earmarked for dinner at a nice restaurant
- Perfume, bubble bath, personalized stationery, scented candles.

8. A single custodial father may need help or at least advice about how to accomplish tasks he may be unaccustomed to. Let him know you're willing to offer help or tips on cooking, shopping, doing laundry, or buying children's clothes.

9. Similarly, a single mother may need help or advice on how to maintain an automobile, file tax forms, buy insurance, or fix something in the house. Let her know you're ready and willing to help and to teach her what she needs to know.

10. Round up a group of friends for a work day at the home of a single parent. Painting, raking, mowing, trimming shrubbery, making car repairs, washing and vacuuming out her car, or chopping wood for her fireplace or woodstove are tangible ways to say, "We really care about you." Send out for a pizza or have a picnic afterward.

11. Write the single parent's birthday on your calendar and be sure to send a card or call. You might want to provide a free evening of baby-sitting, take him out for dinner, or just drop by with a cake and ice cream.

12. If money is tight, leave an anonymous bag of nonperishable groceries on the doorstep with an encouraging note. You might include items like vitamins, seeds for a garden, or a favorite recipe or two.

13. Holidays can be especially hard on a family just after divorce. If they have no extended family nearby, why not invite a single-parent family to join you for the day?

14. When appropriate, consider gifts or loans of money, buying a tank of fuel oil or a load of wood, or paying a bill to take some of the financial pressure off a single

parent. These gestures may be most helpful during the Christmas season or after an unforeseen medical or dental bill.

15. Offer to give the family a ride to church services or to a church event, to take the children to Vacation Bible School if the parent will be at work, or to baby-sit in order to free the parent to participate in a singles' group activity.

16. Pray for the family specifically regarding their financial needs, spiritual growth, emotional healing, and social needs.

HOW TEACHERS CAN HELP

"I was upset being away from my father," said a girl named Suzy. "More than anything, I was ashamed. Ashamed of living in that crummy place, and ashamed of my parents being split up. I didn't tell a soul. One day in class I had a kind of breakdown. The teacher kept me after class and I told him the whole thing. He became my confidant. Every day I went to him. He took a real interest in me. If he hadn't been there, I don't know what I might have done."[2]

Teachers can be vitally important in the lives of children from divorced homes, primarily because they are often the most constant adults in their lives. Because this is so, and because a child may already regard him with respect, a teacher may be in an ideal position to help in significant ways. Male teachers in particular may be especially influential when the father is absent from the home. One teacher told author Linda Francke,

> I'm often the only man in their lives and the kids bring me the incredible needs that wouldn't be there if there were a father present. . . . I feel a tremendous responsibility to them and a tremendous anger toward the fathers. I cannot believe the number of fathers who refuse to parent, either through desertion, neglect, or the withholding of affection.[3]

In some cases, school policies may restrict teachers in what they can do and say concerning divorce. Some schools maintain that their role is purely an educational one and that what happens in the child's personal life should be of no concern to the teacher. Many teachers feel this way too, since they already have more responsibilities, paperwork, and student problems than they can handle. Other schools and teachers take the approach that unless a child can somehow be helped to cope with his personal problems, education will not occur. That is, if the child is too exhausted, depressed, or distracted to concentrate or to care about learning, he won't learn at all.

In *Education Digest,* Robert D. Allers put forth these suggestions for teachers who have the freedom to work creatively with their students concerning the topic of divorce:[4]

1. Plan classroom discussions on divorce. These can serve a dual purpose. They allow the children with divorced parents to see that other classmates have the same problems that they do, which may be a very liberating discovery. These students can then trade ideas and suggestions about how they handle Christmas vacation, visiting with noncustodial parents, and other important issues. At the same time, students whose parents are not divorced will gain understanding about their friends and the problems they face. Allers suggests informing the principal of discussion plans ahead of time and preparing the parents by sending a notice home with the students.

2. Discuss feelings. Often a child cannot verbalize his emotions because he does not know the words to describe what he is feeling. There are many words in the English language that convey specific nuances of thought and emotion. A class period spent discussing some of them will not only enrich a child's vocabulary, but may also help him take another step toward self-understanding and emotional healing.

3. Stock the classroom with age-appropriate reading materials that deal with divorce. (See appendix A for some suggested titles.)
4. Form discussion groups for children whose parents are divorced. A school psychologist or counselor may be an ideal resource person or discussion leader.
5. Define your own feelings about divorce and deal with any anxiety, nervousness, or negative attitudes that would hinder your efforts to help children of divorce.
6. Recognize the need and plan how to avoid the three potential pitfalls of discussing divorce in a classroom setting: airing "dirty laundry," forcing a child to share his feelings before he is ready, and overkill—having too many classes devoted to the subject of divorce.

Even when school policy discourages a teacher from helping children deal with the divorce of their parents, there are some quieter ways you may be able to help.

1. Initiate a private discussion that allows a child to air his feelings about what is happening at home. Perhaps the teacher could invite the child to have lunch with him in the classroom instead of in the cafeteria, or take some time to talk after school or during a study period.
2. Deal with unruly behavior or falling grades with as much understanding as possible, striving to reinforce desirable behaviors with compliments and praise. Extending deadlines or alleviating certain requirements may help in some circumstances.
3. Boost sagging self-esteem by selecting the child for special jobs like erasing chalkboards, taking a message to the office, or collecting papers. Don't overdo it, however, and risk making his classmates jealous.
4. Pray specifically for the needs you see in the child's life.
5. Keep in mind that Mondays and Fridays may be bad days for some children who must migrate from one

household to the other on weekends. Plan calmer activities for these days when possible.

6. Arrange for the child to talk with a school counselor about his problems.

What Church Teachers and Staff Can Do

Sunday school teachers, children's choir directors, scouting and mission club leaders can have an important influence on a child of divorce. From his interactions with them a child may generalize what he supposes to be the reaction of church people as a whole to his parents' breakup. If these special adults are supportive and concerned, he may well come to view his church family as true sources of comfort and encouragement.

In his book *Children & Divorce,* Archibald Hart points out that his Sunday school teacher was greatly encouraging to him after the divorce of his parents. He writes,

> What really impressed me was her ability to give love unconditionally. She never became irritated or angry at us, no matter what we did. She was a beautiful person all through.
>
> She obviously knew about the breakup of our home, although she never embarrassed me over it or made it a big issue. But I could feel her love and concern; it was in her eyes and in the way she touched me—gentle but firm. Her message was very clear: there is more to life than raiment, and more to live for than parents.[5]

Even though this teacher had relatively little time with him, it is evident that her impact was positive and lasting. It is especially interesting that Hart felt and still remembers this woman's love and concern, which was communicated not verbally, but nonverbally, through what she did. She treated him kindly and patiently, made positive eye contact, and expressed her concern through touch.

Teachers and leaders who are able to go the extra mile and spend some time in ministry during the week as well as on Sunday have an even greater potential for making an enduring impression. Here are a few ideas on how to have a more lasting impact on a child's life.

1. Visit the child at home.
2. Call and let him know he is missed when he is sick or cannot attend for other reasons. Or send a "We missed you" postcard from the group.
3. Assure him from time to time that you are available any time he would like to talk.
4. If there are several children from single-parent families in the class, consider memorizing together verses of Scripture that emphasize God's love and care or deal with concerns expressed by the children.
5. Send birthday cards, valentines, and other special-occasion cards during the year.
6. Establish a good relationship with the child's parent. In many cases, a child is a single parent's only tie to a church, and that parent's own desire for involvement may be based on how well the child seems to enjoy his church activities.
7. Demonstrate agape love no matter how the child behaves. Recognize that he may be testing you to see if your love is real. Realize too that misbehavior may be a by-product of the anxiety, fear, or grief he feels as a result of the divorce.
8. Define for yourself your innermost feelings about divorce and know your church's position on divorce-related issues. Evaluate how your personal feelings, if evident to the child, would help or hinder your relationship with him. Do they motivate you to reach out to him, or to pull back?
9. Pray daily for the specific needs you see in a child of divorce and ask God for wisdom and creativity as you seek to touch his life.
10. Give the child personal attention outside your normal contact with him if you can. Take him out for ice cream or a hamburger or invite him to your home.

Remember that your family can serve as a positive example of a Christian home and can make a lasting impression.

11. Male teachers and leaders should be aware of the important role they can play in a child's life. A child who lives with his mother and has only female schoolteachers may have no other man in his life. When this is the case, having a mature Christian man to relate to in the context of the church helps to prevent a child from perceiving Christianity as feminine.

12. Suggestions for how the church can help equip teachers and leaders to minister to children of divorce are in chapter 21.

KID-TO-KID HELP

Sometimes the very best person to lean on during a crisis is someone who has experienced the same thing. Adults can offer children maturity, patient understanding, role models, and other things. But unless they themselves experienced divorce as *children,* they can only imagine what the child must really be feeling. Peer support from those who have experienced parental divorce or are going through it often fills a need as nothing else can. In addition, because they really know what it means to have their homes break up, children of divorce are often highly motivated to reach out to other kids. The experience of comparing notes with others and offering an empathic ear can facilitate their own adjustment.

My panel told me how they would help or have helped other kids and how they have actually received support from others.

SARAH: First of all I would tell them, yes, it's going to be hard and there are going to be nights when you cry yourself to sleep, when you're scared, not knowing what's going to happen next. And

> I'd tell them, "You know I'm here. If you ever want to talk or just need somebody to listen to you to give you some emotional support, I'm here." Every morning in my quiet time I pray for all the kids who are going through the same thing I am because especially if they're non-Christians and they don't have a good church and good support, they're going through just too much that they shouldn't have to go through.

Sarah's desire to help undoubtedly arises from the help she was given by a friend, who coincidentally showed up just after Sarah received the news of divorce. She shared, "You know, I just couldn't stop crying. And if it hadn't been for my friend Abby and seeing her drive by, I don't know what I would have done. It must have been God's perfect timing that He allowed her to drive by so I could talk to somebody. We walked around the neighborhood for a while. Basically she just listened. It was just good to have somebody there to listen and give some support."

KIMBERLEE: Well, there's one girl at school whose parents are getting a divorce, and I said, "If you need anybody to talk to, call me. Just whenever, it doesn't matter; it can be two in the morning. It doesn't matter. Just call me." One time she couldn't cope with it and I said, "I know the feeling." She had to go home from school because it was the day her parents were getting divorced. She was feeling really sick.

PAIGE: I'd tell them that my parents were divorced and how I got through it: Just trust God and He'll work it out somehow.

BRETT: I could tell them I definitely knew what they were going through. I could sit down and relate to them. Our youth group went on a retreat a couple weeks ago. I met a girl there from Atlanta, Georgia and we've been writing. Her parents are getting a divorce. I don't know if I'm helping her or not. I'm just telling her I understand what she's going through and I'm praying for her.

JODY: It scares me when I think about what kind of adults the kids will be that are growing up in divorced families. The children have to take on more responsibility than they are ready for. My heart goes out to kids in broken homes. I wish I were trained to better deal with problem our society has.

JENNIFER: Someday I hope to counsel with children of divorced parents.

ANNA: I feel fortunate to have as many friends as I do, especially friends who are going through what I am.

Kids helping each other is a natural phenomenon as they interact socially on a peer level. Kid-to-kid help can also be intentionally structured, as through a guided discussion in a classroom or a group counseling session. Both means are valuable.

COUNSELING

Counseling, both before the divorce and after it becomes final, is being increasingly recommended for both parent and child. More and more legal and mental health professionals believe there is simply too much at stake *not* to seek guidance at this critical time. Asked about counseling, family law attorney Christine Gale responded,

> I am 100 percent in favor of counseling, especially whenever there's a divorce with children involved, because when there's a divorce you're automatically dealing with a lot of shattered dreams, disappointments, bitterness, revenge, hatred. There is still some love, still some caring, but a real confusion as to how to deal with all those different emotions. And the one that really hurts the most is the child. If the child is to be spared a lot of grief, the parents have to put aside a lot of those bad feelings and learn to deal with each other maturely and peacefully. I really think the only way to do that is to get a lot of those feelings out in the open and to deal with them.

Wallerstein and Kelly found that the counseling intervention given to the families in their study was influential beyond their expectations. Five years after the study began, two-fifths of the men and even more of the women were still following suggestions that had been made during their *initial* sessions. Many who have had counseling now heartily recommend it to others.

Brandon is one single parent who felt especially helped by the counseling he received, so much so that he has come to view periodic counseling as an almost necessary aspect of maintaining healthy interpersonal relationships. "One thing I hope to instill in my children," he said, "is not to be afraid of counseling, not to think that counseling is only for those who are 'sick'—people who have real problems. The best illustration I've heard for counseling is that people go to the doctor for physicals, to be checked. And I try to look at counseling as preventive maintenance in any relationship, because relationships are difficult and the pressures need to be resolved."

Predivorce counseling works best if the whole family—both parents and the children—can be present. This, of course, requires maturity on the part of the parents, but according to Steven E. Goldston, a psychologist with the National Institute of Mental Health, the benefits for the children are many. He feels that in predivorce counseling, "a minimum amount of professional help can have a maximum payoff."[6] A trained counselor such as a psychologist, psychiatrist, marriage-family therapist, or pastor skillfully moves the family through six-to-eight sessions designed to make the divorce as painless as possible and to teach the parents ways to help their children adjust most easily. Sometimes more sessions are called for, and sometimes children are seen separately.

Counseling with the whole family is the best approach to take whenever there is any kind of family problem, according to counselor David Martin. The reason for this, he says, "is that if you've only got part of the family there, you're only going to get part of the story." He feels that children should be included because they too have "part of the story." Another reason why he feels children should not be excluded from predivorce counseling is that they deserve to know how their lives are going to be affected by the decision their parents are making. "When I counsel a family," he explained,

> if the children are old enough to understand what's going on—usually anyone over five years of age—I'll want them in the session. If they're going to be taken through the divorce and they're going to be put to the test of having to cope with it, then they need to know from the very beginning what's going on. If the parents are considering divorce, they're not only involving themselves; they're involving the whole family.

Postdivorce counseling can be very valuable too. Psychologist Archibald Hart has said, "I strongly recommend that every parent seek some form of counseling or therapy immediately following a divorce."[7] Individual or group sessions can be used to ease adjustment for adults and children. Some psychologists have found that grouping custodial parents together works well because they can share their common experiences and help each other. Group sessions for children have proved successful too, especially in groups of five or six and with age spans of three years.[8] These children share their problems, talk about their parents, and swap tips for handling the various aspects of life in a divorced family. The therapist's job is basically to help them help each other.

19 Prescription for Parents

> *It is my goal that when my children are grown adults, their childhood will not have messed up their lives. They're going to be the fullest and the richest that they can possibly be because of their childhood.*
>
> —Sandy, 37, single parent of three

A major premise of this book is that life is relationships. Divorce, because it changes relationships, also changes the lives of those whom it touches. Children of all ages are more dependent on family relationships than adults and therefore more vulnerable when those relationships change. Divorce unquestionably changes the parent-parent relationship, which greatly affects the child. But it also changes the mother-child and father-child relationships, which can have an even greater impact. Wallerstein and Kelly write,

> As the family breaks apart, each parent-child relationship essentially swings free of the structure that has held it in place. The chain of reactions so abruptly set off may reverberate for several years and lead to new relationships greatly at variance with those obtained when the family was together—relationships, indeed, that have no counterpart in the intact family.[1]

Relationships with "no counterpart" include a parent who visits his children rather than lives with them, the hostile alignment of a child with one parent against the other (see chapter 6), various types of custody arrangements, boyfriends or girlfriends of the parents, and stepparents.

How a child is confronted with the relationship

changes wrought by divorce and how he responds to them depends largely on how the parents handle their divorce and its aftermath. Psychologist Steven E. Goldston told *Business Week,* "The parents—their attitudes and how they treat the kids from the first word spoken about separation to the awkward 'visitation' stage—can mean the difference between night and day to a toddler or a teenager."[2]

TELLING CHILDREN

The recollection of being told that one's parents plan to divorce is likely to be a moment in time forever frozen in a child's memory. Ten-year-old Ben recounted,

> I remember the day I found out my parents were getting a divorce. I had spent the night at a friend's house because my sister was having a slumber party. I came home to see if I could go to my friend's grandpa's house. My mom told me about the divorce and I cried for about fifteen minutes and went with my friend to his grandpa's to see if it would take away some of my feelings. That night I had completely forgotten it. The next night I remembered. I stayed up all night crying that night and two nights after.

Kimberlee, twelve, was seven when her parents separated. She recalled,

> My father told me, "Now don't you cry when I tell you this," and we had no idea what was coming. He had me and my sister on each side of him. He had already told my brother about it. I thought my sister was gong to run out of the room, she was crying so hard. I thought, "How could he tell us this right now?" I mean, the way things were going right then. He said, "I don't love your mother anymore and we're going to be separated for a while, so you won't be able to see me." It fazed me there for a minute. I couldn't believe what he was saying. In my mind I was almost furious after a while.

Sarah, fifteen, said,

> I remember I was sitting in the car with my mom and she knew about it before I did. I remember ... first it was

shock, and then I started crying. That's just something I'll never forget and it still hits me sometimes and it upsets me.

The news that parents plan to divorce is never good news. Most children will predictably respond with shock, anger, denial, tears, protests, or creative alternatives that they feel the parents should try. By planning exactly how and when to tell their children, parents can help soften the impact their disclosure is sure to have. Here are a few suggestions:

1. *Tell them a week or two before the actual separation occurs.* This may cause an uncomfortable interim period, but when the actual break comes, it will be easier for children to accept. They will have had some time to get used to the idea and to prepare for the time when the parent actually leaves the home. Experts advise that whenever it is possible, a couple should try to time their separation so that it does not coincide with other major adjustments children have to make. For example, if parents can put off their separation until children have made a transition to a new school, recuperated from an operation, or passed a big exam, the children will have a somewhat easier time dealing with the loss.

2. *Choose a good time to tell them.* Don't spring the news when children's friends are present, or when they are physically tired or cranky, or when tension between parents is running high. Select a time for this critical discussion when family members are most likely to be feeling calm and will be able to talk without interruption.

3. *Tell all the children at the same time.* This way all family members will know that every other member is aware of what is happening. If children are told separately each may think he is the sole guardian of a terrible family secret. Telling them all together enables them to draw strength from one another.

4. *Tell the children when both parents are present.* This way neither Mom nor Dad is left looking like "the bad guy."

5. *Be honest.* This does not mean that children should be told all the sordid details, but they do deserve to know, at least in general terms, why their parents are breaking up. Parents should be truthful about the status of their relationship and what is going to take place as a result. Children can be told that the parents have given very careful thought to what should be done and that they now feel that divorce is the best solution to their problems.

6. *Be as specific as possible about the changes that will occur.* Children need to be told where each parent will be living, whether they will have to change schools, who will care for them after school, how often they will see the parent who is leaving, and any other important information that can be given. Younger children may benefit by seeing a simple hand-drawn map that shows where Daddy or Mommy will be living relative to where they will live and the route they will take to visit him or her.

    When children are old enough to express their preferences, their wishes should be taken into consideration. Whenever possible, allow them to voice opinions about the decisions that will affect their lives. But *never* force a child to choose between parents. According to experts, it is important to shield children from custody disputes. If the child's testimony is needed in court to determine custody, a private talk with the judge is recommended rather than a court appearance. Even in this private discussion, it is vital that the child not be put in the position of having to choose between parents.

7. *Emphasize that the children are not responsible for your decision in any way.* This should be clearly stated and restated so that there is no doubt in the children's minds about this. Younger children may be difficult to con-

vince, and parents should be sensitive to their tendency to blame themselves.

When a spouse leaves suddenly or when the divorce is bitter and not well thought out by the parents, the task of telling the children sometimes falls on the shoulders of one parent. He or she must not only break the news but also explain the absence of the other parent. This is difficult, and the parent may be tempted to be somewhat less than honest.

Brandon used this approach first but then realized that this was not the best course of action. He recalls,

> The first thing I told them was that their mother had to be away for a little bit—that she was sick and had to be away. I felt that was something they could understand at their age. They knew what it was to be sick. This is what I said until I realized that the situation didn't seem to be turning around.
>
> When we first separated, I thought there was a chance it wouldn't be permanent. That's what really made it hard. I didn't know what to tell them. I had talked with counselors and the doctor. They said that the biggest thing is that you're honest with them, because they can see right through you if you're not leveling with them. They told me it was better to tell them the truth, that they could handle that better than if I tried to make up all kinds of stories.
>
> After I realized that we were going to move toward divorce, I started telling them that Mommy was never going to live here again, and that sort of thing. I used the word "divorce" and said we wouldn't be married anymore, because kids will always fantasize about their parents someday getting back together. Even now I still have to keep reinforcing that this is the way it's gong to be because they still fantasize once in a while: "Mommy's coming home again," and that sort of thing. I continue to tell them we're not married anymore, and I talk about the future.

Sandy remembers,

> The kids kind of saw that something was going on, but I really didn't say anything to them. When it came time that they had to know, I knew the best thing to do was to be honest. The thing that parents do not realize is that if you aren't honest with kids, if you don't tell them the truth, then the only thing they can do is imagine. And usually, if they

imagine, it's the worst or the wrong thing. I knew that the key thing was that the kids needed to know that it had nothing to do with them. It had absolutely nothing to do with them. I simply told them that their father was out of fellowship with God and that he was leaving—also that he wasn't leaving us as much as he was leaving God's will.

SOFTENING THE IMPACT OF DIVORCE

Wallerstein and Kelly discovered that what happens after a divorce affects a child's adjustment more than any conditions present in the home before the event. They also found that the ultimate impact of divorce depends not only on what the child has lost, but more so on what is created to take the place of the failed marriage in his life. Five years after their parents' divorce, the children in their study were felt to have been influenced most by these factors:[3]

- How successful the parents had been in defusing the anger and conflict between them
- How well the custodial parent was able to handle the child and the quality of parenting he was able to give the child
- The quality of the relationship between the visiting parent and the child and the regularity of the visits
- The child's ability to use his personal resources—intelligence, capacity for fantasy, social maturity, and the ability to turn to peers and adults
- Availability of support from other people
- Absence of anger and depression in the child
- Age and sex of the child

The first three factors indicate that the relationships between the parents, between the child and his custodial parent, and between the child and his noncustodial parent are of monumental importance after divorce. These relationships even affect the child's ability to gain support outside the family. Wallerstein and Kelly note,

The child's capacity to rely on friends and to turn to them for help was dependent on the child's relationships within the family. We soon learned that children with good relationships at home were those likely to make friends more easily and to sustain these friendships.[4]

It follows, then, that the single most important thing that parents can do to help their children adjust to divorce is to work hard at establishing a friendly, cooperative relationship between spouses. The next most important thing is to strive to make their parent-child relationship as meaningful and nurturing as possible. Let's examine briefly these two imperatives.

MAKING PEACE WITH A FORMER SPOUSE

One psychologist has gone so far as to label the strain that warring parents put on a child as a "form of child abuse."[5] His point, of course, is that if arguing and fighting and hostilities continue after the marriage has ended, the divorce will have served no purpose at all in terms of alleviating stress and unhappiness in a child's life. It is critical that both parents lay down their weapons, since no one stands to gain anything from prolonging the conflict.

Resentment, hatred, bitterness, and an unforgiving spirit are guaranteed to damage at least one person—the person harboring these poisonous emotions. Those next likely to feel their devastating impact are the children. Ironically, the former spouse—the person against whom these weapons are aimed—is least likely to be hurt by them. When both parents fire heavy artillery, the only people sure to be wounded from both directions are the children who must dodge their crossfire.

How do we end the war?

Patti Roberts, whose divorce within a well-known Christian family was painful and much publicized, found the way to lay down her weapons. It takes determination, and it may take time and tears as well; but every Christian, with God's help, can do what Patti Roberts has done: forgive.

In an interview with *Today's Christian Woman* magazine, Patti said,

> Forgiveness has been a real illusive concept. It seems like such a waste of good passion. When you feel just in your anger, it seems like such a waste to do something so wimpy and defeatist as forgive. . . . Forgiveness seemed passive to me. But it's the most aggressive act of love there is. . . . There is no excuse for not forgiving. I don't care how you hurt me or how right I am. In God's economy there is no excuse for a lack of forgiveness. If you live without love in your heart and you say all those God words, it's more sinful, more evil, uglier, and more like Satan than the worse skin flick you can find. It's more damaging than drugs or booze.
>
> I have seen my children, when they were far too young to have to go through something so heavy, agonize about injustices perpetrated on them, lack of love or loss of love, and all of it done in the name of God. And I have not been able to throw my arms around them and say, "You have a right to be angry. You have a right to hate." When you cast that vote and say, "I will not love," you have handed Satan the reins and voted yourself to be a hopeless case. You have taken on practical atheism. You are saying there is no God.[6]

When we cling to bitterness or resentment, the wrong done to us plays through our minds over and over, like a continuous-loop tape. Each time the offense crosses our consciousness it hurts us afresh and etches deeper into our memories. We are miserable until we snip the tape with forgiveness. Failure to forgive results in wounds that never heal. Every time an emotional scab forms, we rip it open with our bitterness and anger. Forgiveness is God's will, partly because He does not want us to inflict ourselves with emotional pain again and again.

Until we forgive, we are unable to help our children to forgive. We must set the example. Until we forgive, the emotional and psychological freedom that our children might otherwise gain may never come. Working hard to arrive at the point of forgiveness ought to be a top priority for every divorced parent.

Romans 12:18 says, *"If possible, so far as it depends*

on you, be at peace with all men." If we believe in the Lord Jesus Christ, we are under a mandate to forgive (Romans 12:19–21; Matthew 6:14–15; Ephesians 4:32; Colossians 3:13). Our former spouses may or may not do the same. God will not hold us responsible for what they do or don't do. But when we forgive, we are kept from destroying ourselves. And we ensure that our children will have the best chance for a good adjustment that we can give them.

Forgiveness means making a conscious, willful decision no longer to harbor resentment against an ex-spouse. It means affirming before God that we no longer wish to hold anything against him or her. Negative feelings and bad memories will rise up to challenge our decision to forgive, but with God's help, each day will be more victorious than the last. You should talk with a pastor or counselor if you have trouble putting forgiveness into practice.

Quality Parenting After Divorce.

Many suggestions have been given in this book for ways that parents can understand and meet the needs of their children after divorce. Here is a summary of some important do's and don'ts.

DO . . .

1. Make spending time with your child one-on-one a high priority. Plan ahead. Mark your calendar well in advance, setting aside time on his birthday and for special school events or recreational events that would be meaningful to both of you. Spur-of-the-moment time is important too. Sandy's efforts in this are worthy of mention. She related,

    The first couple years, especially, kids can get lost in the mass of problems. And kids—especially when you've got three—tend to lose their identity and their individuality with the parent. The Lord gave me real wisdom on this: each one needs to spend time alone with mother. So what I do is, my son and I go somewhere and we'll stop and get ice cream and stop at McDonald's but we won't tell the other two what we did while we're gone on the trip. And then another time when I have somewhere to go or something to do, I'll just take my daughter. And we'll go get a cookie at the mall or something and we don't tell the other two what we did. And then the next time I'll do something with my other child. That way I'm maintaining relationships with each one individually as well as a whole unit which is a very key factor in the really critical first years.

2. Work at establishing a cooperative relationship with your ex-spouse.

3. Encourage the relationship between the child and his other parent.

4. Foster security by disciplining consistently and maintaining a regular schedule of mealtimes and bedtimes. For younger children, keep the same baby sitter and the same bedtime routine—bath, story, prayers, etc. Let older children keep the same outside activities such as clubs at school, Little League, or scouting.

5. Keep the lines of communications open. If you are the noncustodial parent, make a real effort to stay involved in the child's life.

6. Guard against showing preference for a child of your same sex and guard against making a child who physically resembles his other parent a scapegoat. Research shows that this tends to happen.

7. Keep your promises. If you promise you'll be there, be there. If you say you'll call, do so. You are teaching the child whether or not he can trust you.

8. Build the child's self-esteem. (See chapter 8 for some ideas on how to do this.)

9. Allow the child to grieve over his losses and be patient and understanding as he regains his stability.

10. Keep as much of life the same after divorce as you can, for as long as you can. Make major changes—

such as moving to a new house or beginning to work for the first time—slowly if possible.
11. If the child's other parent is not involved in his life, encourage relationships between the child and trustworthy adults of the opposite sex who could serve as role models or surrogates.
12. Reinforce the fact that the child is in no way responsible for the divorce.
13. Find an adult support system of your own.
14. Obtain good predivorce and postdivorce counseling.
15. Build common interests with your kids. Hobbies, sports, and crafts make excellent ground in which to grow a meaningful relationship.
16. Be positive verbally about the other parent, remembering that the child's self-image is derived from both of you.
17. Be aware of these potential problem areas.
    - Schoolwork may suffer for a while. (See chapter 10 for some ideas on how to improve this.) Teachers should be told that parents are divorcing. Parents should decide which of them will stay in touch with the school and instruct the teacher to contact that parent whenever parent-teacher conferences are needed.
    - Children are often resistant to parental dating. They may feel either that the new person is taking attention that rightfully belongs to him or that this person is standing in the way of reconciliation between parents. Older children may feel uncomfortable with the knowledge that parents are sexual beings.
    - The rules at both the custodial and noncustodial parents' homes should be basically the same. Bedtimes, chores, guidelines for TV, and so forth should not vary widely, no matter which parent the

child is with. When parents are unable to agree on these matters, each should at least strive to be consistent with his own rules.
18. Reaffirm your relationship with Jesus Christ and take your children to a Bible believing church that welcomes and ministers to single-parent families. (See Appendix B if you are unsure of your relationship with Christ.)

DON'T . . .

1. Don't put the child in the middle of any disagreements with your ex-spouse. Don't ask him to relay messages, spy, or deliver or ask for checks.
2. Don't jump into a serious new relationship with someone of the opposite sex for at least one year after divorce. Instead, rebuild your life and concentrate on your children. Begin to date only when you fully understand your part in the failed marriage.
3. Don't make your child an emotional substitute for your missing partner.
4. Don't ask a child to take on more household responsibilities than he is ready for.
5. Don't bring a boyfriend or girlfriend along during visits with your children, at least for the first several months. When you do, let it be the exception, not the rule, especially if the visits are the only times your child can be alone with you.
6. Don't cut off a child's relationships with his relatives on the other parent's side of the family.
7. Don't let your children go unsupervised for long periods of time after school or during evenings.
8. Don't substitute money, gifts, or treats for quality time with your children, and don't try to buy their affection. You can't.

9. Don't hesitate to ask for help, for yourself or for your children, when you need it. There is a growing number of loving, concerned people who want to be there for you—emotionally, spiritually, financially, and in the very practical, nitty-gritty areas of life.

THROUGH THE EYES OF CHILDREN

Children are astute observers of parental behavior. They are uncannily perceptive and can be scathingly critical or quite complimentary and appreciative. Usually they strive to be fair, carefully weighing mitigating circumstances in their own minds. Above all, they are candid. They have strong feelings about divorce, about their families, and about what their parents have done right or wrong in handling the breakup. In the end, they are the final authorities on what it means to be a child of divorce, and thus they are our best teachers.

The following is a potpourri of comments, both positive and negative, regarding Mom, Dad, and family life after divorce. Think about the circumstances and feelings that lie behind the words.

"I'm happy that both my parents still love me."

"My father is a nice guy, but he has built resentment against my mom."

"My family has always been there for me when I needed a helping hand or a shoulder to lean on."

"My father needs to understand that for a relationship of any kind to exist, you need to show genuine concern about the other person's needs, desires and expectations. In order for me to take his suggestions seriously he must show—not tell—a concern for my life."

"I'm happy that my parents get along fairly well. It makes it easier on us kids."

"Our family is great, all but my dad. I don't like him."

"What upsets me most about my parents' divorce is that my father, who originally wanted a divorce from my mother, now regrets it."

"My father is such a gentle, loving man. He was always a good provider and spent time with us. He had trouble expressing himself, which I am sure led to many of my parents' arguments. My mother left one day, taking nothing with her. It was sad. A lot of loneliness took her place. My dad didn't talk about it, which made it even worse because we never knew how he felt."

"Our family is close, considering the circumstances, but sometimes resentful. We argue too often."

"Mom never claimed to be perfect. She knew she had made mistakes in her marriage, but by the time she knew what they were it was too late."

"I wish my parents would get back together and stop fighting."

"Basically, I just want my dad to know how I feel and to try to understand. I think he knows what I've said to him; I just don't think he'll accept what I feel."

"I wish my father would come and visit me, but he can't."

"It upsets me that my parents are not friends and don't have any communication between them."

"The hardest part about having divorced parents is they always fight."

"My dad tries to treat me like when I was real little. Now, maybe he wishes I were back at that age, but I'm not anymore. I know he's really uncomfortable; I can just sense it. If I did that to my kids, I would feel guilty about leaving them and I'd probably act the same way."

"Our family has to deal with a lot of problems that can be traced back to the separation of my parents."

"My father needs to understand that he has the permission to come and see me."

"It's very hard for me to trust my mom after all the things she's done."

"I got extremely mad when my dad was separated from Mom and he came and asked her for sexual favors. He'd come over for lunch and then they'd go back into the bedroom. That used to make me so mad, and it still does when I think about it."

"My family has always been there to lend a helping hand."

"I'm happy that they're not fighting, because my dad left."

"I wish my father would remarry. I always feel sorry for men that are alone. My dad does well by himself; I just think he needs someone to love him, like a wife."

"My father likes to play mind games to make me doubt the love of my mother."

"Mother understood that no good could come from downing my father in front of the kids. She always said she could see where she had failed as well as my father. Although she may have had very bitter feelings, she never passed them on to us."

20 Divorce and the Great Commission

I think divorce is Satan's way of attacking a Christian stronghold and God-given institution, the family.

—Melodie, 31

Two thousand years ago, God's objective in sending Jesus Christ to earth was to make the free gift of salvation available to all by Jesus' death. God's objective remains the same in this generation, and it is to us that He has entrusted the task of communicating the Good News. Satan's objective has always been to thwart the progress of the gospel. He is diametrically opposed to God's purposes; whatever God hates, Satan loves. As the conflict between Christ and Satan intensifies and we draw closer to the second coming of the Lord, Satan seeks to distract us from our evangelistic task any way he can. I believe that our runaway divorce rate is a part of his strategy. Because God hates divorce, Satan loves it.

Divorce is especially useful to the enemy of our souls because, for varying lengths of time, it keeps people from thinking about anything but their own problems. When our pain is intense, we become self-focused, unable to reach out to others. Divorce between believers is a special delight to Satan because it temporarily—sometimes permanently—sidelines many Christians whose impact for Christ has been or could have been significant. Who can think about the unsaved in the Middle East or across the street when his own family and his own life appear to be falling apart?

If your spouse told you this morning that he or she wanted a divorce or if you just found out that your parents were splitting up, what would you pray about tonight? As you read these words, millions of people across the country are preoccupied with the turmoil in their own hearts and homes and seeking to deal with the emotional emergency. And this is really as it should be. First Timothy 3:5 says, "But if a man does not know how to manage his own household, how will he take care of the church of God?" Satan, of course, knows this and uses it to his full advantage. He welcomes strife in the home, whether it leads to divorce or not, because it short-circuits our spiritual vitality and saps our emotional energy.

No one is more aware of the spiritual dimension of family life than children whose Christian parents have divorced. They make a direct connection between what happened to the marriage and what happened to one or both of their parents' relationships with Christ. I asked ten-year-old Paige, "Why do you think your mom and dad got divorced?" She answered, "'Cause my father didn't really want to be a Christian. He just didn't want to be around. They could've talked it out if he would've wanted to be a Christian. I don't think he wanted to be a Christian anymore." Paige perceptively views her dad's rejection of his wife and family as a reflection of a waning faith in Christ.

Sarah, fifteen, sees the divorce of her parents in much the same way. She said of her father, "I know I shouldn't judge his spiritual life, but I think he's way different than he used to be, because he used to be so close to God. I just see it personally as him falling away, and so far away that it scares me."

After years of observation, Terry has concluded that divorce is essentially a spiritual problem: "God defined the cause of divorce as it actually is—hardness of heart and putting self first."

The perceptions of these three children of divorce are correct. There is a direct link between the degree of intimacy one has in her relationship with God and the degree of intimacy she experiences in her relationships with others, most notably in the family. Hardness of heart toward God is at the root of most divorces, whether the divorcing parties are Christians or not.

As we have already seen, however, there is no evil that God cannot turn around for ultimate good. There is nothing that He cannot use in some way to bring glory to Himself. He is able to turn even the cleverest of Satan's schemes into a spiritual victory. Accordingly, there is another aspect of divorce, a joyous one that delights not Satan but God.

FRUIT FROM FAILURE

Happily, ironically, the brokenheartedness of a newly divorced person—adult or child—sometimes produces an unexpected benefit: a new humility toward God and the things of God. Newly divorced people are newly plowed up in heart and often suddenly receptive to the seed of the gospel. The ground that was previously hard and headstrong may now be crying out for something good and positive to be implanted. Similarly, believers who have long been spiritually adrift may now suddenly realize that they are not in a proper relationship with God. Steve was one of these.

"I credit my divorce for most of my turnaround, if not all of my turnaround in the spiritual area," Steve said. "My kids might not even be going to church now if it weren't for the divorce. I don't condone divorce. I certainly don't recommend it as a way to get spiritual. But I can see that with the way my life was heading at that time and with the friends we had, it would have just continued that way and I may not have turned back to God and to church at all."

Kathy said, "God used my divorce to draw me closer to Him and to give me a greater knowledge of His love than I ever had before I learned my need for Him."

Divorce is a spiritual paradox. On the one hand, it is a

tragedy. It tears apart a bond that God said should not be torn apart. It causes misery and anguish and suffering in the lives of all who are touched by it. But on the other hand, divorce is a golden opportunity for cultivating eternal fruit. In its wake, apathetic Christians can be revitalized. Because of it, the kingdom of heaven is enlarged as men, women, and children who might never otherwise have entered begin asking, seeking, and knocking in an effort to learn whether God is real and whether He cares for them. Psalm 119:71 affirms this paradox:

> *It is good for me that I was afflicted,*
> *That I may learn Thy statutes.*

THE ROLE OF THE CHURCH

We see that divorce is not merely an unfortunate social malady of our time, but also a spiritual battleground. Satan's purpose is to defeat and destroy everything good, using divorce as a tool toward that end. God's purpose is to stimulate growth, faith, and purpose, using the same tool. There is much at stake.

While divorce is laden with potential for producing eternal fruit, it must be nurtured before it can be harvested. Therefore it is imperative that the institutional church, as well as individual believers, enthusiastically embrace the task of ministering to survivors of divorce in practical, tangible ways.

As an organization the church can provide a framework for its members to carry out their personal ministries, often more effectively than they could do on their own. There are three reasons for this.

1. *Training.* Churches can offer their laypeople specialized training in how to help.

2. *Resources.* Churches offer greater financial resources, teaching tools, and perhaps staff members with special expertise. All these can be employed to enhance individual efforts.

3. *Motivation and Structure*. When the desire to minister to single-parent families is a common objective, creativity often breeds creativity, and people are more likely to be motivated to put their plans into action. When those plans are structured into a curriculum or an overriding philosophy of ministry, those seeking to help will find it a more manageable, feasible task because they have a road map to follow and others to compare notes with.

Ministry Philosophy

In seeking to minister to single-parent families, churches should develop a philosophy of ministry that will form the basis for all that they do. This philosophy will necessarily vary from church to church, depending on the number of people needing their ministry, the specific needs of those people, the resources of the church, and perhaps its doctrinal stance. I would, however, like to suggest two essential components for any church philosophy regarding helping adults and children of divorce.

First, the task of helping should be viewed as a redemptive task. It is part and parcel of our calling to function as salt and light in the world. It goes hand in hand with proclaiming salvation in Christ and serves to open doors to do just that in many cases. Churches can be used of God to help as many as possible suffer as little as possible in the aftermath of divorce. Beyond that they can stimulate spiritual growth, emotional wholeness, and social acceptance—all of which redeem individual potential that might otherwise have been lost in the ordeal of divorce.

Second, I suggest that church membership should never be made a criterion for receiving help. A church's outreach should have no strings attached. Those who sense genuine concern and love from the church will no doubt respond with commitment to the people and the organization, and, hopefully, to Christ Himself. There is no justification for demanding someone's loyalty before we have earned his or her friendship and respect.

The book *Growing Up Divorced* relates a pathetic story about a little girl named Emily.[1] Emily's parents broke up just as she was beginning first grade. Things at home were very bad. Her father left home and then returned repeatedly, only to fight viciously with her mother each time. Emily grew quiet and withdrawn, but no one at school noticed because no one there had known her before first grade.

By second grade, her parents had parted company permanently. The father provided no support at all for the family and never came to see Emily and her brother. Her mother couldn't find work, grew increasingly depressed, and began drinking. Emily would come home from school to find her passed out in front of the TV. By the time Emily reached third grade, her problems were obvious to everyone. She came to school in dirty clothes with uncombed hair. She began to steal from her classmates, who ostracized and taunted her, calling her "El Disgusto."

Emily's withdrawal became complete, and she would no longer even respond to her own name. Her teacher tried sacrificially to help. She scheduled a conference with Emily's mother, but the woman never showed up. She asked the school principal to attempt to locate Emily's father, but his efforts proved fruitless. She spoke to the school psychiatrist, who recommended psychiatric help for Emily. Armed with this recommendation, she contacted Emily's mother again. The mother insisted that Emily didn't have a problem, and even if she did, how could they pay for any help? The teacher then contacted a local family counseling agency and found that their funding had been cut back and there was a three-month waiting list to boot. As a last resort, the teacher called a local church to see if they would help. It certainly wasn't their problem, they said: Emily was not a member.

"Just whose problem is Emily, anyway?" the author concluded rhetorically. I wonder what answer Jesus would give.

WAYS TO HELP

There are numerous ways that churches can help single-parent families like Emily's long before their problems reach the critical stage.

Counseling

One of the most important services any church can offer is free or low-cost counseling. In many cases the pastor can be the counselor, provided he has ability and training. Not all pastors make good counselors, however, and sometimes a pastor's schedule does not allow for a significant counseling load.

Ideally a church should have a full-time professional counselor on its staff, particularly if there is a high divorce rate in the community or if the church seems to be gaining a large number of single-parent families needing counseling intervention. When a staff arrangement is impossible or impractical, several churches can pool their resources and employ one or more counselors to meet this need. In addition, churches should be aware of professional Christian counselors in the community who will accept referrals. The drawback in this approach, however, is that the cost may be a deterrent to some who stand to gain the most from the counseling.

An alternative might be to select several laypeople who could be trained as lay counselors and serve on behalf of the church. This does not make them professionals; it means that they will have been taught basic counseling techniques and how to be good listeners. These skills alone can sufficiently meet many needs. Lay counselors should also be trained to identify warning signals of more serious problems that require professional help and should be able to make appropriate referrals.

Help From Within

The church's membership is likely to include a number of people who could provide single-parent families with advice about money management, legal matters, or community resources and programs for which they may qualify. Pastors, counselors, and lay counselors should be aware of these people and also aware of health-care services, job-training opportunities, and other local, state, or federal programs that might benefit single parents and their children.

The church can also organize a pool of homemakers or retired nurses within the congregation who could be called on short notice to stay with sick children when parents must be at work or are hospitalized.

Minister of Outreach

In large churches where there are many single-parent families within the community to whom the congregation could extend itself, appointing a minister of outreach may be a practical course of action. This person might be a deacon or deaconess or someone within the body who has a special concern for single-parent families. He or she would keep in touch with them on a regular basis, by phone or in person, and keep abreast of their financial and other needs and how they are doing. He or she could then present pressing needs to the church leadership or to the whole congregation as appropriate.

Adopt-A-Kid

Children who live with only one parent may be lacking in relationships with adults of the absent parent's sex. Providing these children with a big brother or big sister or even a couple who would spend time with them regularly could meet a real need in their lives.

Working Through Sunday School and Other Groups

Churches ought to do all they can to prevent children from developing a feminized concept of Christianity. The most potent solution to this is to begin to recruit more men and more couples to work with children, from the nursery on up. In many churches, children have exclusively female teachers year after year. Those from father-absent homes may be especially affected by this, rarely having significant contact with a man in the context of church and Sunday school. Placing men in positions of leadership in the nursery, preschool, and children's departments where they can function as spiritual role models is one thing every church can do.

This kind of ministry is not done more often because some men in the church view it as insignificant or feel inadequate or uncomfortable in dealing with young children. This problem can be alleviated with good teacher training, especially when the one providing the training is a well-respected man in the church.

Educating all children's workers to the special needs of children from single-parent families is one of the most important steps a church can take toward meeting their needs. Great care should be taken, however, not to communicate the information in a way that causes workers to view these children as abnormal or in need of pampering.

Christian Schools

Churches that operate Christian schools should avoid exposing their students to an exclusively feminized classroom. Children from broken homes need male authority figures; male teachers can be highly influential. The classroom setting itself tends to foster quietness, obedience, conformity, and passivity. Male teachers provide a balance that is especially needed by children whose fathers take little interest in them.

A major reason for the lack of men teaching in Christian schools and many public schools is the low pay and low status the positions afford. To attract highly qualified Christian men as teachers and principals, Christian schools will need to upgrade their pay scales, keeping in mind a man's responsibility to support his family.

Christian school teachers in particular need to be educated about divorce. They should be familiar with the needs of children of divorce and should know how to respond when a child's behavior or schoolwork begins to show signs of stress at home. A half-day seminar with a psychologist or counselor might be very helpful in equipping teachers to deal understandingly with these students.

Day Care and After-School Care

One of the greatest needs for many single parents is finding quality day care at a reasonable cost with flexible hours. Churches that provide this service render invaluable help to both parent and child. When working parents know that their children are in the hands of trustworthy Christian people, they worry less. They know their children benefit from the loving nurture, stimulation, and one-to-one attention. They are far less likely to get this same attention in day-care centers that are overcrowded and understaffed with workers who have no deep desire to minister to those whom they serve.

After-school care is equally important to the parents of school-age children. Those who would otherwise go home to empty houses or apartments can benefit greatly from a supervised after-school gathering in the church fellowship hall or gym. Games and other recreation can be provided, as well as tables and chairs for those who wish to do homework until Mom or Dad arrives to pick them up.

Single-Adult Sunday School

If a church wants to minister to single parents, the best place to begin is by establishing a single-adult Sunday school class. Placing people who are single again in a couples' class makes them feel like square pegs in round holes. It intensifies their sense of loss. They need the companionship of others who have gone through the same experience. They also benefit from rubbing shoulders with those who have never married or may be separated. All are spouseless at the moment and can provide friendship and encouragement for one another. Social events where a date or a mate are not required are especially important, and only a singles class can provide the right framework for these kinds of gatherings.

The four singles classes at my church are divided

according to age, and the 260 single adults who actively participate in them range from the late teens and early twenties to over sixty years of age.

Retreats, Conferences, and Seminars

Periodically scheduling special church programs that address the specific needs of single parents or children of divorce is another helpful ministry. Youth retreats or single-adult retreats can be expanded to include elective sessions that address the special concerns of people touched by divorce. These can take a workshop approach and allow for sharing among the participants. Those who lead the sessions should be familiar with the problems and needs of divorced families.

Churchwide parenting or single-adult conferences can bring in outside speakers with special expertise in single parenting. These too can provide special elective sessions or workshops that stress practical solutions to common problems and provide education about how divorce affects children.

One-day seminars or a short-term series of classes can be held just for children. Speakers might include a family law attorney, a counselor, or others who can help the children understand concepts like "alimony" or "best interests of the child," while giving them the opportunity to ask questions. Discussion groups, role playing, and creative expression of feelings can be part of the programming, all of which should be couched in a perspective of helping children trust God with their feelings and problems. The book *Helping Children of Divorce* by Neal Buchanan and Eugene Chamberlain (Broadman Press, 1981) contains a special appendix with step-by-step instructions for holding this kind of seminar for children in grades three to six.

Church Library

If your church already has a lending library, it can be stocked with helpful books and cassette tapes that deal with divorce adjustment for both adults and children.

(Appendix A has recommendations for books you may want to include.) Parenting or single-adult magazines often carry helpful articles. Churches can subscribe to these kinds of publications for members and visitors.

If your church does not have a lending library, why not start one? Don't limit it to the needs of single parents and children of divorce, however. This is an educational ministry that can touch everyone in your congregation.

Sensitivity in Corporate Worship

Pastors need to keep in mind that a significant number of church members and church visitors have been touched in some way by divorce, either in their own families or by friends.

It is imperative that the biblical view of marriage, divorce, and family life be clearly proclaimed from the pulpit, never muted or watered down to accommodate those who are seeking to justify another viewpoint. Yet we can and must be sensitive. The way the truth is proclaimed—the tone of voice, the choice of words—can make a difference to one who has known the sting of divorce. He can be further hurt or further healed by the message, depending on the attitude he senses in the speaker.

Most people receive truth best when they know that the one who proclaims it loves them and has their best interests at heart. People from broken homes and marriages need to sense that the overwhelming stance of the church toward them is characterized by love and acceptance. Solid assurances of this ought to come from the pastor himself and from others who have leadership.

Seeking to reverse intolerances of the past, some Catholic churches now strive to be sensitive to the divorced in their liturgy. The following is used in the Mass throughout the Archdiocese of Detroit:

> For all families who have suffered the pain of separation or divorce—Let us pray to the Lord.

For single parents who need strength to carry through on their responsibilities alone—Let us pray to the Lord.

For the Church, that we may offer to welcome and support, as well as learn from, the separated and divorced persons in our community—Let us pray to the Lord.

For all who suffer rejection, alienation, oppression, poverty, and hopelessness—Let us pray to the Lord.

For all who mourn the loss of their family members through divorce, that they will depend on the strength of God and others in the Christian community during this trying time—Let us pray to the Lord.[2]

Evangelicals can accomplish the same objectives implied in this litany by making mention of these special needs in public prayer during the worship service or at other times.

21 An Ounce of Prevention

If my husband and I had gotten to know each other better, if we had heard the truth from our parents, from the church and from society, then I'm not sure we would have gotten married. But we did. And when the weak foundations of our relationship wobbled, we had no Christian base on which to repair it.

—Barbara Spence, single mother of three[1]

Growing up in a small Pennsylvania town, I was not aware of divorce. As far as I knew then, no one in my family had ever been divorced, and I knew of only one child who had divorced parents. The topic of divorce rarely entered my thoughts or conversations. It was not part of the world in which my friends and I lived.

Today life is different. My own parents divorced four years ago, and other members of my family have also divorced. Friends from high school and college are now divorced, and the parents of some of those friends are also divorced. A large number of the people with whom I have worked since college have been through divorce, and so have many of the people who attend my church. Divorce seems to be everywhere now. I am told that in my city there is a school in which 80 percent of the children come from divorced homes. We are fast approaching the day when living with both parents will be the exception rather than the rule.

PREVENTING DIVORCE

Amazingly, many churches are virtually silent, not only about divorce, but about marriage also. They do nothing to beautify and strengthen marriage in their own congregations. They offer no guidance or preparation to young people about to wed. When divorce occurs, within or without the church, support and encouragement are lacking. This is highly regrettable, because in their passivity and silence these churches are contributing to the problem rather than serving redemptively.

Proverbs 3:27 says, "Do not withhold good from those to whom it is due, when it is in your power to do it." Along the same theme, Galatians 6:10 exhorts, "So then, while we have opportunity, let us do good to all men, and especially to those who are of the household of the faith." In this day of rampant divorce, part of the good that is well within the power of the church to do is tending to the dual priorities of keeping existing marriages together and preparing young people—especially children of divorce—for marriage. Preventing divorce is a greater responsibility and challenge than reaching out to minister when it occurs.

There are at least five ways every local church can inject divorce prevention into the life of its congregation.

1. Teach People How to Live Daily in the Power of the Holy Spirit

Galatians 5:14–16 says,

> For the whole Law is fulfilled in one word, in the statement, "You shall love your neighbor as yourself." But if you bite and devour one another, take care lest you be consumed by one another. But I say, walk by the Spirit, and you will not carry out the desire of the flesh.

If marriage is a spiritual union, then there are spiritual principles that must be followed for the marriage to stay healthy. Learning to walk by the Spirit is the foremost of these principles.

When God's Spirit is in control of both husband and wife, there can be no divorce, for the Spirit cannot be at enmity with Himself. Filled with the Spirit, we fulfill the whole law in loving our spouses as we love ourselves. Allow sin and self to reign and we bite and devour one another, and marital unity is lost. Walking in the Spirit is the most pivotal and potentially life-changing concept any church can impart to its members. Yet remarkably few churches emphasize this, and many pastors do not understand how to live a Spirit-filled life themselves.

A number of fine resources on this subject have been published by Campus Crusade for Christ and are available at most Christian bookstores. An inexpensive booklet titled *Have You Made the Wonderful Discovery of the Spirit-Filled Life?* (Campus Crusade for Christ, 1966) provides a clear, simple explanation and should be read by every Christian. *The Holy Spirit, The Key To Supernatural Living* by Bill Bright (San Bernardino: Here's Life Publishers, 1980) provides a good overview. Other excellent materials written especially for study groups are also available.

The concept of walking in the Spirit is not hard to understand. Children grasp it easily, and it should be part of their Christian training from an early age. A clear understanding of what it means to walk in the Spirit and live in obedience to God may in itself be enough to prevent many divorces.

2. Teach the Truth About Marriage and Divorce

Barbara Spence, who is quoted at the beginning of this chapter, has insightfully written,

> I would say that our marriage went wrong in the year of courtship before we were married. To put it simply, we weren't prepared. And the blame for that goes to our parents, society, the church and, of course, ourselves.
>
> I had a good example of a strong marriage in my home. My mother and father have an ideal marriage. They are an institution in and of themselves. Their love for each other is so strong that I assumed marriage was that way for everyone. I was never exposed to any of the work that held their marriage together. It just *was*. I expected mine to be the same.
>
> Right before we were divorced, my husband said to me, "Marriage should not have to be work. You fall in love, get married, and that's it." He was partly right. You get

married and that's it. But now I know that is where the work begins—after the commitment. I wish our parents had shown us that.

Some of the blame for the failure of our marriage goes to society. Even Christians often believe that false view of marriage that society projects. To society, love is a euphoric state. Television and magazines emphasize the romance—the pretty china, the cozy home life and, of course, the wedding bed. They don't show newlyweds what to do when reality sets in. They don't show the financial struggles, the stretch marks or the dirty kitchen sink. So when the newness of the marriage wears off, the couple often feels jilted. They didn't expect what they got. So they naturally want out. When they vowed that their marriage would last through good times and bad, they didn't understand what an enormous statement they were making. . . .

No one told us that growth, children, health and jobs would change us. No one told us how hard it would be to adapt. No one told us that joy rarely comes without work. And no one mentioned divorce.[2]

In seeking to teach the truth about marriage, part of the task before the church is that of infusing a heavy dose of reality. People who fantasize about marriage meeting all their emotional, physical, and social needs and living happily ever after with that unbelievably perfect mate need to be rescued from the marriage-is-the-answer balloon that has floated them off the ground—preferably before the wedding. That idealized concept of marriage is guaranteed to prove disappointing.

We need to replace society's deceptive, sugar-coated myths with perspectives rooted in reality. We must begin to teach people that marriage is a rugged climb up a steep mountain—because that's what life is. Two people who commit themselves to climbing together will not necessarily have an easier journey than those who choose to climb alone. But they will have companionship, encouragement, help, and a great many joys along the way if they climb the path that God has mapped out for them.

We don't need to let all the air out of the marriage-is-the-answer balloon, but we do need to temper it with the truth. This is crucial to preventing people from substituting one false idealization for another. Those who thought that marriage was supposed to be heaven on earth and then discovered that it was something less may go on to blow up a divorce-is-the-answer balloon, only to become even more sorely disillusioned.

People in unhappy marriages sometimes fantasize about the freedom that divorce would bring. They envision a gala social life, new sexual adventures, time to explore new interests, and freedom from mundane responsibilities. Once divorced, they are greeted instead by loneliness, guilt, lowered self-esteem, and a mountain of worries and responsibilities. The divorce-is-the-answer balloon never fails to burst.

Divorce creates so much unanticipated stress and disappointment that in one study an overwhelming majority—97 percent of the women and 81 percent of the men—felt one year after divorce that the whole thing might have been a terrible mistake.[3] They regretted the fact that they had not tried harder to preserve the marriage. They were not happier, and their lives were not more fulfilling. This is the truth about divorce, and we need to help both young people and married couples face the fact that divorce commonly creates more problems than it solves. We need to instill in them a problem-solving mentality rather than a mindset that naïvely views divorce as a convenient escape hatch.

In our throwaway society we have grown accustomed to simply tossing aside anything that no longer seems useful. Because this tendency sometimes carries over into human relationships, we need to emphasize the lesson of the amaryllis plant.

The amaryllis' bloom is glorious—one or more white, purple, pink, or red lilylike flowers atop a single skyward stem. Once its blossoms fade, however, the amaryllis enters a period of dormancy. Impatient gardeners might be tempted to throw it out, thinking it dead. But it is not. It is full of life and can bloom again, every bit as glorious, if the gardener will only be patient.

When marriages are not in bloom they may seem as dead as a dormant amaryllis. But nurtured with tenderness and patient wisdom, they too can bloom again if they are not hastily cast aside.

We need to underscore the idea of commitment in marriage, emphasizing what it means to be "a friend who sticks closer than a brother" (Proverbs 18:24). Actor Alan Alda has said,

> Most married couples never take the time to learn the great enjoyment people experience from working through all their problems. Just because difficulties occur, you shouldn't say, "Well, I didn't plan for this, so let's get a divorce." A deal is a deal, and marriage is a deal for good and bad times.[4]

3. Elevate the Status of Marriage and Family

More and more, the most compelling witness we have to offer the world is Christian marriage—a living analogy of the relationship between Christ and His bride, the church. The louder our society applauds divorce, the higher the church ought to lift marriage and the family. Franky Schaeffer has said,

> Today in America, the most radical thing a person can do is to be the husband of one wife or the wife of one husband. Things have gone so far that just living an ordinary Christian life, in the real sense of the word, is radical and will have an impact.[5]

Programming. One way by which churches can make marriage and family concerns a priority is by reflecting those needs in their programming. People today need practical help in a multitude of areas that have the potential for enriching their family living. Financial management, parenting, dealing with in-laws, establishing a family worship time, and learning effective interpersonal communication skills are just a few of the needful topics. Some churches have dismissed such topics as irrelevant. They see "Bible teaching" as their sole purpose. Yet biblical truth must be applied to life to be useful, and this is where many believers—hence, marriages and families—are weak.

An Ounce of Prevention

The road to a successful marriage and a happy family is paved with scriptural truth, but not limited to it. There is much helpful truth that comes from places other than the Bible. But all truth finds favor with God and can ultimately be traced to Him.

Marriages and families need all the help they can get in translating scriptural truths into real life. Biblically based seminars, films, workshops, conferences, books, and many secular resources as well, can be creatively used by churches to strengthen the marriages and families in their congregations.

Curing Churchaholics. Child psychiatrist James P. Comer has written,

> Today there are many families in which both parents work, and their jobs may require much more commuting or travel time than they did a generation ago. If parents attempt to keep their religious, social, and public-service activities at the same level they did when one parent worked in or near the home, something is bound to suffer. Too often, it's time with children—particularly those in preadolescence or adolescence.[6]

Because of the hectic pace of modern life, it's not unusual to find families spending more time away from home in separate pursuits than at home together in common pursuits. As Dr. Comer has pointed out, when both parents work outside the home it takes only a few additional commitments to risk placing quality family time in jeopardy.

A church can serve its families well by encouraging people to say no to overcommitment. Most church leaders have no trouble identifying a member who is overcommitted to his job or his hobbies, but few seem able to recognize a person who is overcommitted to the church. Overcommitment, no matter where it is directed, has the same deleterious effect on family life. Unfortunately, because most people find it too easy to say no to opportunities for service, the overcommitted person is a joy to every pastor's heart. Overcommitted fathers and mothers are often publicly praised as faithful even when their church commitments are having an adverse effect on their marriages and taking precedence over the well-being of their families.

Pastors and other church leaders ought to be concerned enough to ask, "Do both you and your wife work? How many nights a week are you at church? How much time do you spend together as a family each week?" The answers may reveal a churchaholic. This seemingly devoted individual may in fact be unable to say no to anything that is asked of him. He may have trouble establishing priorities. He may not fully comprehend the importance of spending time with his family, failing to see that this is also a ministry and one that only he can perform. He may be serving out of a sense of guilt. There may be much more behind his untiring devotion to service than meets the eye. We do him and his family a grave disservice if we encourage him to think that his wrong priorities actually please the Lord, or that he is indispensable to the Lord's work. A wise and discerning pastor will seek to understand and then gently tell the churchaholic, "Go home and spend time with your family. God will provide someone to take your place."

Teaching people how to balance their lives and determine their priorities is one of the most important ways a church can help its people. The result will be a body of believers who are experiencing more personal fulfillment and richer, stronger family living, while rendering service that is truly pleasing to God.

The Pastor. If there is one person who sets the pace for making marriage and the family a priority it is the pastor. His personal convictions are readily perceived and imitated. Overcommitment among pastors is common. Just like other churchaholics, however, the reasons are not always what they appear to be. One divorced ex-pastor admitted,

> The pastorate is a dangerous place to be if one has marriage problems. Whenever I wanted to withdraw from my wife I

could always find plenty of necessary activities, and I could justify spending time there by feeling I was serving the Lord. I knew in theory and am now firmly convinced that a pastor's family is his primary God-given responsibility. If the relationships in the home break down (even short of divorce) his ministry will suffer.[7]

Pastors and their families have the same needs as other families. They are not immune to the effects of overcommitment. Marital disharmony, a lack of strong emotional bonds between family members, and rebellious, insecure children can just as easily characterize an overcommitted pastor's family as an overcommitted layperson's. One pastor's daughter said,

> My father's congregation would have been astounded if they knew how neglected I felt as a child. "Your father's a man of God," my mother would always tell me. "He has to be there for people who need him." But he was never there for me. It never seemed to occur to my parents that I might be one of those "people."[8]

Church members can discourage pastors from overcommitment by willingly embracing ministry themselves within the body. The work can and should be shared by shepherd and sheep alike. Why should the pastor have to attend every committee meeting, every evangelism class, every covered-dish supper, and every Sunday and Wednesday evening service every week? If the prevailing sentiment is that the church would fall apart without the pastor's personal presence at every single function, then the pastor has never caught and taught a vision for multiplying himself through lay leadership. Every pastor ought to have key leaders whom he can disciple, confide in, and call upon to assume some of his duties on occasion.

4. Make Marriage Enrichment a Priority

From the viewpoint of many children, there is something infinitely worse than having divorced parents. It is having parents who seem locked in an eternal conflict with one another, day after day, month after month, year after year. While there is much disagreement on this issue, some noted authorities believe that a child who witnesses constant tension and conflict between parents may actually be in a worse psychological position than the child whose parents have learned to be tolerant of one another after divorce; with constant conflict, there is no end and no way to escape it.

The following are some thoughts from people who hold this view:

Dr. Lee Salk: "Children who live in such an atmosphere receive little emotional satisfaction and frequently try to spend time in other people's homes where there is warmth and communication. Many of my adult patients whose parents stayed together under these circumstances tell me they couldn't wait to grow up and get away from home. These people developed a very negative view of marriage, and many of them said to me that they wish their parents had gotten divorced instead of remaining in a tense and empty marriage."[9]

Dr. Irene Goldenberg: "Sometimes I'm asked, 'What about staying in a marriage for the sake of the children?' And I feel very strongly that any relationship where you have to live a lie, where you are not honest to yourself or can't be honest to children, is extremely destructive."[10]

Wallerstein and Kelly: Neither unhappy marriage nor divorce are especially congenial for children; each imposes its own set of stresses."[11]

Hetherington, Cox, and Cox: "Our study and previous research show that a conflict-ridden intact family is more deleterious to family members than a stable home situation in which parents are divorced."[12]

Obviously a miserable, strife-torn, loveless marriage in which the couple are technically together but emotionally divorced is hardly better than divorce itself. What then is the answer? Is there an answer? I believe there is.

The only real answer is no easier than either of the negative options. In fact, it is much more difficult because it requires commitment and hard work from both husband and wife. The solution to a bad marriage is turning it into a good one. That means healing the marriage. Healing occurs slowly, as husband and wife are taught how to communicate in noninflammatory ways, how to express love for each other, how to resolve conflicts, how to meet each other's emotional needs, and how to give and receive forgiveness.

If this sounds impossible, consider that there can be nothing which God wills or has commanded that is truly impossible. Change is possible. Learning new patterns of behavior is possible. We are capable of doing the will of God and capable of changing our outlook or our attitudes at any time because we are made in the image of God. Part of our God-given legacy is the ability to make decisions and to learn. Since marital harmony is God's will, a couple can count on His unflagging help if they seek to align their marriage according to His principles. Only an unwillingness to grow and change renders marital renewal impossible.

No marriage is perfect. Every marriage needs support, practical help, and godly guidance, and every church ought to be providing it in some form. Enriching existing marriages is powerful insurance against divorce.

Marriage enrichment can take many forms, depending on the depth of the couples' needs, but the underlying emphasis should be one of viewing marriage as a ministry. This means that each spouse deliberately seeks to build up the other, offering support and encouragement and doing all that can be done to help that spouse develop emotionally, socially, spiritually, and intellectually and to cultivate his or her own unique talents and gifts. Emotional intimacy and friendship are implicit in this concept of marriage. According to one divorce lawyer, the biggest reason that couples end up divorcing each other is "the inability to talk honestly with each other, bare their souls and treat each other as their best friend."[13] Teaching couples to do exactly this should be the goal of any marriage enrichment efforts by the church.

Some aspects of marriage enrichment include

- Helping couples learn to communicate their feelings honestly and lovingly, whether those feelings are positive or negative;
- Teaching couples to spend quality time together on a regular basis, not permitting other activities and commitments to take precedence over the marriage;
- Teaching couples how to resolve the big and little conflicts of life, including those dealing with money, sex, and child-rearing practices;
- Helping couples discover their individual personality strengths and weaknesses and how to work together as a more effective team to utilize this knowledge;
- Helping them establish mutual goals and priorities on which they can base decisions;
- Teaching them how to grow together spiritually through shared Bible study and prayer times.

A weekend retreat in a recreational setting away from children and phones provides an ideal environment for a marriage-enrichment seminar. A pastor, counselor, or psychologist can help couples learn new communication and decision-making skills using a variety of exercises and teaching methods designed for fun as well as education.

Back at home, churches can offer films, evening seminars, and Bible studies designed to enrich marriages.* Church-sponsored activities especially for couples such as Valentine banquets and social and recreational events can help build marriages too. Marital counseling should be made available to couples with special problems. All these things should be done with sensitivity toward single parents whether previously married or not. If their special needs are ignored in favor of boosting marriages, a proper balance has not yet been reached.

5. Prepare Young People for Marriage

Howard Hendricks has said, "The greatest decision a young person makes in life next to his commitment to Jesus Christ, I believe, is choosing a life partner. Yet we are

---

*An excellent thirteen-week couples' Bible study called "Building Relationships" is available from Marriage and Family Life Consultants, Inc., P.O. Box 10285, Winston-Salem, NC 27108.

failing our young people miserably in not helping them develop sound attitudes toward the problems and potentials of married life." [14] How are we failing, and what can we do to correct these failures?

False Ideals. One of the ways we fail is by perpetuating the myth of the perfect Christian marriage. This is supposedly a marriage in which there is no conflict or problems. Husband and wife live in perfect harmony all the time. This sanctified version of riding off into the sunset of marital bliss does little more than set young people up for the biggest disappointment of their lives, because no such marriage exists.

Setting forth God's standards of perfection is fine, but young people need to know the additional truth that no couple on earth embodies those ideals 100 percent of the time. Conflict is a normal part of every marriage relationship. Two people from different backgrounds have different ideas about how to do almost everything. Personalities differ and clash on occasion. Spouses sometimes irritate each other. They will not always feel well. They will not always want to talk or listen. There will be good days and bad days, ups and downs. We need to stress that real intimacy in marriage does not come from an absence of conflict, but rather from the resolving of conflict.

People from divorced families especially need to understand how to deal in acceptable ways with normal conflict. How to forgive and how to express feelings honestly yet kindly should be taught as a matter of course in preparing people for marriage. Many of these same concepts can be successfully applied to dating relationships also. A young person who is taught to view dating as a ministry will have no trouble understanding the concept of marriage as a ministry, that is, a relationship based on the desire to unselfishly serve the other person.

Singleness Is an Option. Young adults ought to have the opportunity to discover whether or not marriage is right for them. God does not call everyone to be married. It is wrong to assume—or to allow young people to assume— that marriage is always necessary for fulfillment in life.

We fail young people when we refuse to sanction the single state as a legitimate, God-approved option in life. We silently pressure them to marry when we provide no place for single people in the life of the church. Kristine Miller Tomasik writes,

> I think many Christian young people rush to the marriage altar because they have been taught that this is the road to acceptance and legitimacy within the church body. They have heard the jokes about singleness as being "the gift nobody wants." They get the clear impression that the only people who count are the married ones.[15]

This is clearly an unbiblical idea, and in light of our spiraling divorce rate, one that ought to be dispelled with great haste. Singleness is OK with God, and it ought to be OK with His people too. It is surely far better to choose singleness than to marry under pressure and wind up a divorce statistic.

Sex and Dating. The culture in which we live continually contradicts everything the Bible presents about sex, morality, and the sacredness of the marriage bond. Young people today need help in clarifying their standards for sex and dating. The church is an obvious source of this help and we fail when we keep silent on these topics. These are matters that ought to be addressed regularly and opened up for discussion periodically so that teens and preteens can clearly define for themselves a set of standards that will carry them through adolescence and into adulthood whether they marry or remain single.

Kristine Tomasik suggests that

> perhaps another reason many Christians have overstressed marriage is because they think it is the only safe container for the "dangerous problem" of sexuality. They actually fear the single person, whose sexuality, they feel, is uncontained—dangerous, highly explosive. Yet this too is unbiblical and insulting to the single person who has willed that his sexuality be contained by his chaste spirit and the indwelling Holy Spirit. The will to remain chaste—or faithful—is the only safe container for sexuality, not marriage, as too many Christian married people have discovered.[16]

The time to learn sexual self-control is during the teen and preteen years. These patterns will follow every person through life whether single or married. Those from divorced homes may have a special need for solid guidance in this regard.

Premarital Counseling. Preparation for marriage is really a process that occurs all through childhood. Although the primary source of learning remains the home, children are keen observers of the marriages of others besides their own parents. Churches that lift marriage and family life high do much to impress children with their sanctity and importance. When the time comes for more formal marriage preparation, children who have been so impressed will likely be teachable and motivated to prepare for marriage.

Special classes in premarital counseling should be a requirement for all engaged couples. These should serve as a further test for the couple of both their general call to be married and their specific commitment to each other. The topics of sex, money management, children, leadership in the home, church involvement, goals, and priorities could be among those covered in the sessions. Couples also can be given assignments to read and discuss books on marriage or to hear and discuss relevant tapes. These counseling sessions should reinforce the depth and meaning of a lifelong marital commitment and encourage couples to talk through their feelings about divorce and to renounce it as an option. Couples should also be encouraged to return for additional counseling after the wedding should their marriages ever begin to falter.

APPENDIX A

BOOKS TO HELP CHILDREN THROUGH DIVORCE

Beth Goff, *Where Is Daddy?* (Boston: Beacon Press, 1969)

> This sensitive story was written by a psychiatric social worker for a child who had become severely withdrawn after her parents divorced. It touches on the basic fears of every preschooler and is written in a way that endears the main character, Janeydear, and her dog, Funny, to children and adults alike. The pen and ink artwork is equally appealing. This is a story with which children can easily identify and one which will help adults experience divorce from a small child's point of view. (Preschool)

Sarah Bonnett Stein, *On Divorce: An Open Family Book for Parents and Children Together* (New York: Walker and Company, 1979)

> This book takes a unique approach to parent-child communication in that it provides side-by-side sections, one for the parent and one to be read aloud to the child. No actual divorce takes place, but Becky, the little girl in the story, experiences anxiety about divorce when her parents have an argument. Her playmates' parents have just divorced, which has heightened her awareness. The story is accompanied by interesting photography, and the section for parents is especially insightful. (Preschool–grade 3)

Terry Berger, *A Friend Can Help* (Milwaukee: Advanced Learning Concepts, 1974)

> This easy reading book is most useful in helping children whose friends' parents are breaking up. The emphasis is on being a good friend by being a good listener. Children from divorced homes may be prompted to share their feelings with their friends after reading this book. (Early school grades)

Appendix A

Francine Susan Spilke, *The Family That Changed: A Child's Book About Divorce* (New York: Crown, 1979)

> This book might be a good choice if you are looking for something to read to a child to help prepare him for an impending divorce. It takes a positive attitude toward continued good times with both parents after divorce. It may help a child begin to visualize what life will be like when parents live apart. (Preschool–grade 3)

Doris Wild Helmering, *I Have Two Families* (Nashville: Abingdon, 1981)

> Patty and her brother Michael have two homes, one with their dad and one with their mom. Although divorce has changed the way they live, Patty discovers that having two homes isn't so bad after all. This book takes a positive approach even when it touches on some of a child's common responses to divorce. Custodial fathers may be especially interested in this book since the children in the story reside primarily with their father, visiting their mother two days a week. (Early school grades)

Linda S. Chandler, *David Asks, "Why?"* (Nashville: Broadman, 1981)

> David has both good days and bad days, good feelings and bad feelings after his parents divorce. Both his mother and father try to help him understand that while they no longer love each other, they will always love him. This book includes two chapters about facing the first Christmas after divorce. (Elementary school children)

Matilda Nordtvedt, *Daddy Isn't Coming Home* (Grand Rapids: Zondervan, 1981)

> This especially realistic and well-written book successfully illustrates how the pain of divorcing parents can result in positive things, most notably, faith in Christ. Ten-year-old Faye's pain is evident as she copes with her parents' breakup, meeting her dad's new girlfriend, her emotionally distant relationship with her mother, and the disappointment of seemingly unanswered prayers. Yet, in the end, she is stronger, happier, and best of all, Jesus' friend. (Ages 9–12)

Carolyn E. Phillips, *Our Family Got a Divorce* (Glendale, Calif.: Regal, 1979)

When Chip's parents get divorced, he wonders if it is his fault. He feels irritable and angry for no reason. He misses his dad a lot but has to face the fact that he isn't coming home. His dad even has a new girlfriend! Chip learns many things with the help of his special confidant, Gram. She helps him see that it helps to talk about your feelings, that Jesus is a special friend, and that his mom has feelings too. (Ages 7–11)

The Unit at Fayerweather Street School, edited by Eric E. Rofes, *The Kids' Book of Divorce* (Lexington, Mass.: Lewis Publishing Co, 1981)

This book is unique in that it was written by a group of twenty eleven-to-fourteen-year-olds and is intended for other children of divorce. It zeros in on all the common concerns that this age group experiences when parents divorce and offers kid-to-kid advice on how to cope. Both parents and children can benefit from this book. It should be noted, however, that it does contain advice for kids whose parents are homosexual and those whose dates spend the night. It also incorporates a bit of rough language. Parents should read this book before deciding whether to give it to their children. (Ages 11 and older)

Paula Danziger, *The Divorce Express* (New York: Delacorte, 1982)

When Phoebe's parents divorce, her time is divided between them due to the joint-custody arrangement. As a result, she spends a lot of time on "the Divorce Express," the bus that carries her back and forth between her parents' homes. Phoebe has to deal with many of the common struggles of teens with divorced parents: changing schools, making new friends, coping with feelings of loneliness and anger, feeling responsible for her parents, and finally, the remarriage or her mother to a man she does not like. The book is witty, realistic, and enjoyable. It does contain some references to parents having dates spend the night, but these are carefully handled. (Teenagers)

Other Books About Divorce

Terry Berger, *How Does It Feel When Your Parents Get Divorced?* (New York: Julian Messner/Simon & Schuster, 1977).

Appendix A

_____. *I Have Feelings* (New York: Behavioral Publications/Human Sciences Press, 1971).
Judy Blume, *It's Not the End of the World* (New York: Dell, 1972).
William L. Coleman, *What Children Need to Know When Parents Get Divorced* (Minneapolis: Bethany House, 1983).
Joyce Ellis, *The Big Split* (Chicago: Moody Press, 1983).
Barbara Shook Hazen, *Two Homes to Live In: A Child's-Eye View of Divorce* (New York: Human Sciences Press, 1978).
Joan M. Lexau, *Emily and the Klunky Baby and the Next Door Dog* (New York: Dial Press, 1972).
_____. *Me Day* (New York: Dial Press, 1971).
Peggy Mann, *My Daddy Lives in a Downtown Hotel* (Garden City, N.J.: Doubleday, 1973).
Carol Nelson, *Dear Angie, Your Family's Getting a Divorce* (Elgin, Ill.: David C. Cook, 1980).
Marcia Newfield, *A Book for Jodan* (New York: Atheneum, 1975).
Jeanne Whitehouse Peterson, *That Is That* (New York: Harper & Row, 1979).
Helen S. Rogers, *Morris and His Brave Lion* (New York: McGraw-Hill, 1975).
Janet Sinberg, *Divorce Is a Grown Up Problem* (New York: Avon, 1978).
Bernard Waber, *Bernard* (Boston: Houghton Mifflin, 1982).
Leslie Williams, *Which Way Is Home?* (Nashville: Thomas Nelson, 1981).
Charlotte Zolotow, *A Father Like That* (New York: Harper & Row, 1971).

APPENDIX B

HOW TO KNOW GOD IN A PERSONAL WAY

Christianity is a very personal faith because God is a very personal God. God knows everything there is to know about every person alive—including you. He understands your personality, your problems, your questions. He knows all about your past and all about your future. He loves you completely. He does not put conditions on His love for you. He loves you whether you have been aware or unaware of Him, concerned or unconcerned about Him. He loves you no matter what you have done or what you have not done. He just loves you.

God desires to have a meaningful personal relationship with you. He wants to become your closest friend—involved in every aspect of your life. He wants to be someone in whom you can trust and on whom you can rely whether times are good or bad. In short, God wants you to respond to His great love for you: He wants you to know Him.

What the Bible Says About Knowing God Personally

Many people react positively to the idea of knowing God in a personal way, but they don't know how to go about establishing a relationship with Him. If you are one of these people, there are three things you need to know.

First, you need to understand that there is a barrier between you and God that keeps you from knowing Him personally and from experiencing His love. This barrier is the result of man's natural tendency to rebel against God and go his own way—what the Bible calls sin.

Second, you need to know that there is only one way to remove the sin barrier between you and God. Jesus Christ, God's Son, is Himself the only bridge between God and man. He willingly died on a cross two thousand years ago to remove the

---

Adapted from *Have You Heard of the Four Spiritual Laws?* Copyright © Campus Crusade for Christ, 1965.

Appendix B

barrier of sin between God and Man. When He died, Christ served as a substitute for you and me. That is, the punishment for our sin fell instead on Jesus.

Third, it is important for you to realize that Christ's death does not automatically bring about a relationship between a person and God. Each person individually must accept Christ's payment for his own sins. When he does so, Christ's death on the cross serves to unite that person in a relationship with God by taking the sin barrier away.

The Bible speaks clearly about God's love for us, about the sin that separates us from Him, and about Jesus, through whose death our sins are washed away. Here are some Bible verses that address these things.

God's Love: "For God so loved the world, that He gave His only begotten Son, that whoever believes in Him should not perish, but have eternal life" (John 3:16).

Man's Sinful Nature: "For all have sinned and fall short of the glory of God" (Romans 3:23).

The Consequences of Sin: "For the wages of sin is death," being separated from God, both now and in eternity (Romans 6:23).

Jesus, God's Provision for Our Sin: "But God demonstrates His own love toward us, in that while we were yet sinners, Christ died for us" (Romans 5:8).

Jesus, The Only Way to God: "Jesus said to him, 'I am the way, and the truth, and the life; no one comes to the Father but through Me'" (John 14:6).

"And there is salvation in no one else; for there is no other name under heaven that has been given among men, by which we must be saved" (Acts 4:12).

Accepting Christ's Payment for Our Sin: Jesus said, "Behold, I stand at the door and knock; if anyone hears My voice and opens the door, I will come in to him" (Revelation 3:20).

In this last verse, Jesus lets you know that He is standing at the door of your life and heart, knocking. He wants to come into your life and forgive your sins, but it is up to you to open the door and receive Him as your Savior.

If you welcome Jesus into your heart and life, your sins will be forgiven and the sin barrier between you and God will be removed. John 1:12 says, "But as many as received Him, to them He gave the right to become children of God, even to those who believe in His name." If you receive Christ, accepting His death as payment for your sins, you'll become part of God's own family. God will be your Father and friend. As God's child you will have eternal life: you'll be assured of a place in heaven when you die.

How to Receive Christ

All relationships begin with communication. The way we communicate with God is through prayer. Prayer is nothing more than talking to God. God already knows your thoughts and your attitude, so the words that you say are not as important as the sincerity of your heart. If you would like to receive Christ as your Savior, you may want to pray the following prayer as an expressions of that desire. Or you may want to use your own words.

> Lord Jesus, Thank You for Your great love for me. I acknowledge that I am a sinner and that my sin has placed a barrier between God and me that only You can take away. I accept Your death on the cross as the payment for my own individual sins. I now open the door of my life and ask You to come in. Begin now to make me the kind of person You want me to be. Thank You for giving me eternal life and for making me part of God's own family.

If you sincerely prayed this prayer and invited Jesus Christ to come into your life, He did. You may or may not feel any different. Keep in mind that faith cannot be based on feelings, which waver and change. Instead, Christ and His promises, which never change, are the basis for our faith. Jesus promised to come into your life if you asked Him to. He will never leave you, so you never need to invite Him in a second time. He is already there and will be with you each day of your life from now on. Welcome to God's family!

What's Next?

There are two things you should do now. First, you should obtain a Bible in a modern translation that you will enjoy reading, such as the New International Version. Receiving Christ is the same as being born in a spiritual sense. Spiritual food is found in God's Word, the Bible. You should make a habit of reading a portion of Scripture daily. As you are nourished from

Appendix B

the Bible you will grow with respect to your new relationship with God. It is in the pages of the Bible that you will really come to know God in an intimate way.

The second thing you should do is to begin to attend a church that upholds the Bible and teaches people how to receive Christ, as you just did. You may have some negative feelings about church attendance, depending on your past experience, but it is vital that you now approach church involvement with a new outlook. With Christ in your heart you have a real reason to worship Him alongside others who love Him. Ask Him to guide you in your search for the right church, and don't stop looking until you find one that you really feel at home in.

BIBLIOGRAPHY

Bayly, Joseph. *The Last Thing We Talk About*. Elgin, Ill.: David C. Cook, 1981.
Biller, Henry B. *Paternal Deprivation*. Lexington, Mass.: D. C. Heath, 1974.
_____. *Father, Child, and Sex Role: Paternal Determinants of Personality Development*. Lexington, Mass.: D. C. Heath, 1971.
Biller, Henry B., and Meredith, Dennis. *Father Power*. New York: David McKay, 1974.
Buchanan, Neal C., and Chamberlain, Eugene. *Helping Children of Divorce*. Nashville: Broadman Press, 1981.
Chapman, Gary D. *Hope for the Separated*. Chicago: Moody Press, 1982.
Dobson, James. *Dr. Dobson Answers Your Questions*. Wheaton, Ill.: Tyndale House, 1982.
Dodson, Fitzhugh. *How to Grandparent*. New York: Harper & Row, 1981.
Francke, Linda Bird. *Growing Up Divorced,* New York: Linden Press/Simon & Schuster, 1983.
Hart, Archibald D. *Children & Divorce*. Waco, Tex.: Word Books, 1982.
Kopp, Ruth. *Where Has Grandpa Gone?* Grand Rapids: Zondervan, 1983.
LaHaye, Tim. *Understanding the Male Temperament*. Old Tappan, N.J.: Fleming H. Revell, 1977.
Lamb, Michael E., ed. *The Role of the Father in Child Development*. New York: John Wiley & Sons, 1981.
Mallory, James D., Jr., with James C. Hefley. *Untwisted Living*. Wheaton, Ill.: Victor Books, 1982.
Nelson, Carol. *Dear Angie, Your Family's Getting a Divorce*. Elgin, Ill.: David C. Cook, 1980.
Robson, Bonnie, M.D. *My Parents Are Divorced, Too*. New York: Everest House, 1980.
Stein, Edward V., ed. *Fathering: Fact or Fable?* Nashville: Abingdon, 1977.
Stein, Sara Bonnett. *On Divorce: An Open Family Book for Parents and Children Together*. New York: Walker and Company, 1979.

Stevens, Joseph H., Jr., and Matthews, Marilyn, eds. *mother/child father/child Relationships*. Washington: National Association for the Education of Young Children, 1978.
Swihart, Judson J., and Brigham, Steven L., *Helping Children of Divorce*. Downers Grove, Ill.: InterVarsity Press, 1982.
The Unit at Fayerweather Street School, *The Kids Book of Divorce*. Ed. Eric E. Rofes. Lexington, Mass.: Lewis Publishing, 1981.
Vigeveno, H. S., and Claire, Anne. *Divorce and the Children*. Glendale, Calif.: Regal, 1979.
Wallerstein, Judith S., and Kelly, Joan B. *Surviving the Breakup: How Children and Parents Cope With Divorce*. New York: Basic Books, 1980.
Williams, Leslie. *Which Way Is Home?* Nashville: Thomas Nelson, 1981.

NOTES

CHAPTER ONE

1. "20/20," ABC-TV (March 4, 1982).
2. Cathy Carter, "Children Often Are Among the Victims of Divorce," *Winston-Salem Journal* (11 October 1981): E-1.
3. "Divorce: Kids in the Middle," Showtime cable TV feature (26 March 1983).
4. Armand M. Nicholi II, "The Fractured Family: Following It Into the Future," *Christianity Today* (25 May 1979): 11.
5. Fitzhugh Dodson, *How to Grandparent* (New York: Harper & Row, 1981), 145.
6. Judith S. Wallerstein and Joan B. Kelly, "California's Children of Divorce," *Psychology Today* (January 1980): 68–69.
7. Linda Bird Francke, *Growing Up Divorced* (New York: Linden Press/Simon & Schuster, 1983), 16–17.
8. Judith S. Wallerstein and Joan B. Kelly, *Surviving the Breakup: How Children and Parents Cope with Divorce* (New York: Basic Books, 1980), 36.
9. Ibid., 41–42.
10. Ibid., 42.
11. Ibid.
12. Archibald D. Hart, *Children and Divorce* (Waco: Word Books, 1982), 9.

CHAPTER TWO

1. Bruce Yoder, "My Parents' Divorce Caught Me Off Guard," *Christian Living,* (September 1981): 19.
2. Barbara Spence, "Death of a Marriage," *HIS* (February 1980): 5.
3. Joseph Bayly, *The Last Thing We Talk About* (Elgin, Ill.: David C. Cook, 1981), 97
4. Ruth Kopp, *Where Has Grandpa Gone?* (Grand Rapids: Zondervan, 1983), 129.
5. Leslie Williams, *Which Way Is Home?* (Nashville: Thomas Nelson, 1981), 113–14.

CHAPTER THREE

1. Francke, *Growing Up Divorced*, 61–62.
2. Ross D. Parke and Barbara R. Tinsley, "The Father's Role in Infancy: Determinants of Involvement in Caregiving and Play," in *The Role of the Father in Child Development*, ed. Michael E. Lamb (New York: John Wiley & Sons, 1981), 432, 439, 441.
3. Marie Pichel Warner, M.D., *A Doctor Discusses Breast Feeding* (Chicago: Budlong Press, 1981), 14–16.
4. Frank A. Pederson, "Father Influences Viewed in a Family Context," in Parke and Tinsley, *The Role of the Father*, 310–11.
5. Michael Lewis and Marsha Weinraub, "The Father as a Member of the Child's Social Network," in Parke and Tinsley, *The Role of the Father*, 264.
6. Paul Chance, "Your Child's Self-Esteem," *Parents* (January 1982): 58.
7. Lorisa DeLorenzo and Robert DeLorenzo, *Total Child Care From Birth to Age Five* (Garden City, N.J.: Doubleday, 1982), 362–64.
8. Henry B. Biller, *Paternal Deprivation* (Lexington, Mass.: D. C. Heath, 1974), 70.
9. George Maclean, Letter to *Montreal Gazette* (13 August 1980).
10. Biller, *Paternal Deprivation*, 6.
11. James Dobson, *Dr. Dobson Answers Your Questions* (Wheaton, Ill.: Tyndale House, 1982), 76.
12. Henry B. Biller, "Father Absence, Divorce, and Personality Development," in Parke and Tinsley, *The Role of the Father*, 498.

CHAPTER FOUR

1. Wallerstein and Kelly, *Surviving the Breakup*, 39.
2. Carter, "Children Often Are Among the Victims of Divorce," E1.
3. Henry B. Biller, *Father, Child and Sex Role: Paternal Determinants of Personality Development* (Lexington, Mass.: D. C. Heath, 1971), 6.
4. Wallerstein and Kelly, *Surviving the Breakup*, 61.
5. Ibid., 101.

CHAPTER FIVE

1. Wallerstein and Kelly, *Surviving the Breakup*, 65–66.

2. Francke, *Growing Up Divorced*, 51–52.
3. Wallerstein and Kelly, *Surviving the Breakup*, 71.
4. "Divorce: Kids in the Middle."
5. Francke, *Growing Up Divorced*, 102.

CHAPTER SIX

1. Wallerstein and Kelly, *Surviving the Breakup*, 75.
2. Francke, *Growing Up Divorced*, 119.
3. Ross Campbell, Parenting Seminar, Calvary Baptist Church, Winston-Salem, N.C. (21–22 November 1981).

CHAPTER SEVEN

1. Dan G. Kent, "Adolescent Development: A Primer for Parents," in *Living With Teenagers* (October–December 1979): 23–25.
2. Wallerstein and Kelly, *Surviving the Breakup*, 82.
3. Williams, *Which Way Is Home?* 61–64.
4. Wallerstein and Kelly, *Surviving the Breakup*, 91.
5. Biller, "Father Absence, Divorce, and Personality Development," 504–5.

CHAPTER EIGHT

1. Craig W. Ellison, "The Ugly Duckling Syndrome," *Eternity* (May 1978): 27.
2. Campbell, Parenting Seminar, Winston-Salem.
3. Carin Rubenstein, "The Children of Divorce as Adults," *Psychology Today* (January 1980): 75.
4. Hart, *Children and Divorce*, 108.
5. Bruce Yoder, "My Parents' Divorce Caught Me Off Guard," 18.

CHAPTER NINE

1. Hart, *Children and Divorce*, 21.
2. Leola Archer, "Something Special," *Family Life Today* (November 1982): 24.

CHAPTER TEN

1. Wallerstein and Kelly, *Surviving the Breakup*, 267–68.
2. Dobson, *Dr. Dobson Answers Your Questions*, 186.

3. Biller, *Paternal Deprivation*, 88.
4. Ibid., 121.
5. Ibid., 137.
6. Ibid., 130.

CHAPTER ELEVEN

1. Francke, *Growing Up Divorced*, 16.
2. Gary D. Chapman, *Hope for the Separated* (Chicago: Moody Press, 1982), 56–57.
3. Debbie Barr, "Hope for the Separated: An Interview With Dr. Gary D. Chapman," *Family Life Today* (February 1982): 25.
4. Roger Rosenblatt, "Children of War," *Time* (11 January 1982)): 36–37, 39, 50.
5. Hart, *Children and Divorce*, 10.
6. Dobson, *Dr. Dobson Answers Your Questions*, 43.
7. Tim LaHaye, *Understanding the Male Temperament* (Old Tappan, N.J.: Fleming H. Revell, 1977), 19.
8. Bruce Yoder, "When Divorce Drives Its Wedge," *With* (May 1983): 14.

CHAPTER TWELVE

1. Richard H. Stewart, "Many Discover Divorce Means Economic Woe,"*Winston-Salem Journal* (10 February 1983): 10.
2. Ibid.
3. Wallerstein and Kelly, *Surviving the Breakup*, 151.
4. Ibid., 185.
5. "World News Tonight," ABC-TV (11 April 1984).
6. Biller, *Father, Child and Sex Role*, 125–26.
7. Wallerstein and Kelly, *Surviving the Breakup*, 172.
8. Biller, "Father Absence, Divorce, and Personality Development," 531.
9. Wallerstein and Kelly, *Surviving the Breakup*, 230–31.
10. Henry B. Biller and Dennis Meredith, *Father Power* (New York: David McKay, 1974), 139–40.
11. Wallerstein and Kelly, *Surviving the Breakup*, 124.
12. Francke, *Growing Up Divorced*, 210.
13. Biller and Meredith, *Father Power*, 140.
14. The Unit at Fayerweather Street School, *The Kids' Book of Divorce*, Ed. Eric E. Rofes (Lexington, Mass.: Lewis Publishing, 1981), 90.
15. Francke, *Growing Up Divorced*, 209.

CHAPTER THIRTEEN

1. Marsha Weinraub, "The Myth of the Second-Class Parent," in *mother/child father/child Relationships*, ed. Joseph H. Stevens, Jr., and Marilyn Matthews (Washington: National Association for the Education of Young Children, 1978), 126–27.
2. Rothbaum, Zigler, and Hyson, "Modeling, Praising and Collaborating," in *Journal of Experimental Child Psychology*, vol. 31 no. 3 (June 1981): 418–21.
3. Wallerstein and Kelly, "California's Children of Divorce," 76.
4. "Divorce: Kids in the Middle."
5. Hart, *Children and Divorce*, 54.
6. Benjamin Spock, "Joint Custody and the Father's Role," *Redbook* (October 1979): 80.
7. *Marriage and Divorce Today. The Professional Newsletter for Family Therapy Practitioners*, vol. 8, no. 28 (14 February 1983): 1.
8. "The Superiority of Mother and Daughter, Father and Son Custody," *Psychology Today* (September 1980): 28.
9. Wallerstein and Kelly, "California's Children of Divorce," 72.
10. Ibid., 71.
11. Biller, *Paternal Deprivation*, 74.
12. Nicholi, "The Fractured Family," 11.
13. Biller, "Father Absence, Divorce, and Personality Development," 500.
14. Hetherington, Cox, and Cox, "The Aftermath of Divorce," in *mother/child father/child Relationships*, 170.
15. "Why So Many Marriages Fail," An interview with Herbert A. Glieberman in *U.S. News & World Report* (20 July 1981): 53.

CHAPTER FOURTEEN

1. *1985 U.S. Statistical Abstract*, 46.
2. *Women's Place*, Winston-Salem (N.C.) YWCA (February 1984).
3. Biller, *Paternal Deprivation*, 98.
4. H.S. Vigeveno and Anne Claire, *Divorce and the Children* (Glendale, Calif.: Regal, 1979), 56.
5. Arnold B. Kanter and Carol Kanter, "Innocents in Divorce," *Chicago Lawyer* (1982); 5(6):18–21 as quoted by La Leche League in "Custody and Visitation Arrangements."
6. Biller, "Absence, Divorce and Personality Development," 532.

7. Hetherington, Cox, and Cox, "The Aftermath of Divorce," 174.
8. "Small Boys Worst Victims of Divorce," in *USA Today* (June 1979): 1.
9. Hetherington, Cox, and Cox, "The Aftermath of Divorce," 164.
10. Kris Beckvall, "My Turning Point," in *Home Life*, (March 1983): 37.
11. Chapman, *Hope for the Separated*, 101–2.
12. Carol Nelson, *Dear Angie, Your Family's Getting a Divorce*, (Elgin, Ill.: David C. Cook, 1980), 102–3.

CHAPTER FIFTEEN

1. Francke, *Growing Up Divorced*, 250.
2. Ibid., 251.
3. Ibid., 252.
4. Weinraub, "The Myth of the Second-Class Parent," 120.
5. Toba Korenblum, "Probing the Father-Child Connection," in *MacLean's* (22 June 1981).
6. James C. Young and Muriel E. Hamilton, "Paternal Behavior: Implications for Childrearing Practice," in *mother/child father/child Relationships*, 141.
7. Harry Finkelstein Keshet and Kristine M. Rosenthal, "Fathers: A New Study," in *Children Today* (May–June 1978): 15.
8. Ibid.
9. Dick Thompson, "In California: Unswinging Singles," in *Time* (15 June 1981): 8.
10. "Kramer vs. Reality," in *Time* (4 February 1980): 77.
11. Thompson, "In California: Unswinging Singles," 8.
12. Benjamin Schlesinger, "Single Parent Fathers, A Research Review," in *Children Today* (May–June 1978): 37.

CHAPTER SIXTEEN

1. Nell Perry Barbee, "Youngsters Respond to 'How Did Divorce Affect You?'" in *Winston-Salem Journal* (4 April 1983): 18.
2. Williams, *Which Way Is Home?*
3. Bob Colacello, "Why Jodie Foster Won't Quit," in *Parade* (11 December 1983): 6.
4. Cathy Carter, "In the Aftermath, Stress and Strain Face the Family," in the *Winston-Salem Journal* (11 October 1981): E1.

5. Deidre S. Laiken, "Daughters of Divorce," in *Glamour* (November 1981): 286.
6. Young and Hamilton, *Paternal Behavior*, 142.
7. Rubenstein, "The Children of Divorce as Adults," 75.
8. James D. Mallory, Jr., with James C. Hefley, *Untwisted Living* (Wheaton, Ill.: Victor Books, 1982), 131.
9. Biller, *Paternal Deprivation*, 162.
10. Ibid., 115.
11. Francke, *Growing Up Divorced*, 26.
12. Rubenstein, "The Children of Divorce as Adults," 74.
13. Ibid., 75.
14. Carolyn Males and Julie Raskin, "The Children Nobody Wants," in *Reader's Digest* (January 1984): 65.
15. Williams, *Which Way is Home?* 134–35.
16. "Little Orphan Genius," *Human Behavior* (April 1979): 51.
17. Biller, "Father Absence, Divorce, and Personality Development," 512.
18. Dobson, *Dr. Dobson Answers Your Questions*, 180.
19. Ibid.
20. Kenneth S. Wuest, "Bypaths in the Greek New Testament," *Wuest's Word Studies in the Greek New Testament*, vol. 3 (Grand Rapids: Wm. B. Eerdmans, 1973), 73.

CHAPTER SEVENTEEN

1. David Krech et al., *Elements of Psychology* (New York: Alfred A. Knopf, 1969), 498.
2. John MacArthur, Jr., "Jesus' Teaching on Divorce," part 1, cassette series (Panorama City, Calif.: Word of Grace Communications, 1983).
3. Kristine Miller Tomasik, "Divorced But Not Defeated," in *Today's Christian Woman* (Spring 1982): 98, 109.
4. Ibid., 109.

CHAPTER EIGHTEEN

1. Gloria Ichikawa, "Words Fail Me," in *Moody Monthly* (June 1984): 97.
2. Vigeveno and Claire, *Divorce and the Children*, 115.
3. Francke, *Growing Up Divorced*, 235.
4. Robert D. Allers, "Helping Children Understand Divorce," in *Education Digest* (March 1981): 20–23.
5. Hart, *Children and Divorce*, 21–22.
6. "The Children of Divorce," in *Business Week* (2 April 1979): 103.

7. Hart, *Children and Divorce*, 61.
8. "The Children of Divorce," 104.

CHAPTER NINETEEN

1. Wallerstein and Kelly, *Surviving the Breakup*, 99.
2. "The Children of Divorce," 102.
3. Wallerstein and Kelly, *Surviving the Breakup*, 207.
4. Ibid. 206–7.
5. Hart, *Children and Divorce*, 38.
6. "Life in the Spotlight: Lessons of a Christian Celebrity," in *Today's Christian Woman* (January–February 1984): 72, 74.

CHAPTER TWENTY

1. Francke, *Growing Up Divorced*, 222–23.
2. *Marriage and Divorce Today. The Professional Newsletter for Family Therapy Practitioners*, vol. 8 no. 25 (24 January 1983): 1, 3.

CHAPTER TWENTY-ONE

1. Spence, *Death of a Marriage*, 4.
2. Ibid., 1, 4.
3. Francke, *Growing Up Divorced*, 41.
4. "Family Happiness Is Homemade," in *Family Concern*, vol. 7 no. 1 (January 1983).
5. "It's Time to Repair Our Sinking Ship," in *Moody Monthly* (July–August 1984): 21.
6. James P. Comer, "Are You Too Busy for Your Child?" in *Parents* (April 1980): 96.
7. Alice Fryling, "So Many Divorces," in *Eternity* (October 1980): 86.
8. "I Couldn't Live Up to My Father's Expectations," in *Good Housekeeping* (September 1978): 22.
9. Lee Salk, "Helping Children Deal With Divorce," in *McCall's* (October 1983): 88.
10. "Divorce: Kids in the Middle."
11. Wallerstein and Kelly, *Surviving the Breakup*, 307.
12. Hetherington, Cox, and Cox, "The Aftermath of Divorce," 175.
13. "Why So Many Marriages Fail," 54.
14. Howard Hendricks, "Prepare Your Children For Marriage," in *Moody Monthly* (June 1973): 38.
15. Tomasik, "Divorced But Not Defeated," 101.
16. Ibid.

MATTHEW AND STEPHANIE

A Read-Aloud Story for Children

CONTENTS

1. Bad News! 327
2. Is It My Fault? 331
3. Why Do I Feel So Bad? 335
4. Will Mommy and Daddy Get Back
   Together? 339

This story is designed to be read aloud to preschool or early school-age children, preferably with separate sittings for each chapter. The discussion questions can be used as teaching aids and also as a means for discovering how a child is feeling. The text is approximately third-to-fourth-grade reading level. Children in these grades may want to read it for themselves.

1
Bad News

Bam! The screen door slammed behind Matthew as he ran into the kitchen.

"Mommy," he called, "can I go next door to play with Jeff?"

Mommy was coming up the stairs from the basement. She was carrying a basket of laundry in her arms. When she got to the top of the stairs, she set the basket on the floor. Then she sat down on a kitchen chair.

"Matthew," she said, "come here a minute."

Matthew walked over to where Mommy was sitting. She put her arm around Matthew's waist. In a soft voice she said, "Your daddy and I have something very important to tell you and Stephanie. We want to talk to you both in the living room. Would you ask Stephanie to come inside?"

"Sure, Mommy," said Matthew. As he headed toward the door, he wondered what Mommy and Daddy wanted to talk about. Maybe it was about the camping trip they had planned!

"No." Matthew thought to himself, "That can't be it. Mommy seemed sort of sad. If it was about the camping trip she would be happy."

Suddenly Matthew felt worried. He tried to remember if he and Stephanie had done something wrong. Matthew stepped outside. His sister Stephanie was playing in the sandbox.

Matthew called, "Stephanie, Mommy says to come inside. Daddy and she want to talk to us."

"OK," said Stephanie. She jumped up and brushed the sand off her jeans.

Soon Matthew and Stephanie joined Mommy and Daddy in the living room. Marshmallow, the family dog, was lying on the floor near Daddy's feet. His tail began to thump on the floor as Matthew reached down to scratch his ears.

Except for the thump of Marshmallow's tail, the room was very quiet. Daddy took a deep breath. Then he put one arm around Stephanie and one arm around Matthew.

"Your mother and I love you both very much," he began. "And we will *always* love you. Nothing can change that. You make us very happy. We always thank God that He gave us two very special children."

Matthew grinned at Stephanie. They both knew how much Mommy and Daddy loved them. It made them feel all warm and good inside whenever they said something like that.

Their daddy continued, "Now, I have to tell you something important. It will be very hard to say, so listen carefully." He had a serious look on his face. Matthew looked at Mommy. She had a serious look on her face, too.

Daddy continued, "Your mother and I have had many problems in our marriage. We have tried very hard to work these problems out for a long time. These are *grown-up* problems. They have nothing to do with you children. The problems are only between Mommy and me. We wish we could solve these problems, but we can't. So, we have made a big decision. This decision will affect all of us— Mommy, Daddy, Matthew, and Stephanie. We feel that

Bad News

the only solution to our problems is for your mother and me to get a divorce."

Stephanie and Matthew could not believe their ears! Had Daddy said "divorce"? For a minute the room grew quiet again. Nobody said a word. Matthew wanted to shout, "No, no! You can't," but the words got stuck in his throat. Stephanie wanted to run up to her room and hug her teddy bear, but she could not move. Her eyes started to fill up with tears. The tears rolled down her cheeks and dropped onto her jeans.

Mommy squeezed Stephanie's hand and gave her a tissue. Then she said, "Next Saturday your father will be moving into an apartment. It's not very far away, just four blocks. You can walk over to see him any time you want to. You children and Marshmallow will live here with me."

When Matthew found his voice again he asked, "But *why?* Why can't we all live together? Why do you have to get a divorce?"

"Sometimes parents can't work out their problems, Matthew," said Daddy. "Sometimes they try very hard, but they fail. That's what happened to us."

Agreeing, Mommy said, "We're sorry it has to be this way. We know this is very sad news for you. We know you feel very upset. Your father and I feel bad and upset too. But we still think getting a divorce is what we should do. We are unhappy being married to each other. We think it will be better if we live apart from each other."

Stephanie asked, "Do you still love us? Will you still be our mommy and daddy?"

"Oh yes!" said Mommy and Daddy.

"We'll always love you," said Daddy. And we will always be your mommy and daddy. We'll always take good care of you."

Mommy added, "Divorce can change many things, but it can never change our love for you!"

Caught in the Crossfire

QUESTIONS

1. What was the bad news that Matthew and Stephanie got?
2. Did you ever get bad news like this?
3. When Matthew heard about the divorce, he was so surprised that he couldn't even talk. Stephanie wanted to run away, but instead she started to cry. When you found out that your parents were going to get a divorce, what did you do?
4. What did the parents in this story say that divorce could never change?
5. Do you think the divorce in your family changed anything? What do you think it changed?

2
Is It My Fault?

Matthew opened his sleepy eyes. The sunshine coming through the window in his room told him that is was morning.

"Today is Saturday," he thought happily. "Stephanie and I can watch cartoons on TV!" Then he remembered, "Today is the day that Daddy moves into his apartment."

Suddenly Matthew felt very sad. He hugged his pillow tightly. Soon the pillowcase was wet with tears. Matthew tried very hard to think of something he could do to make his daddy change his mind about the divorce. He thought for a long time. Then he got an idea.

Matthew jumped out of bed. He got dressed in a hurry. Then he ran across the hall to Stephanie's room. He wanted to share his idea with her.

Matthew knocked on Stephanie's door. There was no answer. He opened the door just a crack. Stephanie was not in her room.

"Oh well," Matthew thought to himself, "no time to waste. I'll just have to do it by myself."

Matthew went to the closet where Mommy kept cleaning supplies. He took out a bucket, a scrub brush, and some soap. He carried them outside and set them down in the grass. He filled the bucket with water from the garden hose. Then he poured in lots of soap. The water got all white and foamy with soapsuds.

Matthew picked up the bucket. The water made it very heavy. It was hard for Matthew to carry. Water sloshed over the sides of the bucket with every step he took. Soon his jeans and sneakers were wet. Finally, he reached the garage. He set the bucket down and took a rest.

Matthew looked at the side of the garage. It was covered with all sorts of different colored splashes of paint. The paint hadn't been there very long, only a few weeks. Matthew had tried to paint a beautiful picture on the garage wall. He wanted it to look like the wall in the bank downtown. It was called a mural. But when he finished painting, it didn't look like a mural at all. It was a terrible mess! And when his daddy saw it he had been very, very angry. He had scolded Matthew and spanked him. Matthew had never seen his daddy so angry!

Now Matthew thought, "If I can just get this paint off of the garage, then Daddy won't have anything to be mad about. Then he won't want to move into an apartment. And Mommy and Daddy won't get a divorce!"

Matthew began to work very hard. He scrubbed and scrubbed. But the paint wasn't coming off!

Just then, Matthew heard a funny sound. He turned around, but he didn't see anything. He started to scrub again. Then he heard the funny sound again. He put the scrub brush down and listened hard. There it was again. It sounded like Stephanie's voice. But where was she?

"Stephanie, is that you?" he called.

"Yes. I'm up here," came the reply.

Matthew looked up into the big tree next to the garage. Stephanie was in the tree house that Daddy had built for them. When she saw Matthew she climbed down.

When she reached the ground she said, "Matthew, I know why Mommy and Daddy are getting a divorce! It's because of me. I'm always losing my toys, and my room is messy. And I don't always come right away when they call me. And I wouldn't go to bed when the baby-sitter was here. I was up in the tree house praying that God would forgive me for being so bad. And for causing the divorce." Stephanie started to cry.

"No, Stephanie," said Matthew. "The divorce is not your fault—it's my fault! Mommy and Daddy are getting a divorce because I painted on the garage and made Daddy mad. And now the paint won't come off!" Then Matthew began to cry too.

Just then Daddy came out of the house. He was carrying a box of things for his apartment. He saw Matthew and Stephanie crying. He put the box into the car. Then he came over to where the children were.

"Let's sit down under the tree," he said. So Matthew and Stephanie and Daddy all sat down. They leaned on the trunk of the big, old tree by the garage.

"Tell me why you are crying," said Daddy.

"I know the divorce is my fault, Daddy!" said Matthew. "But I'm trying to clean the paint off the garage."

"The divorce is *my* fault!" said Stephanie. "But I promise that I won't lose any more toys, and I'll keep my room clean. I'll even come right away when you call me. And I'll be good when the baby-sitter comes."

Daddy looked at Matthew. Then he looked at Stephanie. "You are both wrong," he said. "The divorce is not Matthew's fault *or* Stephanie's fault. It has nothing to do with the paint on the garage or losing toys. In fact, it has nothing to do with anything either of you has *ever* done," said Daddy. "Don't think that Mommy and I are getting a divorce because of you or because of something you did. It's not true."

"I know divorce is hard for you to understand," said Daddy. "But you should always remember this: there is nothing children can do to cause a divorce to happen. Divorce is not your fault."

QUESTIONS

1. Why did Matthew think Mommy and Daddy were getting a divorce?
2. Why did Stephanie think Mommy and Daddy were getting a divorce?
3. Who was right?
4. Have you ever thought that the divorce in your family was your fault?
5. Read the last two sentences in the story again. What did Matthew and Stephanie's Daddy tell them? Is he right?

3 Why Do I Feel So Bad?

It was a hot, sunny summer day. Matthew and Stephanie were at the pool in the park. Their friends, Jeff and Maria, were there, too. Jeff was diving off the side of the pool. Maria was standing in line to go down the sliding board. But Matthew and Stephanie were just lying in the sun. They didn't feel like having fun. They were thinking about the divorce.

Matthew liked to swim. He was a good swimmer. But today swimming seemed boring. He opened a comic book and started to read. He liked to read comic books whenever he came to the pool. But today comic books seemed boring, too. He gave them to Stephanie.

"Want to read these?" he asked.

"No, thanks," said Stephanie. "I don't feel like it either."

Suddenly Stephanie jumped up. She had a mean feeling inside. She ran over to the side of the pool and pushed Maria in.

"What's the big idea?" shouted Maria as she climbed out of the pool. Stephanie began to run away. Maria started to chase her. Maria wanted to push Stephanie in the pool to pay her back.

Both girls knew that running was not allowed. It even said NO RUNNING in big letters right on the cement by the pool. Stephanie read the words as she ran across them. But she didn't care whether she obeyed or not. She just felt mean and unhappy inside.

Suddenly a little girl crossed Stephanie and Maria's path. Maria saw her and stopped running. But Stephanie didn't see her. Before anyone could stop her, Stephanie ran right into the little girl. The little girl fell down and started to cry.

The lifeguard blew his whistle and came running. The little girl's mother came running. Maria and Jeff and Matthew came running, too. Stephanie could see that the little girl had skinned her knees. There was even blood on the cement.

Suddenly Stephanie didn't feel so mean anymore. Instead, she felt very sorry. She even said she was sorry, but it didn't seem to help much. She offered to go inside with the mother to wash the little girl's knees, but the mother said, "No."

The lifeguard took Stephanie and Maria aside. He told them, "You have broken the rules. That means you cannot come back to the pool for the rest of the week. That goes for both of you." When Maria heard this, she got mad.

"But it's not my fault!" shouted Maria. "Stephanie was the one who pushed me in the pool. And she was the one who ran into the little girl!"

"Sorry," said the lifeguard. "That's our policy." Then he walked away.

Stephanie felt very bad about getting Maria into trouble. She knew that Maria was mad at her. Most of all, Stephanie felt sorry for hurting the little girl. She wished she had stayed at home instead of coming to the pool.

Stephanie and Maria went to pick up their towels. They told Jeff and Matthew that they had to leave. The boys said they would leave too.

On the way home, Stephanie told Maria that she was sorry they could not come back to the pool for the rest of the week. Maria smiled and said, "That's OK." Then Stephanie knew that Maria wasn't mad at her anymore. That made her feel a little bit better.

When Stephanie got home, she told Mommy what had happened.

"Stephanie, what got into you?" asked Mommy.

"I don't know," said Stephanie sadly. "I just know I feel bad and mean inside since Daddy left. Sometimes I don't understand why I do the things I do. I don't feel happy."

Matthew had been listening. "I don't feel happy either, Mommy," he said. "Nothing seems fun anymore. I don't even feel like playing with Marshmallow."

"Why do we feel so bad, Mommy?" asked Stephanie and Matthew.

Mommy thought about the children's question. Then she said, "When there is a divorce, everyone in the family feels bad. But not everyone feels bad in the same way. Some people feel very sad. They might want to be alone instead of being with their friends. Things that used to be fun for them might seem boring. That's how Matthew feels.

"Other people feel angry inside. The anger makes them say or do things they wouldn't normally do. That's how Stephanie feels.

"The feelings children get after a divorce are often bad feelings. Sometimes they are the same kind of feelings as the ones we get when someone dies. These are feelings of grief. They come because you miss having Daddy here every day. And you miss the way our family used to be. Sometimes feelings of grief take a long time to go way."

"Do you have grief feelings too, Mommy?" asked Matthew.

"Yes, I do," said Mommy. "Some days I feel very sad. Other days I feel happier."

Caught in the Crossfire

Stephanie said, "Some days I feel scared. I don't know what will happen next."

Matthew said, "Some days I feel lonely, especially if Daddy doesn't call us."

"I'm glad we can talk about our fellings," said Stephanie. "It makes me feel better."

"Me, too" said Matthew.

"Me, too" said Mommy.

"Woof!" said Marshmallow.

QUESTION

1. Who had bad feelings in this story?
2. Why did they feel bad?
3. Matthew and Stephanie felt many things after their parents got divorced: sad, angry, mean, lonely, bored. What feelings do you have?
4. When we have bad feelings we sometimes say or do things we later wish we hadn't said or done. What did Stephanie do that she wished she hadn't done?
5. Bad feelings sometimes keep us from enjoying things we usually enjoy. What did Matthew's bad feelings keep him from enjoying?
6. Was Stephanie right or wrong when she pushed Maria into the pool? Can we help it when we get bad feelings? Do we have to act on our bad feelings? What could Stephanie have done instead?*
7. Matthew and Stephanie felt better when they talked about their bad feelings. Do you feel better when you talk about your bad feelings?

---

*This question can be used to help a child see that in spite of his feelings he is still responsible for his actions.

4
Will Mommy and Daddy Get Back Together?

It was a rainy day. Mommy said that Stephanie and Matthew had to stay inside and play.

"What can we play?" asked Matthew.

"I know," said Stephanie. "Let's color in our new coloring books."

Matthew went to get the crayons. Stephanie went to get the coloring books. Then they lay on the living room floor and began to color.

Stephanie colored a picture of puppies and kittens. Matthew colored a picture of a family having fun on a picnic. The family had a mother, a father, a boy and a girl. They reminded Matthew of Mommy, his daddy, Stephanie, and himself. There was even a dog in the picture that looked just like Marshmallow. Matthew colored the mother's hair light brown, just like Mommy's. He colored the father's hair dark brown, just like his daddy's. And he colored the boy's hair and the girl's hair yellow because he and Stephanie had blond hair. He made the dog white with a black spot on his tail like Marshmallow had. Matthew worked very hard on his picture. When he got done he showed it to Stephanie.

"Matthew, it looks like our family!" she cried.

"I know," said Matthew. "But our family isn't all together anymore like this one is." Matthew's voice sounded sad.

For a moment, Stephanie felt sad, too. Then she had a very happy thought. "Maybe Mommy and Daddy will get back together" she said.

Matthew liked that idea. "Yeh! Maybe they will," he said. Now Matthew's voice sounded excited. "Maybe Daddy will come back home and we can all be together again."

Stephanie was getting excited, too. She said, "Remember the day I pushed Maria in the pool? For a while she was mad at me. But then we made up. Maybe Mommy and Daddy will make up, too!"

Stephanie and Matthew wanted Mommy and Daddy to get back together more than anything in the whole world! They wanted their daddy to come home. They wanted their family to be the way it was before the divorce.

Matthew said, "When I blow out the candles on my next birthday cake, I am going to make a very special wish. I am going to wish for Daddy to come home."

"Me, too," said Stephanie. "Then maybe Mommy and Daddy will get back together very, very soon."

Soon the rain stopped and Mommy said that the children could go outside to play.

"Let's go see Mrs. Green," said Matthew. Stephanie agreed. They liked Mrs. Green very much. She was a special friend who lived next door.

Mrs. Green was sitting on her porch. Matthew and Stephanie walked over and sat down on the porch steps.

"What have you two been up to on such a rainy day?" asked Mrs. Green.

"The children told her about their new coloring books. They told her about Matthew's picture that looked like their family. And they told her that they were going to wish very hard for Mommy and Daddy to get back together soon.

Will Mommy and Daddy Get Back Together?

"Well," said Mrs. Green, "that would be very nice. But a divorce is a divorce."

Matthew and Stephanie were puzzled. "What do you mean?" they asked.

"A divorce is a very final thing," explained Mrs. Green. "When a husband and a wife get divorced it means that they are not married anymore. And they will never be married again. A divorce means that the marriage is over."

Matthew and Stephanie did not like what Mrs. Green said.

"When Maria and I were mad at each other, we made up," said Stephanie. "We're still friends. Why couldn't Mommy and Daddy make up, too?"

"Divorce is different," said Mrs. Green. "Divorce is more than an argument. Divorce means that a marriage has come to an end. You could even say that the marriage has died. Sometimes a mommy and a daddy can be friends after a divorce. But they are not married anymore—and they never will be."

"Oh," said Matthew.

"Oh," said Stephanie.

Mrs. Green gave the children a hug. "I know you feel disappointed," she said. "I know you wish that your family could be together the way it was before. That wish won't come true. But here's a happy thought. Now you have two homes: one with your daddy and one with your mommy. That makes your family very, very special."

Stephanie and Matthew smiled. Mrs. Green was right. Their family *was* very, very special.

QUESTIONS

1. What did Stephanie and Matthew wish Mommy and Daddy would do?

2. Do you ever wish your mommy and daddy would get back together?
3. When a husband and a wife get divorced, are they still married?
4. How is divorce different from an argument?
5. What did Mrs. Green tell Matthew and Stephanie when they said they were going to wish that Mommy and Daddy would get back together?
6. Stephanie and Matthew think their family is very, very special. What makes your family special?